GENESIS
A LIVE GUIDE 1969-1975

PAUL RUSSELL

GENESIS

A LIVE GUIDE 1969-1975

PAUL RUSSELL

First published in 2004
by SAF Publishing

SAF Publishing Ltd.
149 Wakeman Road,
London.
NW10 5BH
ENGLAND

email: info@safpublishing.com
www.safpublishing.com

ISBN 0 946719 58 6

Cover photographs: Janet Macoska.

A CIP catalogue record for this book is available from the British Library.

Printed in England by the Cromwell Press, Trowbridge, Wiltshire.

Dedicated to Helen

Without whom it would have taken even longer.

THANK YOU

This book was made bearable with the help of lots of good friends and several people I have yet to meet.
Genesis – you know who you are – but especially Tony Banks, Mike Rutherford, Anthony Phillips and Phil Collins.
Tony Smith and Carol Willis Impey at Hit&Run Music Ltd, for saying yes and getting people together.
Geoff Callingham and Dale Newman at The Farm for letting me crank it up on a regular basis.
Jon Webster for knowing absolutely everybody and starting the ball rolling, and for a perfect Bataclan.
Peter Hammill for saying no!
Dave Hallbery at SAF for saying yes.
Glen Colson for loads of stuff in a black bin liner.
Helen Russell for some serious speed-typing and not locking me away in the attic.
The many collectors who have traded or just sent me lots of great recordings, names as I think of them but extra thanks and badges to Stuart Downes and Ian Laycock, for tapes beyond the call of duty.
Mick Walker for some serious remasters.
Mal Lord (RIP) for lots of great quality shows way before anyone else had them.
Mike Dolman for endless press cuttings.
Mark Bataitus, Volker Warncke and Dietmar Brunns (nice pics Dietmar).
Adam from genesismuseum.com – a belated credit to a great website.
To anyone I have missed out, sorry.

INTRODUCTION

The idea for this book can be traced back to Led Zeppelin, or should I say an excellent book, *Led Zeppelin Live: An Illustrated Exploration of Underground Tapes*, published by Hot Wacks Press. Now in its third edition, it is based on the mighty Zeppelin live in concert and features reviews of the many live tapes in circulation. Luis Rey, the book's author, came into the record store I was working in at the time with a bag full of these books asking if I wanted to buy them.

After relieving Luis of the entire contents of his bag I acquired a copy and as a collector of Zepp shows I found that I could not put it down. Needless to say the books flew out of the door and I was soon on the phone for more.

The Genesis connection came when I was asked to write a review of the first Archive box set for *Record Collector* magazine. This, with the invaluable help of Jon Webster, almost unbelievably became a seven-man reunion at Heathrow Airport where I was able to interview Messrs Banks, Rutherford, Collins, Hackett, Phillips, Silver and Gabriel. An unforgettable morning when old friends met up for the first time in years, phone numbers were swapped, and plenty of distant memories stirred. I also got to take my own photographs – jammy or what?

That day was completed by the first of many visits to the band's studio hidden away in the leafy lanes of Surrey. The Farm, as it is known, is a secluded retreat where many of the later period Genesis albums have been recorded.

With the seed of an idea already sown, I was pleasantly surprised when my tour of the Farm included being shown three dusty cardboard boxes upstairs in a wardrobe (I kid you not). A quick inspection of their contents caused the old ticker to kick into overdrive for a few minutes as I realised what I was looking at.

Several of the reviews in this book are from the aforementioned wardrobe. Hearing them in the band's own studio was a truly magical experience and one I shall always remember. You ain't heard "Fly on a Windshield" as it should sound unless you've heard it as loud as I did in one of those leather studio chairs. A big thank-you to Geoff and Dale for all their help (and toast).

After the initial success of the Zeppelin book and the Aladdin's cave I had seen in Surrey, a live guide to all the known (and in this case unknown) recordings just had to happen. A second magazine article featuring some of the reviews also included part of an interview with Tony, Mike and Ant. This was a joy to do and revealed many fascinating Genesis moments from those early days. With their kind permission this interview is included at the end of this book.

The live tape-collecting world is a strange place with many different inhabitants many still wearing anoraks, who are presumably after the same thing, (as long as it's a low generation recording with an extra 13 seconds of applause). The internet has brought many of them together and some of the collecting sites are truly amazing pieces of computer wizardry. Unfortunately some collectors try to sell their wares and give the 'swappers' a bad name, this will always happen and a debate on the solutions could go on for hours. The bottom line is you don't have to buy, find someone who will trade they are out there somewhere.

Some of the rarest tapes in this guide came from fans who don't even have a handwritten list, let alone a website. These shows were recorded, possibly listened to a few times then left to gather dust. Some of these old fans I met by chance – some through a friend of a friend, but between them several 'new' shows have come to light.

For many Genesis freaks it's a game of two halves. The Gabriel years and the Collins years (sorry Ray). This book only deals with the former for purely selfish reasons, as that's the era I like the most. When you look at an early gig listing you realise just how many of those shows have not and will most likely never appear on tape.

Genesis played the proverbial one man and a dog gig lots of times and the man and his best friend would not have bothered with a tape deck, so we will have to ponder how those very early shows would have sounded, unless of course....

Reviewing the recordings in chronological order was the perfect way to see how the band developed as a live act. The arrival of Phil Collins did wonders for the overall sound and was the kick up the musical backside they obviously needed. Peter Gabriel's position as a storytelling frontman was another continually evolving saga that began with some quaint *Monty Python* style tales and ended with the somewhat bizarre ramblings for *The Lamb Lies Down* tour.

The prospect of reviewing countless *Lamb* shows with their identical track listings was, to say the least a touch daunting, but as the tour progressed, so did the performances. So by the time the band hit Europe there were some simply stunning shows and some of the best "Musical Boxes" I have ever opened.

"Do you have a favourite show or song?" I am frequently asked. The answer is not really. I have a soft spot for those Italian shows from 1972, when things were still a bit wild and some of the more unusual songs were played, or the final show at the LA Roxy in December 1973 (scary or what). As for a song, "The Musical Box" still sends shivers, but then so does '666' – and that guitar solo in "Firth of Fifth" is still the best around.

Genesis from this early period, were the quintessential English progressive rock group. All the parts were in place from the ever so slightly eccentric frontman to the band's complete mastery of their instruments, and of course the odd good tune.

Unfortunately only a couple of the recordings in this book are available in your local record shop, such is the nature of bootleg recording. Current trends have seen several big name acts delve into their archive for some warts-and-all, this-is-how-it-was, style recordings. Many artists loathe bootlegs with a passion, which is one reason traders have to trade them, many artists should just release them, stop moaning and remind the fans how good or bad they used to be.

Like most music buffs, I collect recordings by many different artists and not just Genesis, so after the umpteenth version of "Watcher of the Skies" and enough *Lambs* to start my own flock, perhaps it's time to hang up the cloak, switch off the Mellotron and dig out those Blodwyn Pig tapes.

1. THE THREE GIRLS AT THE BACK YEARS

Endless toiling round the pub and club circuit of London and the surrounding counties, plus the odd sortie 'up north', gave the band much-needed live experience. They did not always play to many people and were often ignored by the disgruntled punter, who found it difficult to dance to the serious-sounding acoustic music emanating from the serious bunch on stage.

The set lists were full of songs now mostly lost in the ether, but one or two future classics were beginning to emerge.

Stage presentation was non-existent due to their inexperience or the ridiculous places they played in.

Gabriel was in his pre- funny hat stage and Rutherford was often to be seen behind a cello.

These early gigs also saw a few line up changes, with Phillips and Mayhew out, Collins and Hackett in, and guitarist Mick Barnard just passing through.

Recordings from this era are thin on the ground, but the Le Ferme 1971 gig from Belgium is as important as any in this book, we know that "The Light" was played quite a few times but this is the only known live recording – so that makes it a must-have.

NOVEMBER 1st, 1969
BRUNEL UNIVERSITY, ACTON, LONDON, UK.

Personnel: Peter Gabriel, Tony Banks, Mike Rutherford, Anthony Phillips, John Mayhew.

Possible Set List: In The Wilderness, Masochistic Man, Stumble, Build Me A Mountain, In Limbo, Digby, Little Leaf, Babies, Key To Love, Looking For Someone, Twilight Alehouse, Sitting On Top Of The World, Pacidy.

This was the first official gig after months of writing and rehearsing. The set list above is in no particular order and is taken from memory, although Tony Banks is sure they ended with "Pacidy". Some songs might be missing in action.

Anthony Phillips: 'The first disaster was me, because we started with that track "In The Wilderness" and I had re-strung just before the gig, which is something you don't do, and I had a loose machine head. We hit the first break and the string had slipped, everyone was looking and there were all these agents there. I was so nervous. It was the first number of a showcase gig.'

Tony Banks: 'I remember from the word go playing at full volume, I had an organ through a Selmer Goliath amp which had a great big speaker and a home-made Leslie. We had all these subtle little changes worked out at rehearsal, I just put my foot down and played flat out, couldn't hear a thing.

Mike Rutherford: 'There was an argument with Peter about where to put the PA. We sat in two rows as we hadn't really thought about how to set up.'

FEBRUARY 22nd, 1970
BBC STUDIO NO. 4, MAIDA VALE, LONDON, UK.

Personnel: PG, TB, MR, AP, JM.

Set List: The Shepherd, Pacidy, Let Us Now Make Love, Stagnation, Looking For Someone, Dusk (recording lost).

This gem of a session not only features three pre-*Trespass* songs, but is one of only two known studio/live recordings to feature both Anthony Phillips on guitar and John Mayhew on drums. The first three tracks found their way onto the *Genesis Archive* 4-CD set, a later recording of "Stagnation" was included, but the version of "Looking For Someone" sadly remains unissued.

"The Shepherd" has Gabriel in fine voice with plenty of trademark mannerisms that balance nicely with the delicate second vocal, surprisingly not from Phillips, but from Tony Banks. Some nice piano and flute bring this gentle number to a close.

"Pacidy" is all 12-string guitars and is again dominated by Gabriel's pleading vocals, with some intricate organ work hinting at things to come. "Let Us Now Make Love" sounds closer to *Trespass* than the other two, with some stirring harmonies, and even Mayhew's drums get a rare look in, if only in the background. Polite applause follows all these tracks, almost like an afterthought.

"Stagnation", one of their finest ever tracks, immediately dominates the session, the opening 12-strings, the build up to Banks's heavily echoed organ solo, and Gabriel's 'and will I wait forever' section are all Genesis at their best. The ending is different from the album version with some heavy power chords then some more vocals about 'the quest for Gold'. A classic song close to its full potential – with only a few small adjustments to come.

The session ends with an ultra-rare recording of "Looking For Someone", with slightly different lyrics, and at last some forceful drumming from Mayhew. Ant Phillips tries a few lead breaks which sound strangely out of sorts with the whole feel of things, but overall the song points the way to future writing styles and gets quite heavy towards the ending.

"Dusk" was also played at this session but has been sadly lost from the radio archive.

MARCH 11th, 1970
THE ROUNDHOUSE, CHALK FARM, LONDON, UK.

Personnel: PG, TB, MR, AP, JM.

Set List: *Twilight Alehouse (short section only)*

A few brief, but very clear moments are all that have so-far surfaced from this infamous show aired during an American interview with Gabriel. This a fraction of a recording made when the band supported David Bowie at London's legendary Roundhouse.

Genesis played a short set that was filmed in black and white. This film still exists and was even offered to the group for a large amount of money. The footage is silent but the soundtrack must still be in the hands of the makers.

Gabriel's voice certainly sounds very young and some of the lyrics are slightly different to later versions. The snippet is over just as you try to pick out Phillips and Mayhew.

Phillips: 'It's the only proof that I was ever in the band.'

APRIL 10th, 1970

EEL PIE ISLAND HOTEL, LONDON, UK.

Personnel: PG, TB, MR, AP, JM.

Possible Set List: Grandma, Let Us Now Make Love, Little Leaf, Dusk, Stagnation, White Mountain, Twilight Alehouse, Visions Of Angels, I've Been Travelling All Night Long, Going Out To Get You, Shepherd, Looking For Someone, Jamaican Long Boat, Pacidy, The Knife.

An island in the middle of the River Thames, the gear had to be carried over a little bridge, a precious microphone was lost in the water, and they were up against Free who were riding high with "All Right Now" and commanded most of the attention.

Anthony Phillips: 'I had to stand up and move my chair every time someone wanted to go past and have a pee, I had to virtually stop playing.'

Tony Banks: 'I played guitar for the first few numbers and wore gloves, it was so cold."

MARCH 7th, 1971

La FERME, WOLUWE, St LAMBERT, BELGIUM.

Personnel: PG, TB, MR, PC, SH.

Set List: Happy The Man, Stagnation, The Light, Twilight Alehouse, The Musical Box, The Knife, Going Out To Get You.

The band's first overseas gig produces one of the most important recordings from this early stage in their career. A complete show, it features unreleased songs, songs in lyrical and musical metamorphosis, and at this time the only known recorded version of "The Light".

"Happy the Man" is introduced by Gabriel as being about a 'Man who eats his fingernails, probably' and is slightly slower than usual. It has a laidback approach from Collins, who adds a certain swing to proceedings, this feel stays with "Stagnation" which is about people 'with bad breath'.

After several minutes delay and a few attempts at an introduction, that rarest of rare tracks "The Light" finally gets underway. A simple bass intro becomes the verse of "Lilywhite Lilith" with some guitar work that Hackett would later duplicate on *The Lamb*'s version. The rest of the verse is very stop-start prog rock, complete with lengthy jam session where Banks and Hackett get to work out, some nice harmony vocals bring us back to the Lilith section. A unique piece of music, and the more I listen to it, the more un-Genesis-like most of it sounds.

"Twilight Alehouse" is almost an anti-climax after the previous revelation, but this live staple shows the band, especially Banks, in commanding form with his almost Van der Graaf-like organ theatrics at the end.

Gabriel mixes French and English for his intro to "The Musical Box", much to the crowd's amusement. The song itself is perfect Genesis and is easily the most played piece from the Gabriel era. This version is slightly different with some extra music before the 'And the clock' section which is sung twice. There's also more soloing from Banks and less from Hackett who was only two months into his time with the band. Gabriel raises hackles as he screams his way through the closing section that is also slightly different from later versions. Masterful stuff indeed.

Banks ushers in "The Knife" after a long-winded French intro from Gabriel. Rutherford's bass is the driving force here as Hackett wrestles with guitar solos he hasn't quite mastered yet. An unfortunate cut in the recording loses the flute-led middle section, but Hackett seems to be well on top during the metal style thrash ending which is met with enthusiastic applause.

Another very strange number, "Going Out To Get You", is played as an encore, with Gabriel describing it as, 'A very old number about passion.' Banks leads and Hackett all but vanishes on this organ-dominated foot stomper....

... a great end to a very important gig.

MAY 10th, 1971

BBC STUDIO T1, SHEPHERDS BUSH, LONDON, UK, Sounds of the '70s.

Personnel: PG, TB, MR, PC, SH,

Set List: The Musical Box, Stagnation.

An excellent quality two-track session showing "The Musical Box" still in a transitional stage, with a longer middle section which adds to the impact of the band crashing back in. Banks is unusually hesitant on his lead lines here, until the duel with Hackett when things really get going. The studio echo adds an almost church-like sound to the vocals, especially when Gabriel busks his way through the closing section.

The twin guitar intro to "Stagnation" is a Genesis highpoint, with Hackett picking up where Phillips left off with ease. Gabriel makes you hang on his every word no matter how many times the song is played.

This version is more polished than the Nightride session, and is almost identical to the recorded one.

JUNE 19th, 1971

FRIARS CLUB, AYLESBURY, BUCKINGHAMSHIRE, UK.

Personnel: PG, TB, MR, PC, SH,

Possible Set List: Happy The Man, Stagnation, The Fountain Of Salmacis, The Light, Moss, Twilight Alehouse, The Musical Box, The Return Of The Giant Hogweed, The Knife.

Over 700 Genesis freaks packed into the Friars club, which by now was a band stronghold, to witness a stunning performance, the power of which obviously got to the band themselves. Gabriel ended the evening with an impromptu attempt at stage diving, the band went down a storm and everyone left on a high. Gabriel was left on the floor with a broken ankle.

Tony Banks: 'He was just lying there while we all went off, he had gone white and was complaining that he could not get up.'

Mike Rutherford: 'Friars was always a good gig for us.'

2. NURSERY CRYME AND SOME ITALIAN JOBS

With Collins and Hackett now on board, live Genesis is a whole new box of fish; songs like "Salmacis" and a revamped "Musical Box" are added to long-term survivors "The Knife" and "Stagnation".

The band venture abroad and go down a storm in Italy, whose fans had the presence of mind to tape several shows for our pleasure.

The Mellotron and Hammond dominate the band's sound. Hackett makes his mark – but still sits down.

Early versions of "Watcher of the Skies" and "Can Utility and the Coastliners" show up at several pre-*Foxtrot* shows.

By now Gabriel has taken to eyeliner and costume jewellery, and shaves part of his head for the Lincoln Festival.

Charisma begin the infamous 'Six Bob Tours' when several of their acts would jump on the bus and tour the country for the princely sum of six shillings (or 30p in new money). Sometimes Genesis would headline, other times it would be label mates Van der Graaf Generator, or Lindisfarne depending whose home town they were in at the time.

JANUARY 9th, 1972

BBC STUDIO T1, SHEPHERDS BUSH, LONDON.

Personnel: PG, TB, MR, PC, SH.

Set List: Harold The Barrel, Harlequin, The Return Of The Giant Hogweed.

Three songs from their latest album *Nursery Cryme*, make up this excellent session hosted by legendary DJ John Peel.

"Harold" has Gabriel in fine character mood, and works well as a brief interlude from some of the longer pieces, it is well played with some driving piano from Banks, who ends with some sombre piano chords. Rarely performed live and only a handful of recordings having so far showed up, notably on the latter stages of the *Selling England* tour when its big brother "The Battle of Epping Forest" was also bemusing audiences.

By contrast "Harlequin" is classic Genesis in miniature, all shimmering guitars and delicate vocals, proving that not all masterpieces have to be ten minutes long. Even more elusive than "Harold", this is only one of two recorded live outings for this piece.

"Hogweed" charges along with Hackett making some great noises, and Gabriel back in character again, not as wild as some of the later versions, this one still raises the hackles with its explosive ending which always gave "The Knife" a run for its money.

JANUARY 23rd, 1972

CHARLEROI FESTIVAL, PALAIS DES BEAUX ARTS DE CHARLEROI, BELGIUM.

Personnel: PG, TB, MR, PC, SH.

Set List: Happy The Man, Stagnation, The Fountain Of Salmacis, Twilight Alehouse, The Musical Box, The Return Of The Giant Hogweed.

An excellent audience recording of just under 50 minutes sees the band on another foray into Belgium, and reveals a rapid improvement in the overall quality of their musicianship, and the power of the material from *Nursery Cryme.*

The now regular opening pairing of "Happy The Man" and "Stagnation" get things under way, with the latter being beefed up nicely by some powerful contributions from Collins. Gabriel then explains to the crowd about Hermaphrodites, before a particularly powerful "Salmacis" is ushered in by Banks and his classic organ/Mellotron combination. The whole band gel for one of the best early versions yet with the Mellotron dominating proceedings – and remarkably staying in tune.

An old live favourite which never made it onto an album "Twilight

Alehouse", sounds a little disjointed and almost out of place, especially after what has just gone before. Halfway through Rutherford's 12-string and some subtle organ pave the way for Gabriel to remind us that he was no slouch on the flute, then there's the usual heavy-handed ending, all protesting organ and scratching strings.

Normal service is restored with "The Musical Box", whose spoken intro is gradually growing into a Gabriel trademark. This version is almost lazy – the beginning is knocked for six by some booming Rutherford power chords and a neat solo from Hackett wakes everyone up. The song then takes on a very bass-heavy life of its own. Classic stuff.

"Hogweed" thunders along, as it generally did, with some nice drum fills and a great vocal from a manic sounding vocalist who would normally end proceedings by throwing his mike stand away in the general direction of the P.A.

MARCH 2nd, 1972

BBC PARIS STUDIOS, LONDON, UK.

Personnel: PG, TB, MR, PC, SH.

Set List: The Fountain Of Salmacis, The Musical Box, The Return Of The Giant Hogweed.

Back at the BBC for another shortish session, they are introduced as the second half of the evening's concert, and launch straight into a very together sounding "Salmacis", which as usual catches Gabriel out with some of the high notes, and a very dodgy sounding flute, the rest of the band are in great form, especially Hackett, who is well on top of the intricate guitar work. After hearing great versions like this one it's a shame the song soon vanished from the regular set.

The man from the Beeb goes on about hearing the Mellotron for the first time, and is pleased that "The Musical Box" has been committed to wax, then trying even harder to be hip introduces Gabriel as 'our court jester,' who wants to say a few words about it.

Gabriel's story, in a series of funny voices went like this:

"'Henry, Henry, Henry, what's happened to our game of croquet?' cried little Henrietta. Henry found croquet completely irresistible so he rushed out onto the front lawn to join his little sister, just as play was about to commence she raised her croquet mallet into the air, and with one fell swoop she removed little Henry's head, this had the effect of killing him. But two weeks later she was in Henry's old room and she found an old musical box which used to play the tune of "Old King Cole", and when she opened the old musical box and the tune began to ring out, a strange and somewhat familiar pair of green knickerbockers, were mysteriously lowered from the ceiling. Into these Henry was dropped, he'd been given a second round,

always a bit on the randy side Henry found himself a young lady, and he led this lady up the old wooden stairs into the attic to show off his very fine water tank.

The nurse was down stairs however, and she heard strange noises, and rushed up, picked up the musical box, and smashed it into the bearded child destroying both. In the middle of this number we've arranged for a small pair of green satin knicker-bockers to be lowered, from the BBC Paris Studios, into which very casually a naked Eddie Waring will be dropped. This is called "The Musical Box"."

The opening section of this piece is very much in-keeping with the album version, although Collins is more active in the vocal department, the heavy section sees the whole band flying with Hackett again leading the way. Not as powerful as some versions but classic all the same.

For once the BBC sound system has some oft-missed clout, and the whole session has a much fuller sound than some previous visits. Mr. BBC gives the band an introduction then tells us about next week's Deep Purple session, before "Hogweed" marches in with a good bass-filled sound to end this short, but very sweet, session.

MARCH 4th, 1972
TECHNICAL COLLEGE WATFORD, HERTFORDSHIRE,UK.

Personnel: PG, TB, MR, PC, SH.

Set List: Harlequin, Stagnation, The Fountain of Salmacis, Twilight Alehouse, The Musical Box, The Return of the Giant Hogweed, The Knife.

A classic case of a show improving with age, from a slightly fast muddy recording, to a crystal-clear correct speed affair. This has now become one of the most important all-round documents of the pre-*Foxtrot* era. And if that's not enough, it kicks off with a gem of a track, which apart from one BBC session, has not been found on any other live recording.

"Harlequin" almost floats by on a wash of acoustic guitars, the delicate balance between Gabriel and Collins who share the vocals, and the gentle rhythm from Rutherford and Hackett [and possibly Banks], is almost perfect. Just as you are enjoying this piece, it is over. Short and very sweet, it deserved a regular place in the set.

"Stagnation" is preceded by a tale of Monopoly and rubber rope, and a rather long pause, the song itself takes up where "Harlequin" left off, all shimmering 12-strings and that simple but devastating organ solo from Banks. The ending is restrained grandeur, or maybe a try-out for forth-coming epics.

Banks dominates "Salmacis", which was dedicated to the Tesco chain of Supermarkets, Hackett gets out some nice solos, but it is Banks, with the Mellotron/ Hammond combination that runs the show, Gabriel gets excited at the end, with some dramatic cries, as Hackett duplicates the solo from the album.

Gabriel then relates the story of the 'tube train girl', that ended up on the back cover of the first live album. He then admits that it has no relevance to the next song – and "Twilight Alehouse" gets underway. As ever the song gets going once the spooky middle eight kicks in, frantic 12-string, dancing flute and some haunting organ set the scene, before Collins and then Hackett crash in with the power-chord section. Banks then wrestles those detuning noises from his trusty organ and Hackett screams down the fret-board.

"The Musical Box" story is embellished with the news that a naked Patrick Moore will be lowered into a pair of green knickerbockers, above the stage during the song, a strange if somewhat unappealing idea before such a serious song.

The shows ends with the "Hogweed" chasing "The Knife" round the hall at a frightening speed, but I think "The Knife" won.

MARCH 20th/21st, 1972

T.V. STUDIOS, BRUSSELS, BELGIUM.

Personnel: PG, TB, MR, PC, SH.

Set List: *The Fountain Of Salmacis, Twilight Alehouse, The Musical Box, The Return Of The Giant Hogweed.*

Back in Belgium, this time in a TV studio, Genesis run through four biggies from their current set, unfortunately they are not as sharp as usual, perhaps suffering from TV nerves – who knows? But the most important thing is that this film footage of Genesis in colour still exists.

A drab studio set with only minimal lighting sees the band arranged in their usual shambolic way. Banks to the right with his trusty Hammond, battered old electric piano, and a mighty twin-manual Mellotron Mk2, later replaced by the more roadie-friendly single-manual 400 version. Next to Banks, and slightly to the front, is Collins flailing away at his smallish drum kit. Gabriel stands behind Collins, whilst Hackett is pushed to the front and hunches over his guitar, almost looking too scared to be sitting there at all. Rutherford is stage left at the back and dares to stand up for a couple of numbers.

All movement is left to Gabriel whose star quality is instantly apparent, rakishly thin and dressed in black with long unkept hair, he mixes camp aggression and moments of melancholy. He oozes charisma which is just as well, as apart from Collins, the rest look like they wish they were somewhere else.

The music is occasionally rushed, especially "Salmacis" where Gabriel struggles on a few high notes. Even "The Musical Box" lacks its usual magic. Gabriel gets all animated during "Hogweed" and swings his mike stand over his head at the end.

This film shows Gabriel to be a star in the making, Collins to be an excellent drummer, and that they need to sort themselves out a bit on stage, but the shots of the big Mellotron are worth the price of admission alone.

APRIL 9th, 1972

LEM CLUB, VERONA, ITALY.

Personnel: PG, TB, MR, PC, SH.

Set List: Happy The Man, The Fountain of Salmacis (cut), Drum Solo, Twilight Alehouse, Can-Utility & The Coastliners [Rock me Baby], The Musical Box (cut).

So far, the earliest of the Italian shows to appear on tape is not complete but very important. "Happy the Man" kicks things off nicely, a fine if somewhat overlooked song that would have enjoyed a much higher profile had it been an album track.

We join "Salmacis" halfway through, but what we get sounds pretty good with everyone handling the tricky sections with ease. The intro to "Alehouse" is followed by an enforced drum solo due to the all-too-common equipment breakdown. Gabriel informs the audience that Collins was taught by a famous Russian spastic, the solo is a rather uninspired thrash, with a few weird noises thrown in by Hackett.

"Twilight Alehouse" has to contend with a somewhat noisy crowd, most of whom had not seen the band before. The vocals tend to fade in and out, but the overall sound is very good. Hackett and Rutherford combine well during the trippy section, and Collins can't wait to wade in at the end, the song is well-received and normal service is resumed.

Gabriel makes an announcement about the previous day's gig in Trieste being cancelled due to police intervention; he dedicates the next song to the town concerned. He calls it " Rock me Baby" but the band then deliver a stunning early version of "Can-Utility", which has Banks taking over with a sea of Mellotron.

Still in the early stages, the song has the beginning and ending from *Foxtrot,* but a marvellous improvised middle section. They almost get lost towards the end, as if no one wants to take it on, then Banks rushes in with the stabbing organ section, Gabriel throws in some different lyrics, more organ, then the familiar closing chords. Only two known recordings of this extended version have so far been found, both from this first Italian tour.

Only the first verse of "The Musical Box" survives on this recording, which is a shame, as they were in fine form. Another rare instance of

Genesis working out new songs on stage makes this a very important recording from a very good show.

APRIL 14th, 1972
PALASPORT, PAVIA, ITALY.

Personnel: PG, TB, MR, PC, SH.

Set List: Happy the Man, The Fountain of Salmacis, Twilight Alehouse, Can-Utility and the Coastliners (Bye Bye Johnny), The Musical Box, The Return of the Giant Hogweed, The Knife.

A clear but distant audience recording which gives a good indication of the sudden increase in venue size the band was playing in Italy. The whole sound gets a bit muddy when things take off, which on this occasion is most of the show. The band often played an afternoon and an evening show and it is often hard to tell which is which.

"Happy the Man" almost gets lost, but is greeted with warm applause. "Salmacis" is epic and goes down a storm, Banks as usual dominates this piece, and Gabriel is in particularly strong voice. This song improves at each show, but maybe would have had more of an effect near the end of the set.

The echo in the Palasport gives the drums an extra kick, and Gabriel's vocals that little bit more menace. An up-tempo "Alehouse" is more together than before, as if everyone is trying a bit harder. The middle section is very atmospheric, then Collins batters down the door to begin the final onslaught. An early try-out for "Can-Utility" which Gabriel introduces as being a new one called "Bye-bye Johnny", sees things proceed normally until the middle eight, when Banks takes flight with some dramatic extended Mellotron work which totally fills the arena, and is absolutely brilliant. Gabriel attempts to bring the song back, but Banks is off again with more swirling walls of orchestral mayhem. Some improvised drumming leads to the stabbing organ finale, again extended, again brilliant. Gabriel soars, Banks keeps going, while Collins nails the whole thing down. Sadly the tape cuts off before the end, but this stunning version is another rare attempt at something different.

After such an bombardment, things calm down with "The Musical Box", with Gabriel more in character than before, Hackett flies through the first guitar section, but 'Old King Cole' slows things right down, before an almost too fast instrumental section, and a slightly frantic ending gets them some lengthy applause.

Back to normal with a more stable "Giant Hogweed", Collins throws in all sorts of drum fills as Gabriel hits all the right notes with ease. The climax of course is frightening, with a blood curdling scream, and all those heavy chords.

The encore, a thundering, not quite out-of-control "Knife", with barely audible vocals, ends up as a Hackett vs. Banks work out. The result is an honourable tie.

APRIL 15th, 1972
HIT PARADE, LUGO DI ROMAGNA, RAVENNA, ITALY.

Personnel: PG, TB, MR, PC, SH.

Set List: Happy The Man, Stagnation, The Fountain Of Salmacis, Twilight Alehouse, The Musical Box, The Return Of The Giant Hogweed, The Knife, Going Out To Get You.

A complete, and top drawer performance from the opening of "Happy the Man", through to the rare appearance of the "Going Out to Get You" encore. This audience recording is either the first or second show, there are no clues, but it is very clear and has been cleaned up to startling effect.

The atmosphere is light-hearted for "Happy the Man", but dark and mysterious for "Stagnation", this version is as good as any you are likely to hear, Gabriel's flute ghosts across the quiet moments, while Banks lays down a note-perfect organ solo for Collins to arrive on. The proverbial pin can be heard dropping as Gabriel, "Waits forever, beside the silent mirror".

A brief explanation on Hermaphrodites, in English and Italian, precedes a stirring "Salmacis", the organ/Mellotron combination is spot-on, as once again Banks leads the way. The frantic middle section has everyone on their best behaviour, Rutherford and Hackett almost have to be held back in this frantic melée.

Gabriel cries to the gods before Hackett brings "Salmacis" to a close, warm applause and a few ecstatic cries signal approval.

"Twilight Alehouse" keeps the atmosphere going, with the vocals getting a little bit lost during the heavy sections. The organ and guitar combine well on this one, with Hackett offering some nice effects.

Some plaintive vocals send shivers up the spine during the opening of "The Musical Box", Collins sings sweetly, Gabriel is all brooding menace mixed with lost love. Hackett and Rutherford hunched over their guitars deliver the Genesis trademark sound. The first heavy section is slightly restrained but still very powerful, and sets up a perfect entrance for 'Old King Cole', who duly arrives before the band take over for some serious soloing.

After the tension on "The Musical Box", things lighten up for a thrash through "Hogweed", but not before Collins has to replace a drum skin, and Hackett is prompted to play the chord of E Major a few times.

Rutherford does battle with the Weed, using a serious bass sound, as Gabriel cries 'giant hogweed lives'.

"The Knife" and "Going Out To Get You" round off a classic performance. "Going Out" still sounds like the odd man out, but as an encore it goes down a storm, and it's a pity it has not surfaced on more recordings.

APRIL 18th, 1972

PIPER CLUB, ROME, ITALY.

Personnel: PG, TB, MR, PC, SH.

Set List: Happy The Man, Stagnation, The Fountain Of Salmacis, Twilight Alehouse, The Musical Box, The Return Of The Giant Hogweed, The Knife, Going Out To Get You.

Another very good audience recording from this rapidly improving Italian tour. "Happy the Man" is as good as it's ever been, with the Collins/Gabriel vocal partnership adding depth to this brief piece. With the audience being prepared to sit and listen, "Stagnation" is presented in all its glory to very attentive ears, and as usual is one of the highlights of the show. There is a nice bass sound throughout the gig, and this adds to the great contrast between most of the songs.

The set list had by now become pretty well sorted, so "Salmacis" takes its regular place in the running order, the Mellotron gives out the odd squeak and is out-played by a particularly loud organ. Rutherford is well upfront and Hackett turns in a fine closing solo.

"This one tells of a man who is very fond of his drink," introduces "Twilight Alehouse", which gets a bit jerky on the stops and starts, and doesn't quite work. Being sandwiched between "Salmacis" and "The Musical Box" is going to highlight any less-than-brilliant material, but it does have its moments, as in the freeform middle section.

Some loud Mellotron tuning and a funky Collins shuffle/drum improvisation precede a variation on the tale of Henry, which this time involves an eight year-old bambino. Hackett all-but-disappears during the heavy section, which is a shame as the whole band is on blistering form, especially Collins who just can't stop being inventive. Gabriel's 'old man' is masterful, with his demands to be touched being most disturbing.

After such a powerful "Musical Box", the "Hogweed" almost seems cultivated. Again Hackett is missing from the first part of the song, but makes a strong entrance for his solo and the big ending, and boy is it big. "The Knife" and "Going Out" complete the show, with Gabriel only managing a brief Graci, before Banks attacks the organ, great effect that, some nice noodling during the quiet section, before a bass-heavy a slightly messy solo section brings Gabriel back to scream "We have won".

The crowd want more, they of course get "Going Out To Get You", nice song but it just can't follow "The Knife", however chaotic it might be.

Some excellent black-and-white film footage also exists from this show, we get to see the band giving interviews, and some stunning live shots from the club itself with the audience sitting down in front of the group while they cast their spell.

The music is dubbed over the top and does not match up with the footage, but it is still essential viewing.

APRIL 19th, 1972

TEATRO MEDITERRANEO, NAPLES, ITALY.

Personnel: PG, TB, MR, PC, SH.

Set List: Happy The Man, Stagnation, The Fountain Of Salmacis, Twilight Alehouse, The Musical Box, The Return Of The Giant Hogweed, Drum Solo, The Knife.

A poor quality audience recording from the last date on the first Italian tour, one of two shows on the same day with a now familiar set list without any of the earlier surprises is greeted with enthusiastic applause, especially "Stagnation", which receives a sudden outburst during the middle section.

Through the haze of this recording the band is again on top form, a fact that is appreciated by the crowd. Gabriel's attempts at Italian during his stories usually result in shorter and somewhat nervous sounding affairs, however "Salmacis" is given its longest English/Italian intro yet, this of course goes down very well with the noisier than usual audience. The song itself is well-played but somewhat uninspired.

During the intro to "Alehouse", someone very close to the tape recorder requests "Harold the Barrel" – alas Harold was not to make an appearance during this show, but did show up later in the year during their second visit.

For a change "The Musical Box" is guitar-dominated, with Rutherford sounding almost metallic during the instrumental sections, Gabriel is encouraged during the 'She's a lady' section, and of course the applause is the longest so far. The end of "Hogweed" is cut off on this tape, and we land in the middle of a drum solo which is usually reserved for power failures and technical problems. It goes down well and leads straight into "The Knife", which sounds a bit laboured towards the end, the tape finishes prematurely, but it's almost safe to say that the crowd went mad.

JUNE 28th, 1972

TOWN HALL, WATFORD, HERTFORDSHIRE, UK.

Personnel: PG, TB, MR, PC, SH.

Set List: Watcher of the Skies, Stagnation, The Fountain of Salmacis, Happy the Man, Twilight Alehouse, The Musical Box, The Return Of The Giant Hogweed, The Knife.

A good audience recording that includes a comedian making strange noises with his mouth, before the audience are encouraged to give a warm Friars welcome to Genesis. This show was put on by long-time fan and promoter David Stopps as a kind of convention to promote the band and unite Genesis freaks everywhere.

An early outing for "Watcher of the Skies" gets things underway, with Gabriel suggesting that it might appear on their next album. The Mellotron echoes its way around the venue, and in one song totally transforms the whole concept of Genesis live. This is powerful stuff indeed, grabbing full attention from the off, and not two or three songs in as at previous shows."Watcher" has Gabriel back in character, as an alien visitor surveying an empty landscape, with staring eyes and a hint of make-up. This early version has slightly different vocal lines in the verses, with Gabriel seeming a little hesitant in places, but still a majestic sign of things to come.

"Stagnation" is magnificent, especially the rhythm section with Collins as usual running the show. It proves what a good drummer he was, even at this early stage. The equipment breaks down before "Salmacis"; so Gabriel prompts Collins into a one-handed drum solo, and adds some Peter Cook style ad-libs as Phil gets funky. "Salmacis" regains the lost momentum, and although a bit rushed, it draws a great vocal from Gabriel, and Hackett takes a rare short solo at the end.

Collins goes percussion-crazy during "Happy the Man", and even throws in a remark or two during the song itself. There's a triangle joke at the start of "Twilight Alehouse", as Collins and Gabriel almost take over the show.

The start of "The Musical Box" is delayed, and again some of the tension Gabriel has created is lost, although this is a great version. The big ending of "Hogweed", and "The Knife", the latter being the much in demand encore and also preceded by a drum solo, sends a 1000 or so happy fans home clutching their custom made Genesis rosettes, and knowing they have just seen another great, if somewhat technically hampered show from Gabriel, Collins and co.

AUGUST 11th, 1972

READING FESTIVAL, READING, BERKSHIRE, UK.

Personnel: PG, TB, MR, PC, SH.

Set List: The Knife, Twilight Alehouse, Watcher of the Skies, The Musical Box, The Return of the Giant Hogweed.

'Talk amongst yourselves for half an hour,' is how a less-than-happy sounding Collins punctuates the endless tuning noises that begin their set. Gabriel then announces "The Knife" and all is well with the world. A rare opening slot for their usual encore, but it's loud and mostly up-tempo, and at a festival, such crowd pleasers are a good way to get you noticed.

The sound balance is very good for the first song, with plenty of bass, and lots of Hackett who is on blistering form, especially during the tricky end section, the power riffing at the close is swathed in echo, and an aggressive Gabriel is right up in the mix, a great start. "Twilight Alehouse", which according to Gabriel, is about a demented alcoholic, seems to fit the festival atmosphere, perhaps the swirling middle section is him staggering home after a heavy session, the ending is as drunken as usual.

'The next number is about a man from the planet Mars who is now living in Clapham – this is called "Watcher of the Skies".' Gabriel then threatens the crowd with the possibility of a one-handed drum solo, but Banks spares everyone with the arrival of the Mellotron. Some strange harmony vocals during "Watcher" give it a new twist, but musically, this slightly faster version sounds fresh and sharp, and not so laboured as some later performances.

A new variation on the Henry/croquet tale, involving some mucus in a box, and Henry's father, leads nicely into a superbly dramatic "Musical Box", everything is right with this song. Gabriel is first calm then frantic, Hackett is on fire during his solos, and delicate during the verses, Rutherford powers the whole thing along with some thundering bass, and his trademark rhythm guitar, Collins is as inventive as ever, and Banks shows perfect restraint, until those famous organ chords at the end.

Despite cries for "Harold the Barrel", the set is wound up with a rousing "Giant Hogweed", Gabriel dedicates it to all the policemen in the audience, and anyone else if there is anyone else. Gabriel really hams up the vocals on this one, and Collins is filling in everywhere, with endless snare and hi-hat antics, obviously a good time was being had by all. Rutherford even throws in some different bass phasing before the solo section. A great recording for an early outdoors show – very well balanced, and very enjoyable.

AUGUST 20th, 1972
PIPER 2000 CLUB, VIAREGGIO, ITALY. (afternoon show)

Personnel: PG, TB, MR, PC, SH.

Set List: Watcher of the Skies (cut), Can-Utility and the Coastliners, The Fountain of Salmacis, Twilight Alehouse, Get 'em Out by Friday (cut), The Return Of The Giant Hogweed (cut), The Knife (cut), Harold The Barrel.

Only the second half of "Watcher" makes it on to this rapidly improving audience recording, which is a shame, as the enthusiastic reception indicates a good performance. "Can-Utility" is now in the *Foxtrot* format with the wondrous improvisations featured during the first Pavia and Verona gigs unfortunately lost forever, however it is a welcome addition to the set and gives Hackett some nifty soloing at the end, the vocals are almost lost in the mix but everyone else is nicely balanced.

A return to more familiar ground now as "Salmacis" powers in, Gabriel's vocals are back on top, although he does have to contend with a booming bass sound as poor old Hackett all but vanishes once again, an increasingly common occurrence during the older material. Gabriel puts a lot more effort into his vocals on "Salmacis", getting more into character and hitting all the high notes with ease.

Phil Collins and his world-famous triangle are presented at the start of "Alehouse", which is slower than usual, and seems more in-keeping with the newer material of which "Get 'em Out by Friday" is the third number from the *Foxtrot* album. Hackett is very much in evidence as he shares opening honours with Banks and his busy Hammond. Gabriel shines on this great storytelling epic, as villain, victim, and the 'Directors of Genetic Control', he also delivers some delicate flute during the quieter passages.

Unfortunately some heavy tape cuts means the end of "Get 'em Out", almost all of "Hogweed" and some of "The Knife" are lost. "The Knife" we do get is bass-heavy but very well played, and received with very loud applause. "Harold The Barrel" makes a welcome reappearance, this time as an encore with Collins contributing his own brand of cockney backing vocals.

A direct if somewhat shaky ending brings proceedings to a close.

AUGUST 20th, 1972
PIPER 2000 CLUB, VIAREGGIO, ITALY. (evening show)

Personnel: PG, TB, MR, PC, SH.

Set List: Watcher of the Skies, Can-Utility and the Coastliners, The Fountain of Salmacis, Twilight Alehouse, Get 'em Out by Friday, The Musical Box, The Return Of The Giant Hogweed, The Knife.

The second show of the day, from an audience recording that gets better halfway through "Watcher", but is still quite distant and a bit thin on the bass side. "Watcher" and "Can-Utility" make a good opening pairing, both giving the show a lot more power and depth, and shifting the emphasis to a dramatic start rather than the gradual build up of before. It also meant that "Stagnation" and "Happy The Man", vanished from the set, never to return.

The downside of this recording is the almost total absence of dialogue, due to the tapers annoying habit of hitting the pause button after every song, which often results in missed beginnings and doesn't do much for the show's continuity. That aside, "Salmacis" is as stirring as usual with Gabriel sustaining some dramatic notes at the end, and Banks running riot with the organ/ Mellotron combination.

"Alehouse" is most compelling with a dreamy middle section, which is then battered by Hackett and Rutherford who power-chord their way towards a very metal ending. Hackett's leap to the front during the *Foxtrot* numbers is again noticeable on "Get 'em Out" where there are less washes of sound, and more complicated time changes and solo work, which suits his style more and demonstrates his increased input as a writer.

The classical sound of Genesis returns for a magnificent "Musical Box", where Gabriel with his part-shaven head and heavily made-up eyes transfixes the audience until Hackett delivers one of his best-ever lead breaks, giving 'Old King Cole' even more suspense, then everyone storms back in with Banks and Hackett racing through their solos to great effect. The climax of this song is breathtaking with Hackett wringing some extra notes from his guitar, and even the taper leaves a few seconds of applause before hitting the button once again.

The familiar big loud ending follows, with a bouncy "Giant Hogweed" leading straight and uncut into a tearaway "Knife", which like "Alehouse" gives Gabriel some flute practice before all hell breaks loose with a certain lead guitarist who is having a cracking gig, finishing it in fine style.

AUGUST 22nd, 1972

TEATRO ALCIONE, GENOA, ITALY.

Personnel: PG, TB, MR, PC, SH

Set List: *Watcher of the Skies, Can-Utility and the Coastliners, The Fountain of Salmacis, Twilight Alehouse, Seven Stones, The Musical Box, The Return of the Giant Hogweed, The Knife.*

One of the best early audience recordings, that sees the band in sparkling form and not afraid to throw in the odd rarity, in a complete and well-appreciated performance. "Watcher" steams in this time, a good upbeat rendition with plenty of punch and loads of drums, some versions tended to be a bit ropey, but not this one.

"Can-Utility" is fast becoming a live highlight, with the sweeping 12-string/Mellotron section showing that it's not all just about power-chords, Hackett having all sorts of fun during his cunningly complicated solo. Gabriel's vocal gets lost at the end as the bass and organ race for the tape. A rather polite audience greet "Salmacis" with less-than-usual enthusiasm, which is strange as the band are on such good form and deliver a very moving performance and even Hackett gets a fair crack of the whip with a stunning solo at the end.

As with several of the Italian shows there are pauses in the recording between the songs – it seems the taper was keen not to run out of tape, but the loss of continuity is annoying and it occasionally causes debate over the authenticity of some set lists.

"Alehouse" gets very heavy especially during the middle section when Collins beats seven shades out of his kit and Banks detunes the Hammond which receives the biggest cheer so far. Another Italian rarity next – the only known recorded version of "Seven Stones", played with controlled restraint, you often feel it is about to explode. Then things calm down and Banks winds things up with that superb Mellotron/organ coda. The appearance of "Seven Stones" is a rare breath of fresh air amongst the more familiar longer numbers and would have been welcomed back anytime.

An old favourite follows the one-off, as Gabriel stays in character for the opening of the "The Musical Box" – a booming version that begins to get slightly out of control with the ever-increasing bass sound overriding a lot of the guitar work.

The gig winds up with a dangerous "Hogweed" with Gabriel in full cry and that foundation-shaking ending literally shaking the foundations. "The Knife" is the subject of some debate as it sounds like it was recorded somewhere else and has probably been added on to this recording to make up the show – maybe the taper left the gig before the ending. Either way it is one of the best Italian shows with a rarity thrown in for good measure.

3. FOXTROT, THE RAINBOW TO READING

With the band almost constantly on the road it was amazing they ever managed to record any albums at all. But with the arrival of *Foxtrot* they introduced their all-time classic track "Supper's Ready" which added another twenty minutes to the set all by itself. The show now always opened with the unique Mellotron fanfare that paved the way for "Watcher of the Skies", this meant an end to the acoustic numbers that used to start the set, as everything got louder and stage presentation became more important.

Gabriel's pre-song rambles were now lasting well past tuning up time and the rest of the band often had to wait for him to finish before they could start the next piece.

By now, dresses and animal heads feature in Gabriel's wardrobe and the band make front-page news and a bit more money. They play a blinding set at the Rainbow Theatre in London, where the UV lights and the gauze sails add to the atmosphere. Likewise the 'Flower Mask' and the 'Red Box Hat' make a dramatic appearance for the first time. They wind up the tour at the Reading Festival.

SEPTEMBER 19th, 1972
MARQUEE CLUB, LONDON, UK.

Personnel: PG, TB, MR, PC, SH.

Set List: Watcher of the Skies, Can-Utility and the Coastliners, The Musical Box (cut), The Return of the Giant Hogweed (cut), The Knife.

The intimate atmosphere of the legendary Marquee club must have seemed somewhat disappointing after the large Italian venues they had just played. Nevertheless this good audience recording features all sorts of strange noises during "Watcher". The sound quality suddenly improves during an almost funky "Can-Utility", which includes a fine Hackett solo and shows the band in great form with everyone getting a fair crack of the whip. Once again the applause and Gabriel's stories have been edited out, greatly reducing the whole feel of the show.

"The Musical Box" is as strong as ever, with the solo sections being particularly aggressive, the vocals tend to drift in and out depending on what Gabriel was up to at that moment. The song being cut, butchers the dramatic finale, then "Hogweed" already started and suffering the same aural affliction as "Watcher" is thrust into the spotlight. Unlike several of the wild Italian versions, this one is controlled but dangerous at the same time, and a good excuse for Gabriel to wave his mike stand about and psyche himself up for "The Knife", which as usual closes the show. It rocks like crazy, and of course is cut off just after the final chord, so we'll have to imagine that the crowd went mad.

As this recording was cut up to fit on a single vinyl LP, the tracklisting might not be complete, especially as "Get 'em Out by Friday" and "Twilight Alehouse" are missing from the setlist.

SEPTEMBER 25th, 1972
BBC STUDIOS, SHEPHERDS BUSH, LONDON UK.

Personnel: PG, TB, MR, PC, SH.

Set List: Twilight Alehouse, Get 'em Out by Friday, Watcher of the Skies.

Broadcast on John Peel's *Sound of the '70s* show on the 7th of November, this 3-track session has the band turning in a highly professional, if somewhat subdued [this was the BBC] performances of regulars from their live repertoire.

"Twilight Alehouse" is very low-key, even the chaotic ending is trouble-free with everyone behaving themselves and hitting all the right notes. Collins counts in "Get 'em Out by Friday", and sets the tone for the whole song with a great display of inventive drumming. Hackett and especially Banks are kept busy during this tricky number, which like "Alehouse" and "The Knife", has a calming middle section before a rather loud finish. Gabriel has fun doing the characters, and even keeps his tambourine in time.

"Watcher" again has Collins in fine form, with lots of percussive interjections that add sparkle to this rather rigid piece. As with most sessions there is a serious lack of power on some of the dramatic moments, with Banks being the victim in the case of "Watcher".

Overall a well-played session if lacking a lot of the excitement and danger of a truly live gig.

SEPTEMBER 28th, 1972
NATIONAL STADIUM, DUBLIN, EIRE.

Personnel: PG, TB, MR, PC, SH.

Set List: Watcher of the Skies, Can-Utility and the Coastliners, Get 'em Out by Friday, The Musical Box, The Return of the Giant Hogweed.

Three days after their last BBC session, the band played a one-off gig in Dublin, before continuing their ever growing schedule of small halls and Top Rank clubs up and down the UK.

This slightly muffled audience recording captures the band in great form, and actually kicks off with Gabriel introducing "Watcher" instead of the usual grand entrance. Collins is driving this show, his drumming on both "Watcher" and "Can-Utility" is inspired, in fact this "Can-Utility" is the most upbeat yet, and swings through the guitar solo.

An almost embarrassing silence follows a Gabriel joke, then "Get 'em Out" crashes in as if to say, 'Ignore that, listen to this.' This is truly a band song, Gabriel takes on the role-playing with relish, Rutherford and Collins play light and dark with the rhythm, Banks stabs, then goes to church on the Hammond, and Hackett is riffing one minute and gone the next.

This version of "The Musical Box" is arguably the most important the band will ever play. Still the set's masterpiece it was further enhanced by the singer leaving the stage, and returning wearing his wife's red dress and the infamous fox's head for what must have been a stunning finale. A great surprise to both audience and the band who had no idea this was going to happen.

One thing that did happen was front-page coverage from the music press, a masterstroke by Gabriel and an idea that would soon dominate each Genesis show. After another lengthy and atmosphere-draining pause, Gabriel screams at the top of his voice the arrival of "The Hogweed", almost as if he is annoyed at how long it keeps taking for the others to tune-up. They eventually deliver a good but uninspired performance, as if the previous song's antics had knocked them all for six.

A very special show, if only for Gabriel's leap into the world of theatre. The result was a lot more people would now be aware of Genesis.

SEPTEMBER 30th, 1972

KENNINGTON OVAL, LONDON, UK.

Personnel: PG, TB, MR, PC, SH.

Set List: The Knife, The Fountain of Salmacis, Get 'em Out by Friday, Watcher of the Skies, The Musical Box, The Return of the Giant Hogweed.

'We'd like to start things off with a little Latin American dance number,' is how their set for this open air concert for the *Melody Maker* poll winner's party kicks off. "The Knife", chosen I suspect to get everybody's attention does just that, with some thunderous Hammond from Banks and plenty of booming bass and screeching guitar. The usual encore makes a great set opener.

A clear and very loud recording captures Genesis in full flight, the restless crowd obviously welcome this different beginning, and are soon telling each other to sit down. "Salmacis" is as majestic as ever, although some of its atmosphere is lost in the great outdoors.

Gabriel precedes "Get 'em Out by Friday" with the line, 'This concerns the fate of two old ladies from Islington.' The number does work outdoors, but has Gabriel skimping on his characters. During the quiet section an annoying humming noise can be heard, but this does not detract from the very high standard of playing, Collins gets in some Bad Company style beats at the end.

There's a long pause before "Watcher", which is dedicated to a large shiny gentleman, or the great god Coca-Cola. Banks is spot-on with his intro, which no doubt had a few fans looking skywards. Rutherford hammers the bass, and Gabriel makes his entrance, shiny gentleman indeed.

The slight change in the running order works well, and is something they should have tried more often. "Watcher" sounds good in the middle of the set, but this occasion was a one-off, and it immediately found its way back as the opening number, where it would stay until *The Lamb* tour.

Other bands at this show included ELP, Focus, and Wishbone Ash. So the rock/progressive fraternity were presumably well pleased. After a storming "Musical Box", the set winds up with "Hogweed" as Gabriel announces 'This is the only number we do which stars Christopher Lee and Vincent Price.'

A touch of Hammer Horror to close this monster of a gig.

OCTOBER 4th, 1972

MUSIC HALL, ABERDEEN, UK.

Personnel: PG, TB, MR, PC, SH.

Set List: Watcher of the Skies, Get 'em Out by Friday, The Musical Box, The Return of the Giant Hogweed.

The show gets off to a slow start, in fact Gabriel and Collins have to do their whistling one-armed drummer routine for about five minutes, until Banks finally kicks the Mellotron into life for the intro to "Watcher". The grand opening effect has been lost by this time, and the performance itself is good, if not inspired. Banks can be heard tuning the Mellotron flutes as Gabriel introduces "Get 'em Out", another small delay kills any atmosphere he has managed to build up, but a fine version of this mini-epic turns things around. The flute tuning worked nicely, as Banks complements Gabriel's playing during the 'genetic control' section, and the song reaches a very satisfying conclusion.

This rather muddy recording is taken from a vinyl pressing, as the appropriate noises can now be heard. So next up is a very average "Musical Box", the vocals are fine, but everyone else sounds rushed, as if they know this is not the best show they have ever done. The "Hogweed" is introduced as "Coming to you courtesy of the House of Hammer," and Gabriel screams out its name in an almost Python-esque manner.

Not the most satisfying of shows, and one, which again highlighted the technical problems that in those days could often scupper a gig.

OCTOBER 11th, 1972

ST. GEORGES HALL, BRADFORD, UK.

Personnel: PG, TB, MR, PC, SH.

Set List: Watcher of the Skies, Get 'Em out by Friday, The Musical Box, The Return of the Giant Hogweed.

An excellent recording from a rare first-generation tape, very well balanced and very well played.

This is a particularly good version of "Watcher", with the vocals being nice and high in the mix, and the Rutherford/Collins engine room driving things along at a fair old pace.

A plug for *Foxtrot* precedes a powerful "Get 'em Out by Friday", with Banks stabbing at the organ and Gabriel giving a fine performance as 'genetic control', only Hackett is lost in the scrum. No surprises there then. A superb Gabriel story for "The Musical Box", is as follows:

'Uncle Bill finally plucked up enough courage to buy himself a dirty magazine, he rushed home with the magazine hidden under his raincoat. As soon as he got

home he slammed the front door, rushed up the stairs and locked the bathroom door. While he was turning over the pages he noticed the strange effect it was having on his head, his hair was moving up, slowly into a vertical position.

"Oh dear," thought Uncle Bill, "what on earth shall I do with my hair standing on end?" So he went down to the kitchen and made himself a cup of tea. He looked very sad, so he pulled a pussy onto his lap, and began to stroke it. As soon as his hand touched the pussy, his hair somehow sank to a normal position.

Well, six weeks later there was a mess on the kitchen floor, and there were kittens all over the place, they looked much like any other kittens except they all had Uncle Bill's face. Little sphinxes he called them, and he gathered them all together in a nice white, clean white bowl, put them inside a Woolies plastic bag, and dropped them at the bottom of the river. Then he went back, ate his cornflakes, and pulled out the musical box, which is the title of this next song.'

An almost ethereal version follows with Gabriel sounding dreamlike during the quieter moments. Hackett makes a welcome, if still distant entrance, and has his usual duel with Banks, which this time he loses.

Gabriel announces the arrival of the "Hogweed", much to the obvious relief of one excitable fan. In keeping with the overall performance it is a fine muscular effort, with Gabriel trying to scare everyone to death, with this tale of the troublesome plants.

The end sequence is room-shakingly loud and most definitely one of their finest endings. Great stuff indeed.

OCTOBER 29th, 1972

ODEON THEATRE LEWISHAM, LONDON, UK.

Personnel: PG, TB, MR, PC, SH.

Set List: Watcher of the Skies, Twilight Alehouse, Get 'em Out by Friday, The Musical Box, The Return of the Giant Hogweed, The Knife.

The show starts with the taper and his friends being told by a usherette that they are in the wrong seats, and that she is only doing her job, voices are raised, Gabriel introduces "Watcher", the taper gets a seat, and the usherette thankfully moves away.

A workmanlike "Watcher" sees Collins shadowing Gabriel on the vocals, while a somewhat muddy sounding organ stabs away. The song is well-received, and is obviously a crowd favourite. The Phil Collins triangle joke is wheeled out again before "Twilight Alehouse", and although the tape as a whole is slightly muffled, this classic piece of theatre still sounds like Genesis of old, in a strange dreamy middle section kind of way. The triangle and some nice flute both make appearances as the piece crashes to its end.

Bang up to date with "Get 'em Out..." Hackett makes an audible contribution at last with some trademark refrains, and Banks again conjures some flowing flutes from his Mellotron box of tricks, adding a somewhat classical flavour to this most Genesis of songs.

The dirty mag story is repeated for "The Musical Box", this time Uncle Henry is the culprit, but the whole thing sounds rushed and loses its usual Gabriel humour. The song itself is wonderfully executed, with Rutherford's 12-string and the vocal backing from Collins being at the forefront. Banks and Hackett battle it out during the solo section, with Hackett just edging it.

The "Hogweed" is more controlled than usual, and is better for it. The organ is more effective, and Hackett's embellishments can be heard, not lost as in the usual charge. The 'giant hogweed lives,' cry heralds the titanic ending with Mellotron power-chords shaking the Odeon to its foundations. Long but somewhat reserved applause is greeted by a reminder to get tickets for their next gig, before the 'one more from Genesis' cry goes up. "The Knife" on this tape sounds like it's from another gig, which is a shame, especially as it's a cracking version

NOVEMBER 18th, 1972

IMPERIAL COLLEGE, LONDON, UK.

Personnel: PG, TB, MR, PC, SH.

Set List: Watcher of the Skies, The Musical Box, Get 'em Out by Friday, Supper's Ready, The Return of the Giant Hogweed, The Knife.

'We'd like to rattle off in our usual manner, with a number called "Watcher of the Skies",' is how Gabriel begins this excellent recording. "Watcher" kicks in almost at once, with no mechanical demons causing the usual delays. The sound balance favours Rutherford and Hackett, the latter's guitar being very dramatic. This is most apparent in "The Musical Box", where Banks is blown away by the twin guitar attack.

Gabriel's vocals are full of expression at this show, the depth during the 'And the nurse will tell you lies' line from "Musical Box", is plaintive and sinister at the same time, whereas the screaming 'Touch me' section is desperation at its most extreme. The dirty mag story is used again, this time with everything being dirty, much to the crowd's amusement, a light-hearted tale before such a sad one.

A rather plodding "Get 'em Out", follows with Rutherford almost throwing in some Dr Who patterns, and the rhythm section in general being a little bit slow. Already requested several times, the next number is the newly-added epic "Supper's Ready". The big one from *Foxtrot*, and one of the greatest Progressive Rock songs ever written. Gabriel would soon develop an intro story of comparatively epic proportions, but for this early performance he informs the excited audience, that the song was, 'Inspired by a shout across from the opposite block of flats.'

A hideous bass note booms out as the delicate guitar/vocal of the opening verses transforms the whole gig onto a different plane. The grandeur of this piece is unlike anything they had done before, and over the next year-and-a-half it would become the focal point of every gig it was played at.

There are a few missed notes here and there, the odd vocal lapse, and some of the sections hadn't quite jelled together yet, but for such a difficult piece, the whole band, especially Gabriel, do a remarkable job. No "Supper's Ready" can be reviewed without mention of the astonishing finale. After the pastoral flute section at the end of 'Willow Farm', the band produce the finest five minutes of their entire career, the relentless pounding rhythm, the endless organ solo, and Gabriel's spine-tingling vocals. This version ends in a more traditional style, the album fadeout will be adopted later.

The "Hogweed" at last gets a mini build-up as Gabriel reports of the Giant plant surrounding the country ready for its return. Hackett shines here, his stuttering riffing leads into a fine solo, which goes a bit bonkers near the end, perhaps a Hogweed....

A manic crowd demand an encore, they of course scream for, and get "The Knife", even though there is a lone cry for "Salmacis". The vocals all but disappear during this slightly restrained romp, which again sees Hackett and Rutherford running the show.

JANUARY 10th, 1973

BATACLAN CLUB, PARIS, FRANCE.

Personnel: PG, TB, MR, PC, SH.

Set List: The Musical Box (cut), Supper's Ready (cut), The Return of the Giant Hogweed (cut), The Knife (cut).

This French TV broadcast from the Bataclan Club is a vital document from an important phase in the band's career. A mixture of live footage and backstage interviews, [dubbed over in French] it is an extremely good piece of film from a transitional era. Most importantly it gives a clear indication as to Gabriel's ideas for the band's visual presentation.

We join "The Musical Box" at the first heavy section, Gabriel furiously attacking a tambourine, wearing a black cat-suit with a heavily jewelled collar, his long hair and eye make-up give him a strange, somewhat feminine look. The rest of the band look painfully '70s, although Collins is wearing shorts and is quite animated behind his kit.

The camera pans slowly around behind Collins and Banks just as the 'She's a lady' section begins, both provide backing vocals to this sequence,

Gabriel resplendent in red dress and fox's head is now in shot, and the effect is quite stunning, as the band kick in during the 'Touch me's' he performs a strange on the spot dance and his voice half breaks with emotion, bringing the song to a chilling climax.

Gabriel stands, arms folded, looking so different from the rest of the band. "Supper's Ready" begins, the camera again pans around the group as the trio of acoustic guitars accompany the opening verses. A nice cross stage shot from behind Banks shows a seated Hackett intent on his playing while the singer lulls the audience. The song progresses nicely until an unfortunate edit takes us from 'The guaranteed eternal...' section, to the last few lines, where a raw-voiced Gabriel now looks like he is covered in flour, as he slowly raises the mic stand aloft.

A rampant "Hogweed" also suffers a painful edit, but everyone lets their hair down, Rutherford even stands up for this one. Gabriel now resplendent in a shiny silver outfit careers across the stage waving the mic stand over his head during the power chord ending. Genesis rock out, the crowd are on their feet, and Gabriel continues to steal the show.

"The Knife" commences from the dreamy middle eight. Hackett, sporting some mighty flares, is also standing now as they work their way to the heavy metal ending. Gabriel pretends his mic stand is a rifle complete with bayonet, and lunges at the front row. Collins with a whistle in his mouth, and Hackett with those flares, both shine during this frantic climax.

The song ends with Gabriel hurling his makeshift weapon into the backline, and stalking off stage, a few moments later the rest follow, though in a more sedate manner.

The fox's head, the red dress, the mock violence, are lasting impressions from this film. All come from Gabriel, who single-handedly was taking their live performance to a different level, a point not lost on the rest of the band. If only the fans knew what was just around the corner.

JANUARY 14th, 1973
FESTHALLE, FRANKFURT TV, GERMANY.

Personnel: PG, TB, MR, PC, SH.

Set List: Watcher of the Skies, The Musical Box.

A rather stiff-sounding German announcer introduces the band for this two-track TV recording. Gabriel just has time to practice his German with the song intro, before Banks gets things underway with "Watcher".

The excellent sound quality is matched by their performance, though not as passionate as some recent versions, the song is delivered with consummate ease. Gabriel seems to be holding back on his vocals, and even Collins isn't his usual all-guns-blazing self.

"The Musical Box" gets a very brief introduction, then Rutherford hits that most famous of Genesis chords. The tempo is back up to speed and Hackett flies through his first solo break. In fact it is the instrumental sections that shine here – while Gabriel is off stage the band catch fire. All the emotions return as Gabriel pleads to be touched, whether it was fox's head or old man mask, I'm not sure he'd get many takers.

JANUARY 15th, 1973

STADHALLE, HEIDELBURG, GERMANY.

Personnel: PG, TB, MR, PC, SH.

Set List: Watcher of the Skies, Twilight Alehouse, Get 'em out by Friday, The Musical Box, The Return of the Giant Hogweed.

The show is built up by the German announcer who mentions *Foxtrot*, and gets wild applause when he introduces the band. Gabriel takes over, plugs the album and "Watcher" and then, nothing happens. Equipment failure, and endless tuning problems seem to be an unfortunate part of many Genesis shows.

Banks eventually gets things underway with a very loud Mellotron fanfare, whereas the organ and Gabriel himself seem rather distant. The song rattles along at a fair old pace, and is a good if not inspired version.

The prowess of Collins and his triangle playing are the source of Gabriel's intro for "Alehouse", but it's the drummer's constant improvisation on this ancient piece that grabs the attention, lots of percussive fills and aggressive tom rolls show a musician not about to sit back and play it by the book.

The middle section is again a highlight, Hackett plucks, Collins uses every cymbal, then powers in for the manic section. The organ is back up front for the ending, as the oldest song in the set crashes to a halt.

Another lengthy pause, some syncopated hi-hat and a seemingly annoyed Gabriel precede "Get 'em Out by Friday". This seems to get the band going, as the performance is the strongest of the night so far. The audience are very quiet during the 'genetic control' build up, but show their appreciation at the song's conclusion.

A simple croquet story brings on a powerful "Musical Box", all raw motion, light and most definitely dark. The echo in the arena adds to the atmosphere, as Collins and Gabriel blend their contrasting vocal talents.

The flute is the perfect instrument for this classical piece, and Gabriel's haunting lines weave amongst Rutherford's 12-string, creating the

Victorian feel *Nursery Crymes* is known for. Hackett and Banks pile on the volume and Collins joins in, while Gabriel gets changed.

A manic scream chases in the "Hogweed", which seems to have attacked Gabriel's mic, as his vocals are so far down in the mix, that some lines are almost lost. He also seems to have cocked up some of the lines, a strange end to a somewhat frustrating recording. "Supper's Ready" and "The Knife" might have been played, but they did not make this tape.

JANUARY 20th, 1973

PALASPORT, REGGIO EMILIA, ITALY.

Personnel: PG, TB, MR, PC, SH.

Set List: Watcher of the Skies, The Musical Box, The Fountain of Salmacis, Get 'em Out by Friday, Supper's Ready, The Return of the Giant Hogweed, The Knife.

The first date of a short three-show Italian tour, saw Reggio play host to a Charisma Festival, with Genesis being joined by Peter Hammill, Lindisfarne, and Capability Brown. 10,000 fans are treated to a fine selection of UK acts. This distant, and slightly muffled audience recording, captures the band in fine fettle, in front of a very enthusiastic crowd.

"Watcher" raises the roof, although the vocals are a bit too distant on this tape, but the image of Gabriel appearing before this manic crowd, while the Mellotron rattles the rafters is a mighty powerful one.

An Italian introduction for "The Musical Box" is another example of Gabriel making the effort to communicate his weird and wonderful stories to as many people as possible. All this attention is not lost on the ever more appreciative fans.

The band canter through the first half of the song, with Hackett and Banks in control, the sound has improved somewhat so the 'She's a lady' section is a lot more defined, and Gabriel's appearance in the fox's head sets many tongues wagging.

A welcome return for "Salmacis", always an Italian favourite, keeps the momentum going. Lots of heavy bass lines and a very strong vocal, turn the clock back nicely. 'Two old ladies get shifted out by a man who has plenty of money and plenty of houses,' is the intro used for a pounding "Get 'em Out by Friday". Gabriel goes straight into caricature, which is where he'll remain for most of the gig. The rigid structure of "Friday" is a stark contrast to the swirling chords of "Salmacis", not easy bedfellows, but a great example of their development, and both classic Genesis.

The first Italian performance of "Supper's Ready" is delayed by some last-minute Mellotron tuning. It finally gets underway, and totally dominates the set, the sheer size of this piece, and its light and dark highs and lows, is breathtaking. From the calm of 'How dare I be so beautiful,' to the apocalyptic climax that is '666' is quite staggering. The second half of "Supper's Ready" has some background noise on this recording, which could be on the tape, or in the arena. It does somewhat detract from the enjoyment of the song, but obviously not the crowd's, who applaud with their customary enthusiasm.

The background noise can now be identified as Van Der Graaf Generator, very strange.

"Hogweed" and "The Knife" round things off in their loud, but not as devastating as usual way, even Gabriel pretending to bayonet the crowd with his mic stand at the end of "The Knife", could never follow "Supper's Ready".

JANUARY 21st, 1973

PALASPORT, ROME, ITALY.

Personnel: PG, TB, MR, PC, SH.

Set List: Watcher of the Skies, The Musical Box, The Fountain of Salmacis, Supper's Ready, The Return of the Giant Hogweed, The Knife.

A clear audience recording, from the first of two nights at the Palasport. The 18,000 Genesis fans packed into this cavernous arena are treated to a vintage show from a band in sparkling form.

"Watcher" sets the scene, all dramatic Mellotron and staccato chords. Gabriel gets a cheer and the sound improves as the song progresses. It is a lot sharper by the time a galloping "Musical Box" takes the crowd by storm. Hackett is flying on this version, his solo work is faultless, as he speeds through the middle section.

An Italian intro for "Salmacis" is warmly received, and the song itself echoes around the arena adding to the splendour of the piece. As always Banks takes the honours here, although this recording also highlights some powerful and inventive bass playing from Mr Rutherford.

"Salmacis" improves with age, and along with "The Musical Box" is most certainly one of their greatest songs. The solo organ sounds cathedral-like, and the sustained vocal at the end is very moving.

Mr Phil Collins and his ding-a-ling are given a round of applause just before "Supper's Ready", which is still without a Gabriel story.

The acoustics of the arena take this epic piece of music to new heights from the crystal-clear 12-strings on 'Lover's Leap' to the madness of 'Willow Farm'. As for the 'Apocalypse', that's almost what it sounds like, there must have been a lot of stunned Italians at the end of this gig.

Gabriel shuffles to the front of the stage screaming '666'. Even though he misses his cue at this most dramatic of moments, the band throw in a couple of spare bars so he can catch up, you can hardly hear the join, and the tension is great.

The song ends with the big finale-style Hackett-going-crazy bit. The applause is annoyingly cut after only a few seconds, and as you catch your breath, the "Hogweed" pops up and grabs you by the throat, or that's what Gabriel would like you to believe.

"Hogweed" triumphs in a wall-shaking cacophony, with lots of heavy bass chords and snare fills.

Gabriel screams his way through an almost out-of-control "Knife", and that man Hackett gets so excited he probably stands up.

A stunning example of Genesis live.

FEBRUARY 9th, 1973

RAINBOW THEATRE, LONDON, UK.

Personnel: PG, TB, MR, PC, SH.

Set List: Watcher of the Skies, The Musical Box, Get 'em Out by Friday, Supper's Ready, The Return of the Giant Hogweed, The Knife (cut), The Fountain of Salmacis (not recorded).

A slightly muddy audience recording documents this very important headline show at London's mighty Rainbow Theatre. After the success of the big Italian gigs, a triumphant band deliver a blistering set full of charged emotion and new costumes.

Gabriel resplendent in batwings and cloak, adds a certain menace to a majestic "Watcher of the Skies", his gradual appearance during the Mellotron fanfare adds to the tension the lengthy build up usually creates. Collins and Rutherford pound out the beat, while Banks stabs the Hammond into life.

This show also saw the first use of the infamous gauze sails which were hung in front of the backline, and became almost invisible under ultra violet light, this added to the atmosphere and helped focus even more attention on Gabriel and his ever-expanding wardrobe. "The Musical Box", and "Get 'em Out by Friday", thunder by in grand style, "Get 'em Out" is now obviously a live favourite judging by the cheer that goes up when Gabriel does his introduction.

But the star of this show is of course the epic "Supper's Ready". Unfortunately Gabriel's story is cut from this tape, and the song gets underway with that most un-Genesis of beginnings, as far from "Watcher" or "Salmacis" as you could possibly get. 'Lover's Leap' leads gently into 'The Guaranteed Eternal Sanctuary Man' section, then things take off with Hackett's stunning solo at the end of 'Ikhanaton and Itsacon', Gabriel is spellbinding during 'How Dare I...' and positively manic for "Willow Farm".

The flower mask is now in use, and as he silly walks across the stage dressed like a giant flower [large plants again] most of the crowd and some of the band must have wondered what was going on. The absolutely staggering 'Apocalypse in 9/8' section must still rank as a pinnacle in the history of progressive rock, and this version is no exception. After spitting out his Magog imagery, Gabriel leaves the stage for Banks to weave his spell, poor old Hackett is out in the cold as the Collins/Rutherford machine lay the foundation for Banks and *that* solo. If that's not enough Gabriel reappears dressed in the Red Box headgear and black cloak to scare the shit out of everyone.

The "Hogweed" arrives unannounced and proceeds to flatten anyone in its path, played with controlled aggression it explodes at the end, and lets Hackett lay down a dirty, if somewhat late-sounding solo.

This pivotal show is blessed with two encores, "The Knife" [beginning only on this tape], and a recall for "Salmacis" which sadly is missing altogether.

FEBRUARY 16th, 1973

GREEN'S PLAYHOUSE, GLASGOW, UK.

Personnel: PG, TB, MR, PC, SH.

Set List: Watcher of the Skies, The Musical Box, Get 'em Out by Friday, Supper's Ready (cut), The Return of the Giant Hogweed.

A raucous crowd get very excited at the band's arrival on stage, and go nuts when "Watcher" finally gets going. This well-balanced if slightly fuzzy audience recording is another fine example of the manic fanbase the band had acquired, and is reminiscent of the adulation they had been receiving in Italy.

"Watcher" is uptempo, with a fine vocal from Gabriel, and some aggressive snare from Collins. The Mellotron is in tune and all-powerful, a fact not missed by the reception the song receives. A little syncopated cymbal work from Collins, and some sarcasm from Gabriel, fills in the time during another keyboard breakdown. The Russian spastic joke, and a run through the whole drum kit, develops into a full-blooded drum solo, while the Hammond is shocked back to life.

"The Musical Box" is credited to Donny Osmond, and begins at last, immediately the mood changes and things get darker. This song never fails to impress, the brooding guitar lines, and the haunting flute almost draw you into the strange world of Henry, and all things dark and mysterious. This version does just that, with the first power chords coming as light relief, but they instantly grab you by the throat and remind you who Steve Hackett really is. The ending is as hair-raising as ever and almost brings the house down.

"Get 'em Out" as usual brings Hackett into the spotlight with some masterful playing, Gabriel of course steals it with his character range, and some sublime flute lines.

The Old Michael story sets things up nicely for "Supper's Ready", which of course raises the roof clean off. Collins turns in some fine vocals on the 'How Dare I' section, and some powerful beats on the 'Guaranteed Eternal Sanctuary Man'. Hackett drowns out Banks and Gabriel for the start of 'Ikhnaton', but the soundman manages to get them back in time for the 'foe to meet their fate'.

The flower gets a laugh, and then things get serious. "Magog" is hit with some dodgy bass noises, and the vocals fade a bit. A speedy '9/8' makes Banks earn his keep, he does so with ease although the organ does get a bit lost in the mix, and goes a bit astray before the big run up the keyboard. Gabriel's arrival is greeted by the crowd, as he sways towards the front of the stage in the red box and cloak get-up. Sadly the ending is cut from this performance.

The "Hogweed" enters and keeps the tension going, the vocals occasionally get lost, but everyone knows the words by now. Hackett turns in fabulous solo, and Gabriel calls the large weed home. A great show, shame about the cuts.

FEB 17th, 1973

CITY HALL, SHEFFIELD, UK.

Personnel: PG, TB, MR, PC, SH.

Set List: Watcher Of The Skies, The Musical Box, Get 'em Out by Friday, Supper's Ready, The Return of the Giant Hogweed, The Knife.

Another muddy audience recording sees things get underway with a powerful, if somewhat lifeless "Watcher". It gets a good reaction but is almost a touch slow. Perhaps this song was due for a rest as the opening number, it is a classic case of the visual effect as opposed the pure musical side.

"The Musical Box" gets through one verse, then grinds to a halt due to a power failure. Being used to such things, Gabriel at once informs the crowd that the album version is longer. Once up and running again "The Musical Box" restores all the lost momentum and then some. Classic song, great performance. Hackett is inspired, and his soloing is razor sharp.

Some unfortunate hiss spoils the quiet passages, but seems to drop out when things get going again.

'This next song is about a Mr John Pebble,' is how "Get 'em Out" is introduced, an established live favourite, it's different sections make it a mini-version of "Supper's Ready", which just happens to be next.

Calls for "Hogweed", are answered with the Old Michael story, which includes the pet shop, worms, and a snatch of Jerusalem boogie. Then that microcosm of all that is Genesis, the 'Lover's Leap' section, which, even with all the tape hiss, is spellbinding. Collins kicks in 'The Sanctuary Man', and Gabriel is a God once more. The quality of any "Supper's Ready" can always be measured by the '9/8' section, this one has Rutherford and Hackett laying down an almost groove-like rhythm for Banks to attack, Collins of course does the business, whilst Gabriel nips backstage for his big hat.

'666' is etched on the foreheads of all who are there. He spits out the marrow from all backbones, and generally sends chills down every spine. That's OK then.

"Hogweed" and "The Knife" jump out of the shadows to continue the aural assault, "Hogweed" is beginning to sound a bit dated, and it just can't follow "Supper's Ready". The crowd go nuts after the "Weed", and Gabriel intros the only possible encore. A strange, almost mechanical, "Knife" tears it up, and features some nice effects from Hackett during the middle section, and builds to the usual manic climax.

Another memorable, if not spectacular show.

FEBRUARY 21st, 1973

BISHOP HOLGATE SCHOOL, YORK, UK.

Personnel: PG, TB, MR, PC, SH.

Set List: Watcher of the Skies.

A brief excerpt from a recently discovered recording which was unfortunately stopped after the opening number. The track is well-received and given generous applause and the band are obviously in fine fettle. Then the taper was spotted by a steward and the recording was halted. Obviously he did not conceal the tape deck well enough.

FEBRUARY 22nd, 1973

CITY HALL, NEWCASTLE, UK.

Personnel: PG, TB, MR, PC, SH.

Set List: Watcher of the Skies, The Musical Box, Get 'em Out by Friday, Supper's Ready (cut), The Return Of The Giant Hogweed, The Knife.

Perhaps the most exciting of the newly-unearthed recordings, this in-your-face audience tape is an excellent example of the *Foxtrot* tour in all its glory. The crowd are loud and the band are louder, so when the Mellotron gets going the resulting response is understandably explosive.

"Watcher" sets the tone for the show and is full of Rutherford's thumping bass and punctuated with some aggressive snare from a razor sharp Collins.

Gabriel waffles on about a little boy in Green Pantaloons, Sainsbury's, and a game of croquet while the usual tuning up noises can be heard, the song is finally introduced with the following half-hearted attempt at humour.

'The part of Genesis this evening is being played by the *News At Ten* team featuring Eddie Waring, that was tedious, this is "The Musical Box".'

The song itself is one of the better versions with Hackett being head and shoulders above the rest in the battle of the solos, Gabriel is his usual creepy self and the organ sounds fantastic.

Gabriel gets carried away during the intro to "Get 'em Out" when he describes how a little old lady, on dealing with Mr John Pebble, thought that he was a c*nt, he then apologises. Collins gets the tale of the aforementioned Mr Pebble underway and Banks adds that classic run on the Hammond and soon the dreaded C-word is all but forgotten.

The calls for "The Knife" have dried up by the time "Supper's" begins and even the most animated of fans sit down and listen as Gabriel weaves his spell. You can hear a pin drop during 'How Dare I..' and an audible gasp as the flower mask appears. The tape is turned over at about the eleven-minute mark so an edit does spoil the continuity somewhat, but all is well in time for the 'Apocalypse'.

The organ solo section is stunning, the almost funky groove set up by the rhythm section is attacked by Banks while Hackett riffs away behind him, Gabriel makes his scary entrance and shouts the place down. Hackett soars during the finale and the Mellotron washes over everyone as the whole thing grinds to a majestic halt.

The "Hogweed" rushes straight in as the intro is missing from the tape, it comes as light relief after the marathon that has gone before but still has its own special magic and Collins even throws in a couple of super fast drum fills to spice things up a bit.

After some lengthy applause the band not surprisingly bows to the one constant request of the night and unleash "The Knife", everyone gets excited and Hackett probably stands up. The middle section is suitably spaced and is full of mellow flute and a hypnotic bass.

Hackett is seriously on the case for his big solo and even throws in some slightly different improvisational stuff. The power chords march in Banks dances over the top while a manic Gabriel struts across the stage and behaves all revolutionary. A manic way to end a great concert.

FEBRUARY 24th/FEBRUARY 25th, 1973
FREE TRADE HALL, MANCHESTER, UK; DE MONTFORD HALL, LEICESTER, UK.

Personnel PG, TB, MR, PC, SH.

Set List: Watcher of the Skies, Musical Box, Get 'em Out by Friday, Supper's Ready, The Return of the Giant Hogweed, The Knife.

These two shows were recorded by the American radio show The King Biscuit Flower Hour [how apt], and were eventually released as the first *Genesis Live* album. "Supper's Ready" was originally intended to be included as part of a three-sided double album, this was shelved so that a budget priced single album could be released instead.

As is often the way with official live albums, lots of the between-song antics that Mr Gabriel got up to are missing, but this stunning quality recording includes a fine tale for "Supper's Ready".

'Old Michael was walking down the street past the pet shop which was never closed, and he sat down on a bench all by himself to feed his words to the birds. But the birds weren't hungry, 'Mmmmm,' thought Michael to himself, 'if I can't get in their bloody brains, I'll get in their bloody stomachs.'

So he took all his clothes off. Then with his ten toes and ten fingers, he began to tap out a little tune; it went something like this. Bom tiddly bom pah... This was the musical highlight in old Michael's life.

The inhabitants of the terrain beneath the ground, commonly known to us mortal beings as worms, they were very turned on by this musical experience. The king worm who was a five-inch slob, declared that the pitter-patter that they were hearing from above, was nothing but rainfall and worms as you know being nothing but dirty creatures, were very partial to bathing themselves when it rains. And within seconds the entire surface of the park, was a sea of swurming warms. Swarming worms.

Old Michael was incredibly happy and he looked up in the sky and began to whistle a tune. Went something like this. [Gabriel whistles a snatch of Jerusalem]. He could fart too, the result of this little whistling tune was astounding, because in bird language the tune just whistled meant supper was ready."

A great cheer greets another fine version of "Supper's", the sound on this recording favours Rutherford a lot, and his masterful 6- & 12-string work is to the fore. Hackett rips into the 'Warlord' solo, and the whole band gatecrash 'Willow Farm,' which rocks rather than bounces. 'Apocalypse' is just that, ushered in by a haunting flute and sly build up, all hell breaks loose.

The organ solo is breathtaking, Hackett and Rutherford slam out that repetitive riff, Collins is kicking ass, and you know what happens next. '666' sends shivers up the spine, then the Mellotron washes in, and cools the whole thing down. Gabriel's voice surges through 'New Jerusalem', and everyone can breath again.

Genesis Live found its way into the charts, but if this version of "Supper's Ready" had been included as originally planned, who knows what might have happened.

MARCH 3rd, 1973

GRAND THEATRE, QUEBEC CITY, CANADA.

Personnel: PG, TB, MR, PC, SH.

Set List: Watcher of the Skies, The Musical Box, Get 'em Out by Friday, The Return of the Giant Hogweed, The Knife, Supper's Ready.

A good quality recording albeit with some crackle during the intro to "Watcher". The song itself is well executed, with the Mellotron sounding as awesome as ever, and everyone as tight as you could wish for.

Gabriel mixes French and English in his shortened story for the "Musical Box". Banks does well in the mix, with the organ to the fore, but he has to compete with an on fire Hackett whose first solo is spot on, in fact his performance on this song is stunning. It's as if he's suddenly decided not to let Banks steal all the solo glory.

The tricky intro to "Get 'em Out" is handled with consummate ease, Banks scuttles up the keyboard for that delicate organ fill, without the slightest hint of a bum note, he continues throughout the song, driving the melody on his trusty Hammond, and filling in some nice flutes from the Mellotron, whilst Gabriel is singing. Hackett again throws in a couple of super-complicated flurries with his eyes closed – these guys are cooking.

A few dodgy tape edits thrust an aggressive "Hogweed" on to an enthusiastic crowd, then "The Knife" is introduced, and Banks canters in for the penultimate number of the evening. Gabriel misses a cue on the second verse, his charging around the stage is the most likely explanation, again the keyboard heavy mix shows all the subtle lines Banks comes up with during the quiet section. Hackett attacks that far too many notes solo with vigour, but it still sounds over crowded, he then ad-libs for a few bars before the metal section. Gabriel screams about dying, and the whole thing staggers to an end.

The 'Old Michael' story is wheeled out for "Supper's Ready", the beginning of which is quite mesmerising.

The song progresses nicely, with Hackett and Banks running the show, Gabriel of course takes over for 'Willow Farm', with a flower on his head, he would! The power of the final section is missing from this recording, although the organ solo is even more manic than usual, and spot on of course. Gabriel removes marrow, as a phased Mellotron brings things home.

MAY 7th, 1973

OLYMPIA THEATRE, PARIS, FRANCE.

Personnel PG, TB, MR, PC, SH.

Set List: Watcher of the Skies, The Musical Box, Get 'Em out by Friday, The Return of the Giant Hogweed, The Knife.

Recorded for the French Musicorama radio show, this audience recording comes complete with an enthusiastic announcer giving it his all [in French] during the intro to "Watcher", and then at every available moment. Most annoying, but it at least confirms the country of origin.

"The Musical Box" has a nice improvement in sound quality and is as captivating as usual. Gabriel's old man voice is well over the top with just the right amount of menace. Some hideous feedback style noise almost spoils things at the start of the loud section, but thankfully normal service is resumed.

They almost lose the plot during the second set of solos which might have something to do with the return of the dreadful noise. The song ends in a less than convincing manner, most unusual for this the most played number in the set.

Gabriel's stories are drowned out by our friendly announcer, so "Get' em Out" piles in as usual, that is until the Mellotron flutes over-power Gabriel's vocals. The song as a whole goes well, but constant level changes in the vocals spoil it a bit, and it lacks its usual punch.

The French commentator once again steps in, and again mentions Peter Gabriel, now there's a surprise. "Supper's Ready" is also mentioned, but not played. Before he can finish his sentence, the "Hogweed" has arrived, and is possibly the best performance of the evening – even some dodgy sounding drums can't stop its advance.

After a lot of end of show waffle, our budding Genesis MC mentions *Tresspass*, and "The Knife", which then duly arrives.

A strange, if unconvincing, performance. It seems the band were never that keen on radio/TV specials.

AUGUST 26th, 1973

READING FESTIVAL, READING, UK.

Personnel: PG, TB, MR, PC, SH.

Set List: *Watcher of the Skies, The Musical Box, Supper's Ready, The Return of the Giant Hogweed, The Knife.*

Another Reading Festival, another muddy audience recording, and the last show with the *Foxtrot* set.

"Watcher" sounds powerful and well balanced, not bad for a festival set, and the fact that our cloak-wearing singer was being raised up on a forklift truck to emerge from a wooden pyramid.

After the applause dies down, several wags in the crowd yell for "The Knife", what they get is "The Musical Box", which suffers from lots of hums and buzzes, but it does shut the "Knife" fans up.

The first loud section has Hackett revving up the guitar before his first solo, all goes well with 'Old King Cole', and 'She's a lady'. Then Gabriel wows the crowd with his plea to be touched, stirring stuff indeed.

Gabriel delivers the Old Michael worm story, 'Swurming Warms' and all. "Supper's Ready" gets underway in its usual spellbinding fashion, 'The Guaranteed Eternal Sanctuary Man' section is a little slow, with a very tight snare sound from Collins, sounding almost like Bill Bruford.

'Willow Farm' has an almost hysterical Gabriel just making the high notes, Collins chimes in his best Artful Dodger voice. The Mellotron takes over with a driving melody line, at the expense of everyone else. 'Apocalypse 9/8' chugs along, with Hackett adding some Echoplex to his guitar sound, a very clear organ solo marches endlessly on with some very interesting chords thrown in for good measure.

A muffled final vocal would indicate Gabriel wearing his box hat, and with the Mellotron back at full volume some of the song's effect is lost.

The "Hogweed" makes its final appearance, and is given a suitably loud introduction, and an even louder finale, with some mighty power chords to bring things to a close.

Of course "The Knife" is wheeled out for the encore, and soon shakes off some rather lame clapping. Hackett staggers through the first solo, and some of the bass notes are out of time. Unfortunately the song is cut just before the end, but you can be certain it went down a storm.

4. SELLING ENGLAND, AND THE USA, CANADA, ITALY ETC, ETC...

The band in full flow play a lengthy tour of North America and Canada, after first bringing the house down at another classic Rainbow gig. The newer, less-structured material brings Hackett into the spotlight.

They film themselves at Shepperton studios for a proposed future release, which of course does not happen, but the film is out there and is another must-have for any fan.

As well as the new *Selling England* material, some dates on the tour feature rare outings for "Harold the Barrel" and Collins sings lead on "More Fool Me".

The sets now are the longest yet with several new epics being added and Gabriel delivering some simply bizarre stories.

Six shows at the Los Angles Roxy Club at the end of 1973 are some of the tightest the band has ever played and are a good indication of things to come.

The set list is pretty much carved in stone by now, each song in its place with only "Harold", or Hackett noodling through "Horizons" rocking the boat.

SEPTEMBER 19th, 1973

OLYMPIA THEATRE, PARIS, FRANCE.

Personnel: PG, TB, MR, PC, SH.

Set List: Watcher of the Skies, Dancing with the Moonlit Knight, The Cinema Show, The Battle of Epping Forest, The Musical Box, I Know What I Like, Firth of Fifth, Supper's Ready (cut).

The first show with the *Selling England* material starts off with a thunderous "Watcher", which although low on vocals more than makes up with sheer power, the Mellotron roars and gets a rapturous response.

The first of the new songs, "Moonlit Knight", is given a simple intro, no stories yet, just Gabriel's solo vocal and then the delicate guitars and piano. The band kick in and the whole song takes the group onto another musical level, stop-start frantic passages, and some wonderful guitar from Hackett. As usual Collins rises to the occasion and keeps everyone in check, then gives way to the Mellotron/12-string coda aided by some nice flute.

"Cinema Show" gets a brief Romeo story then Rutherford delivers the very quiet intro to yet another classic Genesis song, Banks steals the show during the lengthy instrumental section with his ARP solo and Mellotron choirs. Great stuff.

Banks is still tuning up during the long snare drum intro to "Epping Forest", everyone claps along, but soon stop when the difficult verse arrives. This son of "Supper's Ready" has lots of dodgy East End gangsters for Gabriel to take on, as well as a suspect Reverend. Collins joins in for some Cockney backing vocals. Gabriel would often wear a stocking on his head and charge around the stage with a baseball bat during this song, nothing like keeping in character.

After the Black Capped Barons have settled up, Hackett lays down another fine solo, and brings this mini-epic to a close. "The Musical Box" justifiably keeps its place in the set and instantly changes the mood. Hackett tries something different during the first solo and they all charge along a little bit too fast. Gabriel's voice gets lost at the end, until the 'Touch Me' screams receive the biggest cheer so far.

A strange lawnmower sound and some Gabriel mutterings mean "I Know What I Like" makes its first appearance. A Worzel Gummage voice, and a seriously sing-a-long chorus, make it an instant crowd pleaser, short and very sweet, if a touch heavy-handed on the drumming. A brief river story for the last of the new songs – no piano intro – though this will be played at later shows. It's straight in and hang on for Hackett's big five minutes, his solo is the stuff of Genesis legend, and although this one is a bit stiff at first, it soon soars above the rhythm section and sets up Gabriel for one final verse.

Some loud keyboard tuning all but drowns out the start of the worms story, but we do get a brief Jerusalem boogie, and a loud cheer as the song starts. With so many potential epics now in the set, "Supper's Ready" is now the great big cherry on a very big cake, sadly this cherry falls off just as Collins yells, 'All change'.

A slightly muddy recording of a very good show.

SEPTEMBER 29th, 1973
HALLE DES FETES BEAUJOIRE, LAUSANNE, SWITZERLAND.

Personnel: PG, TB, MR, PC, SH.

Set List: Dancing with the Moonlit Knight, The Cinema Show, I Know What I Like, The Musical Box, More Fool Me, Supper's Ready.

Their first Swiss gig is represented by a very distant and muddy audience recording, "Watcher" is missing from my recording, but we can assume it was played.

Gabriel's Romeo story for "Cinema Show" is quite animated, full of silly noises and high-pitched voices. The song itself seems to go well, but it is quite difficult to tell here.

The set listing is a pretty standard affair, with the inclusion of Phil and Mike's acoustic duet "More Fool Me", which really suffers on this recording. "Supper's Ready" was probably fantastic if you were there, it is not here, so we'll leave it at that.

OCTOBER 9th, 1973
GLASGOW APOLLO THEATRE, UK.

Personnel PG, TB, MR, PC, SH.

Set List. Watcher of the Skies, Dancing with the Moonlit Knight, The Cinema Show, I Know What I Like, Firth of Fifth, The Musical Box, More Fool Me, The Battle of Epping Forest, Supper's Ready, The Knife.

A cheer greets Gabriel as he saunters on in batwings and cape, at the climax of the Mellotron fanfare, a solid if somewhat sluggish "Watcher" gets this show underway.

The third show from their first headline tour, it is packed full of goodies from the *Selling England* album, although the muddy recording and varying volume detract from the light and shade that is their trademark sound. The tape even slows down and suffers from occasional dropouts, but as it is only the third show of the UK tour we shall persevere.

"Moonlit Knight" and "Cinema Show", two of the biggies from the album, are given serious workouts, which means Gabriel has a lot of tambourine playing to do. The Banks, Collins, & Rutherford gang take over the fine instrumental section of "Cinema", whilst Hackett steals

"Moonlit Knight". Both are very well received by the well-behaved crowd.

"Firth of Fifth" is also a bit slow, but Hackett does the business again with a sublime solo. "Musical Box" sounds even more menacing than usual. The delicate Collins/Rutherford duo that is "More Fool Me", is almost lost on this recording, unlike "Epping Forest" which marches in, and features lots of nice synth work from Mr Banks, as well as a host of dodgy villains from Gabriel.

Old Michael's arrival causes much excitement, as we all know what's coming next, all twenty-three minutes of it. A very atmospheric opening section leads to nicely restrained 'Sanctuary Man', before Hackett opens up with some energetic riffing, although Banks gives him a run for his money as usual. A good all round version, (there will soon be much better) albeit with a nasty edit during 'Willow Farm'.

"The Knife" which has also been cut, winds things up, and really gets the audience up on their feet, it's a complete version, and although it is the oldest song in the set it still kicks prog rock butt.

OCTOBER 11th, 1973

SOUTHAMPTON GAUMONT THEATRE, UK.

Personnel: PG, TB, MR, PC, SH.

Set List: Watcher of the Skies, Dancing with the Moonlit Knight, The Cinema Show, I Know What I Like, Firth of Fifth, The Musical Box, More Fool Me, The Battle of Epping Forest, Supper's Ready.

A slightly muddy audience recording that improves and is quite clear in places, kicks off with a lively, if somewhat wobbly "Watcher" which cuts in near the start. The trippy ending to "Moonlit Knight" goes on forever; perhaps they felt like jamming. It receives only moderate applause.

Gabriel's comments are often a bit muffled, so we shall not speculate, but as he often used the same story over and over we probably haven't missed much.

The quality of the tape means some of the subtleties of "Cinema Show" and "Musical Box" are almost lost, but "More Fool Me" sounds good with Collins coming on all heartbroken with his three minutes of spotlight.

The band are playing well enough, and of course give "Supper's" a good work out, but things are not as clear as we would like on this recording.

OCTOBER 20th, 1973

RAINBOW THEATRE, LONDON, UK.

Personnel: PG, TB, MR, PC, SH.

Set List: Watcher of the Skies, Dancing with the Moonlit Knight, I Know What I Like, Firth of Fifth, Musical Box (probably played), More Fool Me, The Battle of Epping Forest, Cinema Show, Supper's Ready.

The second of two sell-out gigs at the legendary Rainbow Theatre – a good show for an adoring crowd, broadcast on the radio with the exception of "The Musical Box" which for some reason is absent from any of the recordings (it must have been played?) this is a near perfect example from the early part of the *Selling England* tour.

Several tracks from this show turned up on the first archive box-set, but we all know what happened to them. This is how they really did sound. "Watcher" is far more together than usual, with everyone getting a fair crack of the whip and staying in tune, and "Moonlit Knight" gallops along at a fair old pace, not as frantic as some of the later versions but still top drawer.

'It's knocking off time for the cosmic lawnmower,' is how "I Know What I Like" is introduced. It's a pretty standard version and always seems so short in length. Hackett makes a meal of his "Firth of Fifth" solo, but does have a nice dirty sound on the guitar, there's also some hesitant piano work from Mr Banks, perhaps the old radio session phobia is back.

"Epping Forest" gets underway whilst some Mellotron tuning is going on, a nice measured build up before basher Gabriel climbs through the window with a sack full of dodgy characters, who like the general feeling of this gig are holding a little something back.

With nearly all the pre-song stories missing from my recordings, a lot of the Gabriel-built atmosphere is missing from this show which is a shame as it is such a good recording. At least the Peter & Phil "Supper's" boogie is still there, and this is a fine rendition, especially Hackett who positively flies through his first solo at the 'Waiting for Battle' sequence, 'Willow Farm' bounces along nicely, but Gabriel is still not quite in the mood.

The star of this show is the 'Magog' section, Rutherford, Banks & Collins almost swing their way through the organ solo, whilst Hackett hammers out that repetitive riff that you never normally hear. The importance of Collins during this section cannot be stressed enough, he is the business. Gabriel goes all scary and his voice breaks, and Collins adds a few more fills.

Their second visit to this famous venue produced a good, if not great show, with lots of high points.

OCTOBER 23rd, 1973

EMPIRE THEATRE, LIVERPOOL, UK.

Personnel: PG, TB, MR, PC, SH.

Set List: Watcher of the Skies, Dancing with the Moonlit Knight, The Cinema Show, I Know What I Like, Firth of Fifth, The Battle of Epping Forest, Supper's Ready.

A noisy crowd greets "Watcher", but they've settled down a bit by the time Banks plods through his intro. The Rutherford, Collins entrance is still one of the finest in Progressive Rock, even if this slightly fuzzy audience recording takes the edge off things. There are some bungled lines by Gabriel, mainly leaving it too late before he comes in, which on this ridgid piece is quite noticeable.

"Harold the Barrel" is called for, but he ends up in the English Channel, much to everyone's amusement. There's a long pause before "Moonlit Knight", but Gabriel makes up for it with a fine performance as does a speeding Mr Hackett, lots of great fretwork on a song that seems far ahead of "Watcher" in the enjoyment stakes.

"Cinema Show" is preceded by a Romeo fig leaf story, nothing strange here then, but the audience seem genuinely surprised at this. The song itself suffers a rare false start after a few bars, with Gabriel, declaring that it was a shorter-than-usual version.

Lots of calling out for old songs as Gabriel tells the "Firth of Fifth" story – a nice heavy beginning makes sure there's no hiccups here. Like the second half of "Cinema Show", "Firth of Fifth" comes alive after Gabriel stops singing, Hackett plays a blinder, and Collins comes over all heavy-handed.

"The Musical Box" story is a short one, then there is another long pause for Rutherford's guitar lead to be replaced, or 'My lead is fucked' as Gabriel announces. The song is abandoned and after some snare drum antics from Collins they march into "Epping Forest".

Rutherford is back for "Supper's Ready" which rescues the situation and if anything is a bit bass heavy.

OCTOBER 26th, 1973

CITY HALL, NEWCASTLE, UK.

Personnel: PG, TB, MR, PC, SH

Set List: Watcher of the Skies, Dancing with the Moonlit Knight, The Cinema Show, I Know what I Like, Firth of Fifth, The Musical Box, More Fool Me, The Battle of Epping Forest, Supper's Ready (cut).

A bit of tuning up, a roll around the kit, and we're off. A very enthusiastic crowd greets the bass-heavy opening of a very muscular "Watcher of the Skies". Rutherford obviously has his foot on the pedals here while Collins, Banks and Hackett serenade Gabriel as he shuffles his way to the front of the stage.

This good quality audience recording replaces the muffled tape that first appeared of this show, and between them we can piece together the whole set, and get a much better feel of this hot night in Newcastle.

Gabriel's introduction to "Moonlit Knight" is accompanied by some lengthy and intrusive Mellotron tuning and several shouts from the crowd, which increase once he starts the solo vocal beginning. A good, if not outstanding, version sees them come over all Mahavishnu Orchestra for the stop-start section near the end. And the audience still spellbound by the ease at which they handled the complicated ending, remain silent for the dreamy coda.

A story about Romeo and some fig leaves conveniently ending up in a cinema is joined by several calls from the crowd."The Cinema Show" rushes by in a blur of hi-hat and jazzy guitar, Banks hurries the solo but must have impressed Gabriel as he gives Phil and Tony a namecheck at the end of the song. A West Country Wurzel voice is used for "I Know What I Like", with plenty of time at the end for lawnmower impressions.

"Firth of Fifth" rather plods along, maybe the band are trying to comprehend the bizarre tale about covering the wide river in blankets. Hackett does his thing, although he has changed the first section around quite a bit, and being such a famous solo this does sound strange. Collins perks up during the keyboard section, throwing in some nice jazzy fills before Gabriel returns for the big prog rock ending.

A welcome break from *Selling England* material next with a mood changing and emotional "Musical Box". During the Little Henry story some wag in the crowd calls out Mickey Mouse, A dead pan Gabriel corrects this interruption much to everyone's amusement. The song itself brings that bit extra out of the group, especially the singer.

"More Fool Me" and a rambling but still well-received "Epping Forest" lead up to an epic "Supper's Ready".

Gabriel silences the hecklers with a masterful performance, almost getting hysterical during 'Willow Farm', then after a note-perfect and up-front organ solo, he screams the place down during the 'Apocalypse'.

A strong performance all round, with the crowd just winning on points.

OCTOBER 28th, 1973
HIPPODROME THEATRE, BIRMINGHAM, UK.

Personnel: PG, TB, MR, PC, SH.

Set List: Watcher of the Skies, Dancing with the Moonlit Knight, The Cinema Show, I Know What I Like, Firth of Fifth, The Musical Box, More Fool Me, The Battle of Epping Forest, Supper's Ready.

A fairly clear recording, although the audience are very quiet with hardly any calling out or whistling. "Watcher" is rather laboured and even Gabriel's appearance at the start fails to raise a cheer. The song is performed without a hitch and is followed by a brief Britannia in the English Channel story before the "Moonlit Knight" arrives.

Hackett does a fair job with the first solo, but appropriately it is the dreamy end section that stands out here, lots of nice flute and synth interplay and some odd guitar noises thrown in for good measure.

This gig lacks the energy from the earlier Newcastle show, the songs are executed well, but nothing exciting happens. "Cinema Show", "I Know What I Like" and "Firth of Fifth" are all missing that little bit extra, although Mike, Tony and Phil once again get acknowledged by Gabriel at the end of "Cinema". I wonder what Hackett felt about that?

"Epping Forest" sounds like it was recorded outside the venue, but the sound is restored for "Supper's Ready" which has the story and the first verse missing as well as being cut short at the Guards of Magog.

A recently discovered, if somewhat uninspired performance.

OCTOBER 30/31st, 1973

SHEPPERTON FILM STUDIOS, UK.

Personnel: PG, TB, MR, PC, SH.

Set List: Watcher of the Skies, Dancing with the Moonlit Knight, I Know what I Like, The Musical Box, Supper's Ready.

The idea was to make a live 'in concert' film for some future release, so two specially arranged shows at Shepperton film studios were slotted in at the end of the UK tour. They used their current stage set although budget restrictions meant not enough lights were available and the whole thing is a bit on the dark side.

Gabriel stands resplendent in his floor length cloak and the batwings head-dress, with just a touch of eye shadow and a somewhat distant expression on his face. The Mellotron is joined by Phil, Mike and Steve and "Watcher" gets underway. Apart from a little movement from Gabriel there is not much else visually happening on stage. At the end of the song the Watcher turns his back on the audience and raises his arms up so spreading out the shiny green and blue cloak.

Dressed in the Britannia outfit, Gabriel introduces "Moonlit Knight", a fine up-tempo performance is enhanced by the images of the old-fashioned Green Shield Stamp which are projected on the screens behind the band. Hackett solos nicely but is still welded to his stool, and is wearing a shiny open neck white shirt that would give the singer a run for his money. The coda focuses on Gabriel who alternates between flute and finger cymbals, as well as more moody staring into space.

Sporting what could pass as a First World War German soldier's helmet, Gabriel, with some grass between his teeth, hunches over and does a quite convincing lawnmower impression. Hackett, who must have moved a little bit, is now playing a Coral sitar guitar, and "I Know What I Like" bounces across the screen with everyone except the static guitarist helping out on vocals. This footage was intended to promote the single, but they decided not to use it, which is a shame as it shows a serious band having some fun.

"The Musical Box" shows Gabriel at his theatrical best. The opening verses are all dreamy guitars and plaintive vocals; Banks is playing a 12-string acoustic and Rutherford a classic 12-string Rickenbacker.

Dressed in a plain black catsuit with plenty of white face makeup, Gabriel looks almost sad and clown-like, and he does a strange tambourine dance when things first get heavy.

During the final guitar break, Gabriel leaves the stage for the band to duel it out amongst themselves, he returns wearing the old man mask and makes his way to the mic stand. Dramatic lighting and acting make this a chilling ending to a classic song, as he finally falls to the ground in a most disturbing fashion.

The lack of lights works in the band's favour for most of "Supper's Ready", adding to the tension as the song gradually builds to the hair-raising climax. There's some light relief with the flower mask during 'Willow Farm' and several tranquil guitar sections with Gabriel adding some soothing flute. But this is all shattered when the 'Magog' section kicks in, Gabriel screams the vocals then leaves the stage.

As Banks marches through the organ solo, the atmosphere changes to a flame engulfed battlefield, the lighting against the gauze sails give the impression of flickering flames. The strobe light whirls around, and as the organ runs out of notes, Gabriel, clad in black cloak and the red box headgear sways to the front of the stage. This is rock theatre at its peak, no wonder he grabbed all the headlines, even Rutherford is perched on a stool as if in awe of the approaching apocalyptic vision.

The pyro explodes and Gabriel rushes forward dressed in white for the 'Hey Babe' section, the Mellotron is almost deafening and he has to battle to be heard above it. At the very end he hoists a blue neon tube into the air and the applause begins.

An essential part of any fan's archive, this film gives a perfect view of Genesis in late-'73. It frequently does the rounds as Oxford '73 or Bristol '74, either way this film should be released.

NOVEMBER 7th, 1973

CAPITOL THEATRE, QUEBEC, CANADA.

Personnel: PG, TB, MR, PC, SH.

Set List: Watcher of the Skies, Dancing with the Moonlit Knight, The Cinema Show, The Battle of Epping Forest, The Musical Box, I Know What I Like, Firth of Fifth, Supper's Ready (cut).

The first of a handful of Canadian dates before another crack at the USA. The set list was fairly stable by now with only the odd variation in the running order and the occasional song addition to mix things up a bit.

"Watcher" is well-balanced and very powerful, and gets rapturous applause, although some of the vocals do get lost in the mix or the bat-wings. "Moonlit Knight" flies by in a hail of guitar and some devastating drumming – this piece is easily one of the finest in the set and gives everyone a chance to do their stuff, especially Collins and Hackett.

A brief name check for Romeo before the "Cinema Show", which is well-played and passes by in no time at all. Collins then starts the slow drum roll of "Epping Forest", an odd change in the set but Gabriel's gang of felons duly arrive and cause chaos whilst charging around in a stocking mask wielding a baseball bat.

A few technical problems delay the start of "Musical Box" and Mike Rutherford gets the blame. The opening section casts its usual spell, with a distant Gabriel using his almost childlike vocals to chill the spine instead of trying to break it with violence as in the previous number. The first solo section has Hackett all over the shop as he tries to keep up with the others, he just about pulls it off and the song reaches its old man climax.

The multi-river story that introduces "Firth of Fifth" almost becomes a tongue twister, so Gabriel keeps it brief and the band pile in. Hackett plays a totally different solo and it sounds just right, proof that he was never frightened to break away from the no jamming policy the band have always had. Collins really hams up the ending as Gabriel comes back in – an interesting performance.

The worm story is partly drowned out by a cacophony of Mellotron and organ noises as Banks tunes up, then Rutherford joins in and is still fiddling even after the song has been announced. The song itself gets as far as Gabriel, the railway porter, yelling "all change" then the recording cuts off. If anyone knows how it ended....

NOVEMBER 8th, 1973

MASSEY HALL, TORONTO, CANADA.

Personnel: PG, TB, MR, PC, SH.

Set List: Watcher of the Skies, Dancing with the Moonlit Knight, The Cinema Show, I Know what I Like, Firth of Fifth, The Musical Box, More Fool Me, Supper's Ready.

An excellent recording from the second of the Canadian shows, "Watcher" is greeted with much excitement, especially Gabriel's arrival on stage which the taper and his friends find most amusing. As the song ends someone close by asks where the light show is, Collins replies that it is many miles away.

After some strange high-pitched shouts of 'Hello', the next number is announced, and as per usual the "Moonlit Knight" makes his unaccompanied entrance. Hackett again strays from the album version with his stunning solo, even during the coda he is making all sorts of strange noises as this section drifts into silence.

The next track is a revelation, one of the best "Cinema Shows" so far; maybe the story about Romeo and his sexually stimulating fig leaves got everybody going. If Hackett took the honours in the previous song then Banks most certainly steals them back again with some remarkably fluid fingerwork during the breathtaking instrumental section. Bringing things back to earth Gabriel takes his usual Farmer Giles voice to the point of sounding like Worzul Gummidge on speed, as he goes all cosmic lawnmower for "I Know What I Like".

A brief apology from Gabriel over the missing light show and back projections, he confirms the earlier remark that they are still in transit from Quebec. This might explain the extra effort the band is making on the previous night's show.

"Firth of Fifth" is time for Hackett to shine again, which he does of course, adding some more new phrases to his now legendary lead break. There is an unfortunate edit on this recording but the ending is intact as is the overall feel of this powerful piece. A brief explanation about the game of croquet then "The Musical Box" gets underway, albeit with a mistimed opening chord from Rutherford. Everyone excels himself on this version and it easily gets the longest applause so far.

'This is something a little different,' is how Collins introduces his duet with Rutherford. "More Fool Me" is delicate and brief, and the perfect respite between two of the biggest numbers in the set. As the applause ends, calls for "Harold the Barrel" and bizarrely "Boris the Spider" are met with the 'Old Michael' story, and then of course "Supper's Ready". All shimmering 12-string guitars and excellent harmonies, the start of this masterpiece is often overlooked due to its epic conclusion. Collins is spot on with his harmonies and of course his drumming, as the whole thing marches on through the weird musical hall of 'Willow Farm' to the scary hat ending.

How much visual impact was lost due to the lack of lighting effects is not reflected by the band's stoic performance, Gabriel gives his all for '666' and even with some wildly out-of-tune Mellotron, pulls of a pretty dramatic ending.

NOVEMBER 10th, 1973
UNIVERSITY SPORTS ARENA, MONTREAL, CANADA.

Personnel: PG, TB, MR, PC, SH.

Set List: Watcher of the Skies, Dancing with the Moonlit Knight, The Cinema Show, I Know what I Like, Firth of Fifth (cut), The Musical Box, More Fool Me (cut), The Battle of Epping Forest, Horizons, Supper's Ready (cut).

The last of the Canadian shows takes a while to get going, with lots of tuning up and technical problems keeping the crowd waiting. Gabriel gets his usual cheer as the "Watcher" moves to centre stage.

This fairly clear recording sees "Moonlit Knight" charge by with Hackett once again taking the spoils. The pairing of these songs is a good example of the two main styles of Genesis songwriting, the more rigid chord structure of "Watcher" with its traditional Progressive rock leanings, against the free flowing almost fusion feel of "Moonlit Knight". The latter number has Collins and Hackett written all over it.

Several fig leaves later "The Cinema Show" with its almost apologetic beginning, gradually becomes the Phil, Tony and Mike show, as they stretch out for the sublime keyboard solo. "I Know What I Like" is full of Gabriel overacting and his multi-river and blanket story for "Firth of Fifth" still does not make sense. Hackett strays from his usual solo but it still sounds great, although the ending almost sounds out of tune.

An eccentric and somewhat sinister explanation of the rules of croquet using heads instead of balls, is how Gabriel introduces little Cynthia and Henry, and of course "The Musical Box". This song belongs to Gabriel and his performance here is masterful; painful emotion with plenty of menace backed by those delicate 12-string guitars and Phil's perfect harmonies.

The guitars dominate this version with Banks struggling to be heard, Hackett roars into action and Gabriel does his funny tambourine dance and gets a round of applause. The old man ending brings the house down for the longest cheer of the night.

Collins threatens to sing whatever comes into his head in French, instead he starts "More Fool Me" which on this recording only makes it to the first chorus. "Epping Forest" has a few vocal drop-outs and lots of inaudible mutterings from some of Gabriel's myriad of characters. There is almost too much for him to do, and this time he doesn't quite pull it off.

A rare treat for Hackett fans next with a nice run through of "Horizons" which follows the old Michael story and gets no introduction at all. "Supper's Ready" then starts and takes you back to hearing them both in that order when listening to *Foxtrot.*

Unfortunately the recording is cut short at about seven minutes.

NOVEMBER 17th, 1973
TUFTS UNIVERSITY, COHEN AUDITORIUM, MEDFORD, USA.

Personnel: PG, TB, MR, PC, SH.

Set List: Dancing with the Moonlit Knight, The Cinema Show, I Know what I Like, Firth of Fifth (cut), The Musical Box, The Battle of Epping Forest.

An excellent recording that unfortunately misses out the beginning and end of the show, with "Watcher" and "Supper's Ready" being the casualties. Perhaps the taper was so in awe of Gabriel's alien presence that he forgot to press the record button. "Moonlit Knight" sees Hackett put in a devastating performance as he sticks to the script and turns up the heat, making everyone else play catch me if you can.

The pause button gets hit between songs, so a lot of the atmosphere has been lost, but we do get to hear Gabriel giving the road manager a hard time before asking, "What the hell's happened to my fucking lead?" as there is obviously a delay before "The Cinema Show".

The bass pedals are way too loud during the first half of "The Cinema Show" but have been sorted for the instrumental section, that shows Banks is in top form, even though he seems to be playing a little too fast during his lengthy synth solo.

Gabriel wants to take the crowd to the countryside where it is lawn mowing time, the booming bass makes this a heavier than usual version and is all the better for it. Collins is grooving on the cymbals as Banks plays out with the lawn mower. We join "Firth of Fifth" just before the middle section, which is handled with ease by all concerned.

"The Musical Box" almost sounds like the album version, very dark and mysterious, with some nice dreamy flute and shimmering guitars. Things pick up for the first lead break, when Hackett makes his guitar roar into action, a total mood change in an instant, then 'Old King Cole' brings it all down again. Easily the most convincing song in the performance, it improves with age and still brings the house down every time.

They fight their way through "Epping Forest" without incident, by contrast with the previous epic, this is the least convincing song they play, although Gabriel does try hard to make it work.

The savage editing and the lack of two key songs does take the shine off this generally well played show.

NOVEMBER 22nd, 1973

FELT FORUM, NEW YORK, USA.

Personnel: PG, TB, MR, PC, SH.

Set List: Watcher of the Skies, Dancing with the Moonlit Knight, The Cinema Show, I Know what I Like, Firth of Fifth, The Musical Box, Horizons, More Fool Me, The Battle of Epping Forest (cut), Supper's Ready, The Knife.

One of the better quality recordings from the *Selling England by the Pound* tour which is very clear and nicely balanced. "Watcher" positively swings into action and develops into a pounding groove before Gabriel makes his bat-winged entrance, a slightly different feel than usual but still an impressive start.

The crowd are then asked why are they in the Felt Forum on Thanksgiving Day watching a spectacle with feathers. Someone makes a comment about taking acid, then Gabriel starts "Moonlit Knight". Not as sharp as some of the more recent versions with even Hackett sounding a bit reserved, although he does a pretty good seagull impression during the mellow section.

In stark contrast "Cinema Show" is a revelation – easily one of the best yet, Collins gets very jazzy, Banks flies through the solo and Hackett plays some beautiful lead during the verses perfectly complimenting the vocal lines, and all the way through Rutherford's 12-string work holds the whole thing together. The groove continues for "I Know What I Like", Collins makes lots of noise both vocally and with the sticks, lots of nice fills here.

Gabriel tells his five-river story using various parts of the stage to indicate where the rivers are, after trying to get some crowd participation going he calls the audience dummies and "Firth of Fifth" crashes in. Hackett plays a fine sustained solo holding that long note for an eternity, before the Mellotron washes in and a tambourine waving Gabriel makes his entrance.

The guy who taped this show is determined to talk to his friend for the entire gig, so during the quiet sections of "Musical Box", through all of "Horizons" and "More Fool Me" there is some annoying conversation going on and some of the atmosphere is lost. No problems on "Epping Forest" which thunders by with a van load of villainous characters.

After Old Michael has rubbed himself into the clean green grass, "Supper's Ready" gets underway, a good solid performance which gets up a head of steam for the 'Magog' section which bounces along with some nice echo on the vocals. '666' is also echoed, but is almost drowned out by Banks in a sea of organ and Mellotron. Gabriel's voice is very rough for the end section as he battles to be heard, especially as Hackett has now joined in for his solo.

A rare encore is offered and of course, they play "The Knife". It canters in with Hackett having lost all control of his volume pedal making all sorts of loud noises. Things settle down, but the whole thing is rather messy, with Gabriel out of breath and lost in the mix. The ending is organised chaos with lots of heavy guitar and vocal screaming.

At least it shut the fans up.

DECEMBER 1st, 1973
NEW GYM, STATE UNIVERSITY, BUFFALO, USA.

Personnel: PG, TB, MR, PC, SH.

Set List: *The Musical Box, The Battle of Epping Forest.*

Just a brief two-song section from this excellent sounding gig. A nice atmospheric "Musical Box" with Hackett struggling to keep his guitar volume under control, Collins is very forceful on this piece with some gunshot snare drumming during the 'She's a Lady' section.

"Epping Forest" was always going to be great visual number with Gabriel taking on a whole host of suspect characters, hearing it live without the benefit of his theatrics, it often sounds like there is too much going on and just a little bit messy. This is one of those times, nice try but no stocking mask.

Another recording that has had some doubt cast over its date and venue, and has often been linked with the show from November 11th 1973, also in Buffalo.

DECEMBER 3rd, 1973
KAHN AUDITORIUM, NORTHWESTERN UNIVERSITY, CHICAGO, USA.

Personnel: PG, TB, MR, PC, SH.

Set List: *Watcher of the Skies (cut), Dancing with the Moonlit Knight, The Cinema Show, I Know what I Like, Horizons, More Fool Me, The Battle of Epping Forest, Firth of Fifth (cut).*

One of several recordings that have caused confusion as to their date and whereabouts, this particular show has been passed off as Evanston 17/4/74, but as Gabriel actually mentions the Kahn Auditorium in his story for "Moonlit Knight" I'm confident of this tape's authenticity. This is further confirmed as he does the same thing for the Peace Auditorium at the Ypsilanti gig five days later, so it was obviously a feature of that current round of stories.

We join "Watcher" halfway through the Mellotron fanfare, a good start but things get better with a lively "Moonlit Knight" with its Britannia-in-feathers story. Banks plays a nice solo during "Cinema Show" with lots of great noise from the ARP. The song is slightly delayed as the Mellotron takes longer than usual to tune.

They swing through "I Know What I like" which still sounds like a hit single, then there is a cut in the tape before "Horizons" starts, so it might not be the right running order. Collins then informs everyone that "More Fool Me" was written during the first four numbers. If that was true, he did a bloody good job because with Rutherford's help he turns in a fine performance.

Another cut in the recording before "Epping Forest" which suffers a bit in the sound department, but still sounds complicated enough to keep everyone guessing as to who Gabriel was at any one time.

Without any more tape edits "Firth Of Fifth" follows, minus the piano intro and with the multi-rivers story. Both points indicate that this is the correct date for this show and also a strange change to the running order, a most un-Genesis-like occurrence. Sadly the song is cut short with Hackett in full flow bringing a premature end to this intriguing concert.

DECEMBER 8th, 1973

PEACE AUDITORIUM, YPSILANTI, USA.

Personnel: PG, TB, MR, PC, SH.

Set List: Watcher of the Skies, Dancing with the Moonlit Knight, The Cinema Show, I Know what I Like, Firth of Fifth, The Musical Box, More Fool Me, Supper's Ready (cut).

A clear audience recording although a bit on the hissy side, "Watcher" is tight and for once the organ outguns the Mellotron, so it has new feeling about it. The beginning of "Moonlit Knight" has a feel of *Nursery Cryme* about it, with the plaintive vocal and then the 12-string guitar accompaniment before Hackett arrives in a flurry of notes.

Gabriel recites the following tale before "The Cinema Show":

'So Romeo discovered that he had a strange green growth somewhere above his knees and below his waist, he identified the green growth as a fig leaf and on one Sunday afternoon, with tremendous courage the fig leaf was removed. He placed it underneath his arm which is where he kept all his most precious things and there it stayed for over two weeks. On removal Romeo noticed the fig leaf had changed to a deep maroon colour so he decided to crumple up the fig leaf into a fine powder, place it between his wet lips, chew upon it and digest it.

This produced in Henry (even Gabriel gets confused about his characters) what is known as a high degree of sexual excitation. Fortunately for the entire world, just around the corner on a balcony is standing little Juliet, (Gabriel makes several silly noises) Romeo was much attracted to the motion on the balcony, so he grabbed Juliet off the balcony and took her to the darkness and obscurity of the cinema. What followed is described now as "The Cinema Show".'

Collins helps the lawnmower in with a wash of cymbals and some pretty heavy drumming on the jammed-out ending, which almost stumbles to a halt as if the band suddenly realise that they don't usually improvise. The "Firth of Fifth" rivers story involves Banks leaving the tap on in his Mellotron, a spitting gnome, a urinating hedgehog and a pile of crying bass guitars. Hackett plays another variation on his solo, but all the main ingredients are there and he elevates the song to the level of Genesis live classic every time he plays it.

There are a couple of cuts in the tape during "The Musical Box", and the performance lacks the usual menace.

Only ten minutes of "Supper's Ready" have survived on this recording a common occurrence on this section of the tour – if only the tapers had gone prepared.

DECEMBER 17th, 1973

THE ROXY, LOS ANGELES, USA. (Early Show)

Personnel: PG, TB, MR, PC, SH.

Set List: Watcher of the Skies, Dancing with the Moonlit Knight, The Cinema Show, I Know what I Like, Firth of Fifth, The Musical Box, More Fool Me, Supper's Ready.

The first of six sell-out shows at the legendary Roxy Club. They played two shows a day so cuts were made to the usual set, with "Epping Forest" being the most notable casualty.

The crowd reaction at this first gig is fantastic – every movement by Gabriel is cheered with plenty of cries of 'Alright' spread throughout a faultless rendition of "Watcher". The sound quality on this recording is one of the best yet with everyone getting a fare share of the sound mix.

They gallop through "Moonlit Knight" although Hackett almost gets caught up in some of his own fiddly bits, Collins comes to the rescue with some rapid fire drumming. The Romeo story goes down well with the excitable audience, fig leaves were obviously big in California.

After a good, but not great, "Cinema Show" and a rather straight-laced "I Know what I Like" Gabriel runs through his five rivers story involving the usual Mellotron, urinating hedgehog, bass guitars approach. He calls the crowd dummies and then "Firth of Fifth" crashes in. Hackett of course runs the show but his fine solo is butchered by a nasty edit on this recording.

The intimate atmosphere of the Roxy helps "The Musical Box" work its magic, Gabriel sings his socks off, Hackett wins the solo honours, and the crowd are full of vocal interjections throughout the whole song. The old man mask catches most of them by surprise and brings the biggest ovation yet.

Collins introduces himself as the warm-up act, and "More Fool Me" as a song written during the first half of the set, he sings it well and the everyone behaves themselves.

If the English eccentricities of "The Musical Box" raised a few Californian eyebrows, then the full-blown madness that is "Supper's Ready" certainly made a few wonder what Gabriel was on. The flower mask draws several comments and they freak out over '666'. A good solid performance if a touch organ-light, the 'Magog' section has a nice swing to it and Gabriel is suitably venomous. Hackett adds some nice touches at the end and Collins hams up those tom tom rolls.

A fine start to their 3-day residency which no doubt earned them many new fans in the USA.

DECEMBER 17th, 1973
THE ROXY CLUB, LOS ANGELES, USA. (Late Show)

Personnel: PG, TB, MR, PC, SH.

Set List: Watcher of the Skies, Dancing with the Moonlit Knight, The Cinema Show, I Know what I Like, Firth of Fifth (cut), The Musical Box, Supper's Ready (cut).

Another clear well-balanced recording from The Roxy Club with all the instruments well represented in the mix. A shaky Mellotron gets "Watcher" underway but it soon settles down as the rhythm section kick in. Gabriel's cloaked arrival is greeted with the usual cheers and cries and he delivers another strong performance. The Britannia story is embellished with lots of Englishmen watching the English Channel in case the horrible French come.

"Moonlit Knight" also has Mellotron problems, mainly on the dreamy end section; maybe the exertion of the earlier show has worn it out. Rutherford causes "Cinema Show" to grind to halt after a few bars because as Gabriel informs us, 'He has chosen the wrong guitar'. Banks has more problems this time with his ARP synth which makes all sorts of strange noises during his solo, but as per usual he holds it together and the song continues.

The 'lady on the subway' story makes an appearance, with Gabriel repeating the word knickers in an attempt to get a reaction; he does so and the band then play "Firth of Fifth". Why he chose this story is anybody's guess, as it bears no relevance to the song and sounds very out of place. "Firth" is cut in half by a nasty tape edit, and that Mellotron is still misbehaving itself.

They run through "Musical Box" without any problems but there is a cut at the end of "Supper's Ready" on this recording which is a shame as it is a very powerful version.

A show plagued by technical problems and uninspired performances, perhaps two gigs in one day was not such a good idea

DECEMBER 18th, 1973

THE ROXY CLUB, LOS ANGELES, USA. (Late Show)

Personnel: PG, TB, MR, PC, SH.

Set List: Watcher of the Skies, Dancing with the Moonlit Knight, The Cinema Show, I Know what I Like, Firth of Fifth (cut), More Fool Me, The Musical Box (cut), Supper's Ready (cut).

Show four from the Roxy six, and things are warming up, the recording is the poorest of the lot, the performance is spot on. "Watcher" is compact and powerful, and Collins can't wait to kick-start "Moonlit Knight" with some razor-sharp snare work.

The fig leaf story is still in use for "Cinema Show" which suffers from a brief but annoying edit, Hackett plays some beautiful lines during the vocal section and everyone has fun for the long instrumental. "I Know What I Like" is led by Collins and bounces along nicely, the sound quality of the recording also improves at this point and is even better by the time "Firth of Fifth" arrives. Another bad cut in the tape spoils a great rendition, which of course is dominated by a rampant Hackett.

Phil and Mike do their solo spot, then it's the turn of "The Musical Box" to hypnotise the audience, with those King Crimson sounding guitars and the singer's Victorian menace. The organ gets lost for the first heavy section, but this sudden burst of power wakes the crowd from their Gabriel-induced trance. Another hideous edit and change of sound quality ruin this song, which is a shame as it is a masterful performance. This show was broadcast on the radio which makes the sound quality even harder to take.

Gabriel informs the listeners that Phil is wearing a nice white boiler suit, and he will shake his Christmas balls if they all make enough noise. "Supper's Ready" suffers from vocal dropout during the 'I know a farmer' section but things are soon back to normal with Banks turning in a particularly good 9/8 solo and Collins throwing in more fills than usual.

Dodgy edits aside (commercial breaks), this is a very good performance and sets things up nicely for the last two Roxy gigs.

DECEMBER 19th, 1973

THE ROXY CLUB, LOS ANGELES, USA. (Early Show)

Personnel: PG, TB, MR, PC, SH.

Set List: Watcher of the Skies, Dancing with the Moonlit Knight, The Cinema Show, I Know what I Like, Firth of Fifth, The Musical Box, Horizons, Supper's Ready (cut).

Another excellent recording from the Roxy marathon. "Watcher" is tight, "Moonlit Knight" is majestic, even though the Mellotron choirs sound very close, in fact the recording could have been made inside the beast itself.

Lots of bottom end during "Cinema Show" which works well on the solo section, but does tend to overpower Hackett and all the intricate lines he is playing, the choirs sound fantastic and Collins really jazzes things up with some nice syncopation.

We join the urinating Hedgehog story halfway through, then Collins counts in a powerful "Firth of Fifth" with the vocals being right at the front, and this time Hackett is back for the big one. He throws in some tricky bits at the start, then holds an unbelievably long note before the Mellotron washes over everything. The sound is so clear on this song that Gabriel's breathy flute and the electric piano sound like they have been added on.

"The Musical Box" is almost perfect. The delicate 12-strings, the powerhouse guitar and organ, the sinister vocals and some quite brilliant drumming make up a classic Genesis performance perfect for the small club atmosphere.

Giving the crowd time to draw breath, Gabriel tells the Old Michael story that he ends by introducing a prelude by Hackett. "Horizons" draws polite applause before another of those dramatic pauses slightly kills the intro to "Supper's Ready". Gabriel goes very 'East End' with his accent before things settle down. Unfortunately the tape runs out just after '666' spoiling yet another epic work out.

DECEMBER 19th, 1973

THE ROXY CLUB, LOS ANGELES, USA. (Late Show)

Personnel: PG, TB, MR, PC, SH.

Set List: Watcher of the Skies, Dancing with the Moonlit Knight, The Cinema Show, I Know what I Like, Firth of Fifth, The Musical Box, More Fool Me, Supper's Ready.

The last of the six Roxy shows is an absolute cracker, a great soundboard recording of a stunning performance, the band are on fire, and to top it all, Gabriel wears his Father Christmas outfit to celebrate their last show of 1973.

Things get off to a shaky start with "Watcher" stuttering to a halt after only a minute, a nasty humming noise is soon banished and normal service is resumed, maybe this setback spurred them on, or maybe they were just getting real good.

The best ever (to these ears anyway) version of "Moonlit Knight" follows, after a helium-voiced Gabriel does some gift catalogue promotion, and tells the all-too-brief tale of Britannia with the big boobs. Everyone is on their toes for this one, Collins sets the pace with all sorts of jazz rock fills and machine gun snare rolls, Hackett then charges through that hair-raising solo before the 'Fat old Lady' makes her appearance. The Mahavishnu Orchestra-style ending is handled with ease and the dreamy coda gives everyone chance to draw breath.

Some nice flute and backing vocals ease "The Cinema Show" into the majestic instrumental section, here Banks reigns supreme with his synth and choirs combination. Hackett is a little light on "Firth of Fifth", but all the right notes and a few new ones are there.

Gabriel puts his all into "The Musical Box" the only song that always changes the atmosphere and comes over all dark and Victorian. Gabriel has made this song his own and it still sets the hackles rising. Collins goes all soppy on "More Fool Me"; he offers to do requests, but of course sings his plaintive tale of lost love.

The other star of this set is "Supper's Ready", at last a complete version has appeared and for musicianship and passion this is up there in the top drawer. Hackett and Banks decorate the solid foundation laid down by Rutherford and Collins, Gabriel of course is in character heaven and still has time for some nifty flute playing.

All live performances of this song are measured by the 'Apocalypse 9/8' section and this one is truly scary, Gabriel's echoed voice screams about 'The Guards of Magog' and boy do you believe him, the organ solo is still the best around and the way Collins sets it up is classic. The '666' proclamation must have worried even the most laid-back Californian.

Hackett wails away while Gabriel looks for Jerusalem, a truly moving moment. Progressive rock at its absolute peak and a prime candidate for official release.

DECEMBER 20th, 1973
NBC STUDIOS, BURBANK, CALIFORNIA, USA.

Personnel: PG, TB, MR, PC, SH.

Set List: *Watcher of the Skies, The Musical Box.*

Genesis on the TV was never a perfect match, their performances tended to be a bit stiff, in a similar vein to earlier BBC sessions, TV lighting was always very bright which did nothing to help the atmospheric nature of the songs. This aside, seeing the band in glorious colour with plenty of close-ups is a great insight into their then current stage act.

A close-up of Gabriel – all fluorescent eye make-up and batwings – is a good a way as any to start "Watcher", some nice shots of Banks as he builds up the Mellotron/organ fanfare before the whole band kick in. Hackett resplendent in a silk bomber jacket, and now without those stylish glasses he had always worn, has at least made the effort to look like a rock star, although the rest of the group still look like man at 'Mr Byrite', except of course the singer who looks plain weird.

Gabriel's movements throughout "Watcher" are jerky and exaggerated, he spreads his cloaked arms and then hides behind a tambourine whilst doing an on-the-spot jerky dance, maybe that's what extra-terrestrials do.

Things calm down for "The Musical Box", so much so that Gabriel almost forgets that they are playing a shortened version and reaches for the flute just as the power chords arrive. Banks is in the spotlight again with some lengthy shots of him playing all manner of complicated stuff, including a lot more lead lines than you would imagine.

The entry of Gabriel in the Old Man mask is classic rock theatre, he shuffles to the mic stand bent over and looking like he might not make it – by the end of the song he is bearing his chest begging to be touched before slumping to the floor during the dramatic finale.

JANUARY 13th, 1974

HIPPODROME THEATRE, BRISTOL, UK.

Personnel: PG, TB, MR, PC, SH.

Set List: Firth of Fifth, The Musical Box, Supper's Ready.

The first show of 1974, or a part of it at least, as only these three songs have surfaced. The recording quality is good, so hopefully one day the rest of this show will emerge. We join proceedings near the end of the rivers story, and then get Banks adding the piano intro to "Firth of Fifth". Unfortunately he makes a complete hash of it with bum notes all over the place. The song itself is well played, with Hackett adding his now familiar deviation to the solo.

The mere mention of croquet gets a loud cheer, or a polite English one at least. "The Musical Box" follows in all its glory, not a great version but still enough to bring the house down, with Gabriel stealing the honours this time.

Someone with a Welsh accent is yelling for "Harold the Barrel". He was soon to make an appearance in the set list, but not tonight. Next up is the 'Old Michael' story, followed by "Supper's Ready". Collins is quite heavy during the 'Guaranteed Eternal Sanctuary Man' section playing it straight with the minimum of frills; Gabriel forgets a few words but bluffs his way through it.

The echo Gabriel uses on the 'Magog' section is almost too much and detracts from the tension he has created, it sounds like he is singing everything twice and doesn't really work.

With the London 5-nighter just around the corner this show served as good warm up for some of the epics to come.

JANUARY 20th, 1974

THEATRE ROYAL, DRURY LANE, LONDON, UK.

Personnel: PG, TB, MR, PC, SH.

Set List: Watcher of the Skies, Dancing With the Moonlit Knight, The Cinema Show, I Know What I like, Firth of Fifth, Harold the Barrel, The Musical Box, Horizons, More Fool Me, The Battle of Epping Forest, Supper's Ready.

The fifth show from a sell-out five-night run at the prestigious Theatre Royal, this excellent recording is so far the only one to have surfaced and now exists as two completely different audience recordings, one of which has been cleaned up at the band's own studio. Did anyone tape any of the other nights? If they did, no one has yet owned up. The set list has expanded to include several of the shorter numbers and one very welcome return.

"Watcher" is solid, with the organ adding an almost soothing contrast to the powerhouse rhythm section, Gabriel is slightly back in the mix, but still sounds like he might well have come from another planet. The song's conclusion is greeted with a mighty cheer, and after a few exaggerated shouts of 'Hello', the well-oiled machine that is "Moonlit Knight" gets underway.

With the exception of "Epping Forest", which was always a little too over the top, the material from *Selling England by the Pound* has a free flowing feel to it. "Moonlit Knight" and "Cinema Show" both give the band a chance to stretch out, whilst the singer nipped off to the wardrobe for his next silly hat.

The keyboard solo in "Cinema Show" is magnificent, with Banks on top form, although coming just after another fret-melting "Moonlit Knight" from Hackett, he has to be. "I Know What I like" calms things down a bit and the focus switches back to Gabriel as he does his country yokel routine.

The 'Lady on the Subway' story comes next, it doesn't quite work and Gabriel acknowledges this, as he introduces "Firth of Fifth". Banks makes a fair attempt at the piano solo but it still sounds awful, in fact the odd bum piano note still creeps in during the big Hackett build up. Maybe he was frustrated at the limitations of the electric piano.

A piece of Genesis theatre next as "Harold" makes a welcome return. 'Here's one for the old timers,' says Gabriel before this perfect miniature bundles in, all pounding piano and cockney accents, it gets the loudest cheer so far.

A less-than-convincing "Musical Box" is followed by Hackett's melancholic solo piece "Horizons", all-too-short, but very well received. Then it's the turn of Collins and Rutherford to take centre stage for their lost love duet, some of the high notes almost catch Collins out, but he just about pulls it off.

Hackett is on form for a better than average "Epping Forest", for once the stop-start nature of the song flows nicely into the middle section with its host of dodgy characters, then builds to the cutting guitar solo at the end. "Supper's Ready" crowns a fine all-round performance, the pastoral opening section gradually gets louder, only to drop right away for 'How Dare I Be So Beautiful'.

Banks uses a perfect mix of Mellotron brass and organ for the music-hall mayhem of 'Willow Farm'. The tension builds, then explodes into a stunning 'Apocalypse' – the Banks, Rutherford, Collins engine pumps out that hypnotic rhythm, Gabriel screams about all sorts of unpleasantness, then at the end of the manic organ solo he promptly flies through the air – with the aid of a harness of course. Hackett takes over at the end with some killer guitar to end one of the best performances yet.

JANUARY 26th, 1974
VORST NATIONALE, BRUSSELS, BELGIUM.

Personnel: PG, TB, MR, PC, SH.

Set List: Watcher of the Skies, Dancing With the Moonlit Knight, The Cinema Show, I Know What I Like, Firth of Fifth (cut), The Musical Box, More Fool Me (cut), Harold The Barrel, Supper's Ready.

One of several shows from early 1974 that keeps improving in sound quality as better versions are discovered, this is now a very good audience recording with a reasonable balance for all concerned.

Gabriel gets the usual cheer as he makes his cloaked entrance at the start of "Watcher", the echo in the hall adds to the power of the song with the drums and bass combination being very up-front. "Moonlit Knight" and "Cinema Show" both get the enthusiastic crowd on their feet, as they cheer every move Gabriel makes.

"Cinema Show" has some nice flute from Gabriel, which leads up to the big keyboard section where Banks puts the ARP and the Mellotron through their paces, he totally dominates this piece but is well supported by the rest of the group.

Lots of cheering during "I Know What I Like" – the crowd obviously likes the silly dance and lawnmower impressions taking place. Collins adds lots of nice touches to the play-out of this song before the deafening lawnmower moves away.

The dreaded "Firth of Fifth" piano solo rears up to haunt Banks once more, great on the album, not great live, it just does not work on the electric piano. Unfortunately there is a horrendous edit just as Hackett unleashes another solo and we join the song again for the final verse.

Gabriel whips up the crowd with his half-French, half-English story for "The Musical Box"; he really gets into character and casts a spell over the entire hall with his theatrical mannerisms and dreamy flute playing. Some of the audience sing along before Rutherford hits that most famous chord and is answered by Banks.

After the excitement of "The Musical Box" there is an all-too-brief snippet of "More Fool Me" before the recording jumps straight into "Harold the Barrel". Harold works well in concert with the music-hall vocals and the drawn-out doom and gloom piano chord ending, it also acts as some welcome light relief before the endurance test that is "Supper's Ready".

A good, if not great, "Supper's Ready" suffers a bit with some sound drop-out and that little bit of edge that accompanies the 'Apocalypse' section, but Hackett does shine during the ending.

JANUARY 28th, 1974
EULACH HALLE, WINTERHUR, SWITZERLAND.

Personnel: PG, TB, MR, PC, SH.

Set List: Dancing With The Moonlit Knight, The Cinema Show, I Know What I Like, Firth Of Fifth, The Musical Box, More Fool Me, Supper's Ready.

We join this fairly good audience recording just after "Watcher" has finished which is a shame, as the band play a very good "Moonlit Knight" and a casually stroll through "Cinema Show", so much so that some of the vocals get lost altogether.

The lack of clarity of this recording does detract from the light and shade of most of the songs, Hackett does an admiral job on "Firth Of Fifth" and "The Musical Box" gallops along during the instrumental sections, but loses a lot when Gabriel goes all old man.

Collins shines during an almost guitar-less "More Fool Me", his plaintive voice cuts through the background noise to bring some calm to the proceedings.

Gabriel's 'Old Michael' story almost sounds like he has forgotten the words but still amuses the audience, who he soon has clapping in military time. The song itself is well-played, but not a classic performance – everybody plays his part but that vital spark is missing. 'Magog' has a nice swing to it and the organ solo is still breathtaking if somewhat spoiled by a hideous bass noise which thankfully soon disappears.

JANUARY 30th, 1974

PHILIPSHALLE, DUSSELDORF, GERMANY.

Personnel: PG, TB, MR, PC, SH.

Set List: Watcher of the Skies, Dancing With The Moonlit Knight, The Cinema Show, I Know What I Like, Firth Of Fifth, The Musical Box, More Fool Me, The Battle of Epping Forest, Supper's Ready, Harold the Barrel.

A vastly improved recording with plenty of bass and some nice clear vocals, it's amazing how the quality of these shows improves as lower generation tapes are unearthed.

"Watcher" is fairly sluggish to start, with but soon picks up when Collins and Rutherford get going, Gabriel dressed in full-length cloak and batwing headress must have seemed quite alien to the audience, while behind on the backdrop two giant eyes stare out as the unrelenting rhythm pounds on.

An excellent run through for "Moonlit Knight" begins the usual quartet of songs from *Selling England by the Pound.* "Cinema Show" is all pleasing harmonies and Rutherford's relentless rhythm guitar, topped off with some nice lead from a restrained Hackett, a true classic amongst Genesis classics.

Nothing happens for a few minutes while Gabriel gets his lawnmower out, this done he leads them through a nice bass-heavy jaunt in the back garden. English eccentricity in front of a German crowd must account for the mediocrity of the applause. The usual rivers story sets Banks up for another stab at the "Firth of Fifth" intro, once again he does not pull it off and the pause before the band pile in is just too noticeable. Hackett is a bit down in the mix during his solo and he has quite a different sound this time around, but all those long-sustained notes are there as he tries to match the sheer class Banks turned on during "The Cinema Show".

Croquet is obviously not a favoured sport in Germany, as most of the audience don't recognise "The Musical Box" until it actually starts. Collins powers his way through the first heavy section, and gets a ripple of applause for his efforts. Hackett is on top of his game as he and Banks wrestle the lead lines from each other. Gabriel is just getting into the old man routine when a hideous edit takes us to the 'Touch me' section.

Two more tracks from the latest album contrast the sparse "More Fool Me" with the jam packed "The Battle of Epping Forest", from Collins and his plaintive love song to Gabriel and his cast of thousands. Both songs are executed with ease.

"Supper's Ready" sets off with its usual wash of nicely picked acoustics which for the next four minutes take the audience from Epping Forest to some distant land whose exact location even the singer would be hard pressed to reveal. Things progress through to the pounding finale, everyone gets a bash here, Collins and Rutherford power things along, Hackett wails away, Banks does a Banks and plays that unbelievable organ solo, while Gabriel takes off.

If that isn't enough "Harold the Barrel" rolls up for a rare encore and is a welcome three minutes of slightly sinister musical hall after the epic battle of good and evil that has just finished.

JANUARY 31st, 1974

STADHALLE, OFFENBACH, GERMANY.

Personnel: PG, TB, MR, PC, SH.

Set List: *Watcher of the Skies, Dancing With The Moonlit Knight, The Cinema Show, I Know What I Like, Firth Of Fifth, Harold the Barrel, The Musical Box, More Fool Me, Supper's Ready.*

Another highly impressive recording gets underway with a rather rigid "Watcher", which suffers from a couple of edits in the tape. Collins has to work the audience into responding to his 'Good evening, Offenbach' but gets there in the end.

They cruise through "Moonlit Knight" without any Hackett fretboard gymnastics, although Collins throws in some strange noises during the end section. Gabriel runs through the Romeo and Juliet story much to the amusement of the audience, who obviously appreciate such humour, "Cinema Show" gets very jazz-funk during the long instrumental lead by Collins and expertly backed by Rutherford and Banks.

The lawnmower routine is greeted with some random applause, Gabriel it seems can do no wrong, or maybe they just like men in funny hats.

The five rivers story loses its way a bit as Gabriel tries some audience participation, but then Banks surprises everyone by playing an almost note-perfect piano intro to "Firth of Fifth", the band crash in and deliver a magnificent rendition with Hackett adding all sorts of extras to his already stunning solo.

There is something special about the few occasions "Harold the Barrel" is played, perhaps it is because the set list for this tour was so rarely changed, or the fact that any song from *Nursery Cryme* is worth getting sentimental about. Anyway, his brief appearance before an excellent "Musical Box" totally transforms the atmosphere, taking it back to those early shows of 1972.

Collins and Rutherford set things up for "Supper's Ready" with their well-received solo spot, then Gabriel gives an animated performance as he tells the 'Old Michael' story. His love of *Monty Python* is very obvious here with lots of exaggerated shouting in a high pitched voice. The song is well played, but still not as intense as the late 1973 shows, though I imagine it scared a few Germans during the '666' section.

FEBRUARY 3rd, 1974

PALASPORT, TURIN, ITALY.

Personnel: PG, TB, MR, PC, SH.

Set List: Watcher of the Skies, Dancing With The Moonlit Knight, The Cinema Show, I Know What I Like, Firth Of Fifth (cut), The Musical Box, More Fool Me, The Battle Of Epping Forest, Supper's Ready, The Knife.

The first of four sold-out Italian shows and the band are riding high, *Selling England* is on top of the Italian charts and those adoring fans just love their Mellotron-drenched prog rock.

This recording is a very clear audience tape, which captures the general excitement the band conjured up every time they played there. Some very good colour, but sadly silent, footage has surfaced but it still gives a great indication as to what was happening on stage, especially as far as the lead singer is concerned.

Things kick off with a noisy greeting for "Watcher" which passes without a hitch, "Moonlit Knight" is good, "The Cinema Show" is better, Gabriel leaves the stage for the long middle section and Rutherford turns to face Banks and Collins for the legendary three-way jam.

"I Know What I Like" has Gabriel in the WW1 Prussian helmet with the spike on top, he does his usual funny dance and Rutherford has a big grin on his face. Banks does a Les Dawson (English comedian who played the piano badly on purpose) on the intro to "Firth of Fifth", and there is a nasty edit in the middle of the piece so Hackett's moment is spoiled.

Gabriel gets some laughs with his Italian version of the Henry and Cynthia story, and then gets an almighty roar when he introduces "The Musical Box". There is an almost reverential silence whilst this crowd favourite unfolds.

"Epping Forest" sees Gabriel don a top hat and sparkling dinner jacket as he prances across the stage.

A powerful "Supper's Ready" is followed by that rarest of things an encore, "The Knife" is given a good going over and even gets the crowd clapping in time, Gabriel is charging around so much that his vocal all but disappears for most of the song.

FEBRUARY 4th, 1974

PALASPORT, REGGIO EMILIO, ITALY.

Personnel: PG, TB, MR, PC, SH.

Set List: Watcher of the Skies, Dancing With The Moonlit Knight, The Cinema Show, I Know What I Like, Firth Of Fifth, Harold The Barrel, The Musical Box, More Fool Me, Supper's Ready, The Knife.

Twelve thousand excitable Italians are packed into the Palasport and witness a real peach of a performance, luckily one of them was together enough to make this excellent recording, which has recently been tweaked and cleaned up into one of the most enjoyable from this era.

"Watcher" is very up-beat, with Rutherford and Collins combining for an almost funky rhythm section. "Moonlit Knight" is spot-on with everyone at the right place at the right time, the Mellotron is very dominant during the end section.

Gabriel throws in some Italian during the intro for "The Cinema Show"; not much, but enough to raise him to god-like status with the crowd. Hackett plays some beautiful lines during the verses and Banks gets his fingers caught up in the long middle section, Collins of course is as inventive as ever. "I Know What I Like" has a jovial Gabriel really going to town on the silly voices, a great performance.

The "Firth of Fifth" story again involves a Urinating Hedgehog, a splitting trouser leg and some forced crowd participation. The piano intro is played with only a couple of bum notes, but the song itself is a real tour-de-force; Hackett more than making up for his almost total absence from "The Cinema Show".

As with most Italian recordings they tend to fade out between each song, this is slightly annoying but at least everything is here.

"Harold" flies by with a mixture of 'east end swagger' and *Monty Python* humour. Gabriel must be rushing about as his vocals sound quite out of breath, although he holds some nice long notes for the ending which sounds much better than the album version.

Lots of anguished vocals in the opening section of "The Musical Box", bucket loads by the end. Collins calms things down with "More Fool Me". A few cries from the audience are soon hushed by those who want to listen, which is just about everybody.

'Old Michael' goes Italian, much to everyone's amusement, Jerusalem boogie gets a hand clap, "Supper's Ready" gets a roar of approval and for the next twenty-four minutes the twelve thousand are held spellbound. This is a truly great "Supper's" with Gabriel on top form, pushing every character to the limits, the '666' moment really is scary.

The crowd are finished off with a riotous version of "The Knife" with Hackett in full overdrive mode and Gabriel screaming out the vocals whenever he can. He almost won't let the band end the song as he continues to shout. The only possible way to end this classic gig.

FEBRUARY 5th, 1974

PALASPORT, ROME, ITALY.

Personnel: PG, TB, MR, PC, SH.

Set List: Watcher of the Skies, Dancing With The Moonlit Knight, The Cinema Show, I Know What I Like, Firth Of Fifth, The Musical Box, More Fool Me, The Battle of Epping Forest, Supper's Ready, The Knife.

The big one. 20,000 manic Genesis fans packed into the vast concrete Palasport greet the "Watcher" fanfare with a burst of noise, in fact they greet everything the band does in similar fashion. "Watcher" with its thunderous rhythm and wall-shaking Mellotron must have had the foundations quaking as the crowd roar their approval.

'Ciao Roma' is the greeting, before "Moonlit Knight" gets the customary thumbs up, Hackett shines and Collins keeps things moving along at a fair old pace. In the eyes of the masses the band can do no wrong and they don't. "Firth of Fifth" still has the piano intro and Hackett unleashes a masterful solo.

"The Musical Box" could have been written for the Italians, they even quieten down a bit during the slow sections, although never for long. "More Fool Me" gets a generous reception as Phil and Mike take centre stage and manage to pull off a three-minute ballad in front of their largest audience yet.

Massed whistling and the slow marching snare ushers in the next epic. "Epping Forest" sees Gabriel well and truly back in several saddles, all dodgy villains wielding pick-axe handles and a well-suspect vicar. Gabriel in his black catsuit and stocking mask charging across the stage must have been a sight to behold.

"Supper's Ready" is suitably impressive, Gabriel has a serious echo on his vocal during 'Magog' and Banks has the organ solo for breakfast, there must have been some freaked out Italians as the be-cloaked figure with the scary box headgear shuffled to the front of the stage screaming '666', Hackett wails away after 'Jerusalem" and the crowd go ape.

This legendary gig is topped off with a rampant "The Knife", although somewhat lacking in vocal quality, it still packs a punch and harks back to the Italian tours of 1972.

A good audience recording making up in atmosphere for what it loses in clarity.

FEBRUARY 6th, 1974

PALASPORT, NAPLES, ITALY.

Personnel: PG, TB, MR, PC, SH.

Set List: Watcher of the Skies, Dancing With The Moonlit Knight, The Cinema Show, I Know What I Like, Firth Of Fifth, The Musical Box, More Fool Me, The Battle of Epping Forest, Supper's Ready, The Knife.

The last of the Italian jobs is another good audience recording with plenty of atmosphere and a lot of clout. "Watcher" seems to take forever to get going and there's even a stutter just before the vocals come in, Collins greets the audience with a 'Good evening Naples', and then Gabriel comes on all smarmy with a 'Ciao Napoli'.

Those close to the taper babble on throughout the show, but this adds to the ambience and is not too distracting. Both "Moonlit Knight" and "Cinema Show" lack the usual spark but are still well played and equally well received. Collins has to whip up a funky drum solo as the Mellotron plays up at the start of "Moonlit Knight", he then adds lots of swing to the lawnmower song and it works a treat.

The first part of the piano solo from "Firth of Fifth" is missing, which is a shame as the band pile in with a vengeance, Hackett adds a few frills to his solo and everyone gives a fine solid performance. As usual, the Italians get excited about anything from *Nursery Cryme* and once the 'Henry and Cynthia' story begins they start shouting and whistling. It's a shame "Harold the Barrel" was dropped for these shows.

"The Musical Box" is majestic, Rutherford's 12-string power chords make such a dramatic entrance and they set Hackett up for his first solo, which is note perfect and gets its own round of applause. An annoying tape edit breaks the spell, and then someone finally loses control and shouts out just as the Old Man is doing his thing, very powerful indeed.

Collins threatens the audience with some soul music but of course doesn't fool anyone, they even make 'be quiet' noises to the few that have to call out. "Epping Forest" has a feel of "Get 'em Out by Friday" to it, with all those iffy characters and odd time signatures, but here Gabriel's stage antics cause some of the vocals to sound a bit out of breath.

Some more edits spoil a below-par "Supper's Ready", although Collins does his best with some excellent drumming. Everyone gets excited at the flashpot climax, hadn't they seen anyone fly before?

The encore rattles along with lots of Hackett sounding like a motorbike, the vocals are all over the place, but it's the thought that counts, good job that a certain Hogweed didn't rush in…

FEBRUARY 12th, 1974

T.V. STUDIOS, PARIS, FRANCE.

Personnel: PG, TB, MR, PC, SH.

Set List: *I Know What I Like, Supper's Ready.*

Another European TV show which has survived in glorious colour. Luckily the tapes were not wiped, as they surely would have been if the show had been in the UK.

The bright studio lighting and the very seventies background effects somewhat detract from the music, especially during "Supper's Ready". For the costumes to work properly you need an atmospheric light show with a strobe, and the darkness adding to the scary bits at the end.

Gabriel comes over all camp for "I Know What I Like" sporting what looks like a WW1 German soldier's helmet and some face paint, he plays to the camera and even Collins can't suppress a grin as the human lawnmower passes his kit. Hackett, now minus the trademark glasses and looking a lot more like a rock star, is twanging away on the strange looking sitar guitar, but of course all eyes are on the strangely disturbing lead singer.

It's great to see "Supper's Ready" professionally filmed with lots of nice close-ups, it's not a classic version and the '666' section is nowhere near as effective as the film from the Shepperton Studios back in October '73. This is because of the excessive lighting, which ruins the finale and makes all the costumes look rather silly.

The film is worth seeing if only for Gabriel's gradually changing appearance, his taste for make-up and a really bizarre haircut.

MARCH 3rd, 1974

TOWER THEATRE, PHILADELPHIA, USA.

Personnel: PG, TB, MR, PC, SH.

Set List: *Watcher of the Skies, Dancing With The Moonlit Knight, The Cinema Show (cut), I Know What I Like, More Fool Me, Firth Of Fifth, The Musical Box (cut), The Battle Of Epping Forest, Supper's Ready.*

A very rhythmic "Watcher of the Skies" with plenty of funky drumming and thumping bass gets this nice and noisy audience recording underway with a swagger not normally associated with this generally rigid number. The good folk of Philly make plenty of noise, and Gabriel and Collins give them plenty of shouts of 'Hello' before Britannia makes her entrance. "Moonlit Knight" has lots of Rutherford and the usual array of impossibly quick drum fills.

There are some nasty edits in "The Cinema Show" which is a shame as it is a full-on version with Banks well on top of his lengthy solo. Gabriel throws in some nice flute at the end of "I Know What I Like", otherwise it's a standard version.

The running order might not be correct as "More Fool Me" is too early in the set, but there are breaks in the recording between most songs, so anything could have happened.

The dodgy editing spoils the atmosphere at this show and becomes more annoying as things progress. "The Musical Box" is even separated from its story but still casts its spell, the noisy Americans keep quiet and some atmosphere is restored. Hackett gets off a nice aggressive solo and the organ is well to the fore.

The two closing epics are intact and "Supper's Ready" is a real gem, lots of echo on 'Magog' and after a very nimble organ solo, Gabriel really pulls out all the stops then quite literally takes off, much to the amazement of most of the crowd.

MARCH 7th, 1974

CIVIC AUDITORIUM, FORT WAYNE, USA.

Personnel: PG, TB, MR, PC, SH.

Set List: *Watcher of the Skies, Dancing With The Moonlit Knight, The Cinema Show, I Know What I Like, Firth Of Fifth (cut), The Musical Box, Supper's Ready (cut).*

A muddy recording but still a great performance, Collins is in particularly good form with some powerhouse work during "Moonlit Knight", Hackett dishes out some dirty licks and only the vocals suffer in the mix.

"The Cinema Show" loses something due to the less-than-great quality of the recording, but everyone does their bit with Banks in fine nimble finger form.

Some editing means we lose the intro to "Firth Of Fifth" and the story for "Supper's Ready", but between these we have a nice dark "Musical Box" with some meaty power chords and desperate vocals. Gabriel wows the crowd with the old man dance and for once the recording quality almost adds to the atmosphere.

Hackett plays a blinder on "Supper's" and the Mellotron is put to good use for 'Willow Farm', and Gabriel is seriously menacing during an almost swinging 9/8 which of course has Collins throwing in fills as casually as you like.

Then the unthinkable happens and the tape cuts off at the 'Lord of Lords' end section, a shame to end this great performance in such a sudden fashion.

There might be a couple of songs missing from this recording, as the set list is a bit short.

MARCH 9th, 1974

GUSMAN HALL, MIAMI, USA.

Personnel: PG, TB, MR, PC, SH.

Set List: Watcher of the Skies, Dancing With The Moonlit Knight, The Cinema Show, I Know What I Like, Firth Of Fifth, The Musical Box, More Fool Me, The Battle of Epping Forest, Supper's Ready.

Another good audience recording with plenty of atmosphere and only a little bit of sound fluctuation.

"Watcher" and "Moonlit Knight" hurry by with Hackett in fine fettle, Gabriel drags out the Romeo story before another really top drawer "Cinema Show" arrives.

Collins excels during the solo sections and Hackett plays some beautiful lead lines in the verses, this song improves with age and the band obviously get a kick out of playing it.

The story for "Firth of Fifth" has now changed to one concerning dead bodies. Pigeons and also a Scotsman feature in a tale Gabriel seems to be having fun telling. The piano solo is almost on the mark and the band really hit the spot when they all crash in together. Hackett's solo is sublime even though the recording has an annoying edit in the middle, the Mellotron arrives and a tidal wave of sound washes over the transfixed audience.

A lengthy Henry story with lots of audience interaction is rapidly wound up as the tuning and/or repairs must have suddenly finished, the dream like quality of the opening section is perfectly captured, three guitars and Gabriel standing still at the mic stand, then breaking into that ungainly dance as the heavy stuff kicks in.

It's a shame when tapes get cut between songs, whether it's the taper trying to save tape or just bad editing is any ones guess. It's also a pain when people yell out during quiet bits, this happens at the start of "More Fool Me" so Collins stops the song to ask for some hush. The song is well played and is a nice break before the madness that is "Epping Forest" and "Supper's Ready" back to back.

Gabriel really gives the East End villain a good working over, and screams his head off at the end of "Supper's". Well he did have to follow a stunning '9/8'.

MARCH 21st, 1974

CIVIC REUNION CENTRE, SANTA MONICA, USA.

Personnel: PG, TB, MR, PC, SH.

Set List: Dancing With The Moonlit Knight (cut), The Cinema Show (cut), I Know What I Like (cut), Firth Of Fifth (cut), The Musical Box (cut), Supper's Ready (cut).

Another show that was filmed by an enterprising fan, this is one of the more watchable shows from the tour.

It's in colour and has the original sound, still dark in places but the cameraman pans the stage and even Hackett gets an occasional look in.

The action jumps from song to song but unlike some of the other amateur footage from this era you actually get reasonable sections from each piece and it gives a pretty good idea of how the show ran.

Gabriel's severe haircut comes in for a close-up for a small part of the "Cinema Show" story, lots of nice clear shots of the instrumental section, with plenty of Banks and Rutherford, and a cool close-up of Collins. A big floppy hat is donned for "I Know What I Like" and the lawn mower shuffle is followed across the stage.

Banks plays the "Firth of Fifth" solo and turns to the organ as the band crash in, Hackett gets some spotlight during his solo and some generous appreciation from the crowd.

The "Musical Box" with its old man theatrics gets the biggest applause yet, plus several audible exclamations in the 'Wow' and 'I don't believe that' league. Gabriel is as impressive as ever, as he transforms his catsuit into an off-the-shoulder number whilst offering himself to the baying crowd, his dying swan finale being a truly great Genesis moment.

The few fragments of "Supper's Ready" that survive show Gabriel in a strange domed hat for 'the foe have met their fate' section. Also the excitement of the finale is felt despite the hideous editing. This fragmented recording is very enjoyable to watch and shows a band on top of their game.

APRIL 6th, 1974
STUDENT UNION AUDITORIUM, TOLEDO, USA.

Personnel: PG, TB, MR, PC, SH.

Set List: Watcher of the Skies, Dancing With The Moonlit Knight, The Cinema Show, I Know What I Like, Firth Of Fifth, The Musical Box, Horizons, The Battle of Epping Forest, Supper's Ready.

The excitement of the recorder and his friends sets the scene for this excellent show, one fan declares to a neighbour, 'You're gonna be totally shattered' and they all lose control when Gabriel appears in the batwings as the "Watcher" build-up peaks.

Britannia in water wings charging round a supermarket with several packets of biscuits briefly shuts everyone up for a few moments, that is until they hear the opening words to "Moonlit Knight" then it's 'Wow' and other superlatives.

Hackett and Collins blow the roof off with this version, stunning drumming, and glass-shattering guitar as good as it gets for this unsung Genesis classic. Obviously stunned by the previous song's brilliance Banks makes a couple of howlers during his solo in "The Cinema Show" he also comes over all ham-fisted with the Mellotron choirs, a most unusual event.

Gabriel explains to the crowd that the human body is 98% water, and the piano solo foxes Banks once again. But Hackett saves the day with a sublime solo as the band almost drift off on cruise control.

The Croquet story is wasted on the bemused audience, so Gabriel makes several silly noises to keep them happy. It works, and "The Musical Box" is wheeled out to darken the mood of the evening. It's tranquil beginning with the delicate guitars and the pleading vocals are soon to be lost in a maelstrom of power chords and overdrive guitar. There is an unfortunate break in the recording near the end but it is still a masterful performance.

The applause lasts for a long time until Collins introduces "Horizons" which is duly played, and is well received. For a song so full of characters and costumes it's strange that "Epping Forest" didn't merit a Gabriel story, instead we get the usual snare march before all manner of chaos breaks out.

The Battle is fought and won with Hackett giving more than a good account of himself. He also does well in "Supper's Ready" which is one of the better ones, all pomp and trapeze wires, flash pots and that man Hackett. The song ends and there is a split-second pause before the applause kicks in. A nice show with an enthusiastic audience.

APRIL 7th, 1974

THE AGORA, COLUMBUS, USA.

Personnel: PG, TB, MR, PC, SH.

Set List: Watcher of the Skies, Dancing With The Moonlit Knight, The Cinema Show, I Know What I Like, Firth Of Fifth (cut), The Musical Box, More Fool Me (cut), The Battle Of Epping Forest, Supper's Ready (cut).

Sounds like the person who recorded this show was holding the microphone inside the bass cabinets, which is a shame as the rest of the sound is well-balanced and the performance is another good one. But every time Rutherford hits the bass we get an awful distorted sound.

Collins informs us that it is 8.30 on a Sunday night, the band then rattle through "Moonlit Knight" and "The Cinema Show". "Firth of Fifth" has the 'jumping on dead bodies' story but the song itself is spoilt by the hideous bass noise, as well as being cut in half as the tape runs out.

The tape goes from bad to worse as "More Fool Me" is also cut and the rest of the show is ruined by the distortion.

APRIL 15th, 1974

THE PALLADIUM, NEW YORK, NY, USA.

Personnel: PG, TB, MR, PC, SH.

Set List: Dancing With The Moonlit Knight, I Know What I Like, The Cinema Show (cut), Firth Of Fifth, More Fool Me, The Musical Box (cut), The Battle Of Epping Forest, Supper's Ready.

A reasonable, though somewhat thin-sounding recording, that has unfortunately been messed around with, so that the running order has obviously been changed and there are some nasty edits. "The Cinema Show" suffers from a couple of cuts and "Watcher" is missing altogether.

The band are in good form with Hackett turning in a solid performance on "Firth of Fifth", while Collins holds his own during a nice "More Fool Me" which this time features some strong backing vocals from Rutherford.

We only get a brief snatch of the Henry story before "The Musical Box" weaves its spell. No matter how bad the recording is, this song always manages to shine through, plus it always keeps the audience quiet, no mean feat with some of the enthusiastic American crowds.

There is still a lot of power in this version of "Supper's Ready" and the audience are knocked sideways when the flash pots go off and Gabriel takes to the skies. Very dramatic – shame about the cuts.

APRIL 16th, 1974

THE FORD AUDITORIUM, DETROIT, MI, USA.

Personnel: PG, TB, MR, PC, SH.

Set List: Watcher of the Skies, Dancing With The Moonlit Knight, The Cinema Show, I Know What I Like, Firth Of Fifth, The Musical Box (cut), Horizons, Supper's Ready.

An excellent recording that has seen several levels of improvement as lower generation tapes have surfaced, the sound is crisp and very clear and every hi-hat is perfectly audible.

The Mellotron sounds fragile and a bit rough around the edges, but by the time the rest of the band arrive to back it up the "Watcher" intro is filling up the hall. Collins is hot from the word go and really propels this number along on a bed of funky drumming. Gabriel in an eccentric voice calls out 'Hello' a couple of times before delivering the following tale for "Moonlit Knight":

Thank you very much – ta – delighted, wonderful. We are in the process of doing (unintelligible bit) in front of your very eyes, a small feathered contraption feathered by fear. The young lady (?) the old lady, yes very old, standing before you now. Britannia, pomp and pride of the British Empire. She sinks slowly on the waves on a small pair of water wings, rushes for enlightenment, grabs a trolley in the supermarket marked chariot of the gods. Hurtles down the passageway, grabs a few Buddha biscuits, Krishna cookies, and a small helping of Jesus jumpers, and all of these packets she eats quickly at home until fully masticated and spits them out into a large balloon which grows considerably larger. So large that it's big enough for her to pull a little blunt pocket knife and slit a hole in the bottom, pouring the entire contents onto a small piece of manuscript paper which when rotated at a speed of thirty-three-and-a-third RPM sounds a little like this..."

Before the song starts an equipment breakdown causes an annoyed-sounding Gabriel to ad-lib for a couple of minutes, an interlude he blames on Rutherford and Nick the roadie. 'What has happened to my fucking lead?' We almost get a one-handed drum solo but normal service is resumed and "Moonlit Knight" begins.

Gabriel puts a bit more into the vocals this time, and Collins goes drum roll crazy in a somewhat slower version than usual, Hackett is missing in action during the second half, but the trippy bit is suitably trippy with the guitarist back on board.

"The Cinema Show" takes an age to get going and crawls along at snail's pace through the verses, things pick up when Banks takes over as he drags Rutherford and Collins into the classic three-way jam. The Mellotron choirs miss their cue but the rhythm section are spot-on as usual.

A spacey intro to "I Know What I Like" sounds almost like early Tangerine Dream, before Collins funks things up and farmer Gabriel takes over, even Hackett gets in the swing on the sitar guitar. This song is so loose it could be Kool and the Gang on the stage. The recording has a bit of trouble during the fade out but soon gets back to normal.

Dead bodies and water extraction make up the "Firth of Fifth" story, Hackett makes up some of his solo and steals the show hands-down. This was always going to be a winner once Banks had played a note-perfect piano intro, a rarity indeed. Whilst telling the Henry story, a heckler is put down by Gabriel with the comment 'My mother does not eat shit', Collins then adds that there is 'also a bar'. Suitably chastised, things remain quiet for the first half of "The Musical Box". An unfortunate edit takes us quickly into Hackett's first solo, which is a shame as this sounds like a particularly intense version.

A nice clear "Horizons" is well-received, although there is the lengthy 'Old Michael' story to come before the grand finale. Collins and Gabriel actually sing a verse of Jerusalem in dodgy cockney accents much to everyone's amusement.

Some crackling and buzzing spoil some parts of "Supper's Ready", but like "The Cinema Show", something is still missing. 'Willow Farm' is full of sound effects and *Python*-esque voices, then things get going as the 'Guards of Magog' swarm everywhere. Gabriel really stretches the vocal chords during '666'. A powerful gig if a little slow in places, still plenty of highlights and superb sound quality.

APRIL 20th, 1974
UNIVERSITY SPORTS CENTRE, MONTREAL, CANADA.

Personnel: PG, TB, MR, PC, SH.

Set List: *Watcher of the Skies, Dancing With The Moonlit Knight, The Cinema Show, I Know What I Like, Firth of Fifth, The Musical Box, More Fool Me, The Battle of Epping Forest, Supper's Ready.*

The first of two shows at Montreal University is a mostly excellent audience recording that captures the band in top form once again. The audience had just listened to a solo set by labelmate and Van der Graaf Generator mainman Peter Hammill, and if that wasn't enough, Gabriel announces "Moonlit Knight" in French.

"Watcher" is Collins-driven and therefore quite loose. "Moonlit Knight" starts slowly but gets into gear with the Hackett solo, which dominates the first section, as for once he is higher in the mix than Banks. The coda is full of strange noises and dreamy Mellotron, Collins shakes lots of percussion and gives the tubular bells a work out.

There is a tape edit during Banks' solo in "The Cinema Show", only a slight one but still enough to spoil a superb performance with Collins being ever-so on the case with the snare drum/hi-hat combination.

The organ is mostly buried on this recording, so songs like "The Musical Box" lose some of the dramatic impact during the heavy sections, the old man's appearance is the source of much amusement to the taper and his friends. Hackett romps through "Firth of Fifth" and Banks even gets the piano intro right.

Collins and Rutherford deliver a fine duet and earn themselves some generous applause, Collins then contributes some great backing vocals during a spirited "Epping Forest" which does get a bit bass-heavy in places and the sound quality drops below the rest of the show's high standard.

The story for "Supper's Ready" is also in French and is obviously very funny as it gets more reaction than usual, the sound quality is now back to normal although the vocals do get lost in the first part of the song.

There is an edit early on and the recording wavers in quality again, it sounds like the taper is now further away from the stage. Gabriel really comes alive for all the echoed shouting at the end and gets the usual gasps as he leaves the stage for the flying sequence.

Some nice footage of this concert exists. Shots include the strange headgear that resembles a giant gooseberry that Gabriel wore during

'The Guaranteed Eternal Sanctuary Man' and some film of the band leaving the hall after the show.

APRIL 21st, 1974
UNIVERSITY SPORTS CENTRE, MONTREAL, CANADA.

Personnel: PG, TB, MR, PC, SH.

Set List: Watcher of the Skies, Dancing With The Moonlit Knight, The Cinema Show, I Know What I Like, Firth Of Fifth, The Musical Box, Horizons, The Battle of Epping Forest, Supper's Ready.

A radio broadcast of the second night in Montreal means a crystal-clear recording, in fact one of the best from the whole tour. Peter Hammill's opening set was introduced by a French-speaking Gabriel, much to the crowd's delight.

This much-bootlegged set begins with a fearsome "Watcher", everyone in overdrive from the word go. The vocals are upfront and Collins punches out a powerful rhythm, even the Mellotron is behaving itself for once. Gabriel's French announcement for "Moonlit Knight" includes several references to the radio; his story for "The Cinema Show" causes much hilarity as his voice descends into a lecherous tone as he expands on the tale of Romeo and his amorous intentions.

Both songs are expertly performed; "Moonlit Knight" lacks a little of the aggression from earlier shows in the tour, but Hackett and Collins are still the top dogs here. The Gabriel/Collins harmonies on "Cinema Show" are some of the best yet, Collins sings exactly the right parts to complement Gabriel's ever-changing voice, then Hackett throws in that beautiful riff during the 'Once a man like the sea I raged' line and everything falls into place. Banks gets his fingers caught up during his solo, perhaps Hackett's gorgeous lead put him off.

The sound fluctuates a bit every now-and-then and the audience response the end of every song is a bit slow, but that is probably down to the radio broadcast and editing.

For some reason "Firth of Fifth" lacks any real fire, Hackett plays it safe and even Collins isn't as forceful as usual, perhaps the old 'holding it back when on the radio' syndrome has struck again. The start of "The Musical Box" again showcases the stunning vocals of Gabriel and Collins, and when the ghostly flute takes over, the whole feeling on the concert has changed once again.

Like many radio shows the sound might be crystal clear, but it is not always balanced, this is definitely the case here, as the heavy section kicks in there is a distinct lack of bass guitar and far too much drumming. There is a lot to be said for a good audience recording.

"Horizons" comes and goes with Gabriel announcing 'Monsieur Ackett' then it's straight into the forest all manner of dodgy goings on. The shift in sound towards the vocals means we get an excellent rendition of Gabriel's tale of '70s villainy, Collins plays his part as 'Bob the Nob' and 'Liquid Len' inflict violence on each other. Hackett then winds the whole thing up with one of his most underrated solos, although even he gets a little stuck on a few notes.

The 'Old Michael' story is embellished with some nifty Chinese finger cymbal work and a lot of interplay between the band's two comics. "Supper's Ready" then starts and the whole mood is once again changed.

The shift in sound sheds new light as to what each member does during this epic, Hackett is playing a lot of low-key intricate lines which usually get lost with the audience recordings, and Banks is playing everywhere mostly on the ARP synth, he is constantly coming up with all sorts of complicated harmonies.

The 'Magog' section and the organ solo are so sharp you can hear every hi-hat and almost feel the Hammond stabbing out that greatest of all Genesis solos. Gabriel sings from the depths of hell and shouts the house down with some heavy echo on '666' the faded ending is greeted with polite applause and the house music starts quickly, just to let everyone know that there will be no encore.

APRIL 23rd, 1974

CIVIC CENTRE, QUEBEC, CANADA.

Personnel: PG, TB, MR, PC, SH.

Set List: Supper's Ready.

Only the finale has surfaced from this show, some questions as to the date and indeed the venue, but a general consensus places the band back in Quebec for this night.

A good audience recording presents a workmanlike run through of the 'big one', things start slowly then get worse as Gabriel forgets the words during 'The Guaranteed Eternal Sanctuary Man' he recovers and sounds suitably repentant during 'How dare I be so beautiful'.

There's a serious echo on 'Guards of Magog' with each word repeating to double the menace that the singer exudes. The solo is played out over a solid backing, which demolishes anything in its path. As Banks scuttles up the upper manual of the Hammond, a lone cheer greets Gabriel's becloaked arrival, a dodgy edit spoils the continuity, but the song continues with the Mellotron in complete control and it stays in tune.

The vocals get a bit lost as everyone else plays at maximum volume especially Hackett who blasts out some killer guitar, but at least Gabriel gets to fly through the air.

APRIL 24th, 1974
MUSIC HALL, BOSTON, MASSACHUSETTES, USA.

Personnel: PG, TB, MR, PC, SH.

Set List: Watcher of the Skies, Dancing With The Moonlit Knight, The Cinema Show, I Know What I Like, Firth Of Fifth, The Musical Box, More Fool Me, Supper's Ready.

Another very good recording and another very enthusiastic audience, lots of cries and shouts during the "Watcher" intro and several during the song itself which is up-tempo and full of power.

Someone actually calls out 'Boogie' during the story for "Moonlit Knight", Gabriel then asks the question, 'What has happened to my fucking microphone?' As Nick the roadie frantically sorts things out, normal service is eventually resumed and the very noisy crowd are temporally calmed. Some feedback aside, Gabriel turns in a somewhat lifeless performance, the rest of the band do their best and fly through the instrumental sections.

The audience are thanked for their patience as more technical problems delay the start of "The Cinema Show", the first half of the song puts the band back in control as the 12-string guitars and the vocal harmonies float by and cast their spell over the unusually quiet crowd.

Banks takes over for the long solo section, and with Rutherford and Collins in close attendance, he turns in a mostly classic performance with only a few of the endless stream of notes ending up in the wrong place. Collins is very aggressive on some of the drum fills and even has some phasing on his sound.

The lawnmower effect comes and eventually goes as more problems plague the equipment, Rutherford blasts out a frantic bass solo, Collins says, 'I bet you wish that you'd all gone to the pictures', and Gabriel once more apologizes for the 'fuck up'. The song is played without further incident and ends up as a nice funky number with lots of syncopations from Collins.

As per usual the loudest cheer so far is reserved for a thrilling "The Musical Box" which passes without a hitch, as does "More Fool Me" which has seen Collins growing in confidence as the tour progresses, handling the lead vocals with ease.

More laughter and calling out as the Old Michael and the worms story is told, then a very impressive "Supper's Ready" begins to take shape. Hackett is a little low in the mix but everyone else is alive and kicking, especially Gabriel who seems to be trying to make up for all the sound problems that have littered this show.

After a spirited organ solo and dramatic build up, the vocals almost vanish at the start of '666' they return in time for the flying finale.

A problem-filled show with plenty of highs.

APRIL 28th, 1974

ALLEN THEATRE, CLEVELAND, OHIO, USA.

Personnel: PG, TB, MR, PC, SH.

Set List: Watcher of the Skies, Dancing With The Moonlit Knight, The Cinema Show, I Know What I Like, Firth Of Fifth, The Musical Box, The Battle of Epping Forest, Horizons, Supper's Ready.

An audience recording that, like so many others, seems to improve in sound quality as the first couple of numbers progress. "Watcher" starts a little muffled then soon gets a lot clearer and by the time "Moonlit Knight" arrives the sound is sharper still.

The crowd must have been impressed as Gabriel made his entrance for "Watcher" with batwings and multi-coloured cloak, his eyes painted with UV light receptive make-up to add to the alien look. Behind the band on two giant video screens a pair of eyes stare out as the Mellotron shakes the theatre to the core.

The Britannia costume with its Mohican head dress and red white and blue colour scheme probably meant less to the US audiences than it did to the UK ones, but was still an impressive piece of rock theatre. The song is handled with ease as Collins gets a chance to let off more steam.

The Romeo and his fungus story is told at break neck speed and "The Cinema Show" begins with that most Genesis of intros, Rutherford at his best which is more than can be said of Banks who makes a pig's ear of the Mellotron choirs during his solo. That moment when the choirs crash in and everyone steps up a gear is ruined when the Mellotron fails to work – or is it that he just forgot to play it for a few seconds?

Sporting a suspect white sun hat and still in his black catsuit Gabriel camps his way through the lawnmower song. It sits nicely between "Cinema" and "Firth" acting as light relief before another epic rendition.

The dead body story is now so bizarre that Gabriel even demonstrates how to jump so water can be extracted from said body, this obviously affected Banks as his piano intro has the usual couple of bum notes and with that dreadful pause while he turns to the organ before the band pile in. It just does not work live.

A new twist on the Henry and Cynthia story involves Henry Hamilton Smyth performing the first recorded streak in 1896, he still loses his head to Cynthia and her croquet mallet, and as always she ends up opening "The Musical Box". The importance of Gabriel's flute playing is most evident during the first part of this song, its mellow sound helps set the scene before Rutherford hammers out those chords and the stillness is shattered.

The old man mask finishes the job as he twists and turns and attempts some desperate sexual encounter with the mic stand, before finally dying as the song reaches its dramatic conclusion.

"Epping Forest" is a Gabriel one-man movie, his cast of characters take over the stage once Collins has finished his military drum roll. The sinister Reverend complete with dog collar and stocking mask charging around the stage making threatening gestures with a crowbar must have had those in the first few rows cowering in fear.

At last "Horizons" precedes "Supper's Ready" with only 'Old Michael' in between, the sound also suffers from some bass distortion, perhaps the taper had moved closer to the speakers or maybe things just got louder.

The back screens are put to good use again with two giant flowers for 'Willow Farm' as if a human one isn't enough. The flying sequence is greeted with cheers as this mighty piece reaches its flash pot climax.

APRIL 29th, 1974

ALLEN THEATRE, CLEVELAND, OHIO, USA.

Personnel: PG, TB, MR, PC, SH.

Set List: Watcher of the Skies, Dancing With The Moonlit Knight, The Cinema Show, I Know What I Like, The Musical Box, More Fool Me, The Battle of Epping Forest.

The second show at the Allen Theatre is a rather poor quality recording, very bass-heavy and plenty of hiss, but at least it's authentic, as Gabriel utters those immortal words 'Hello Cleveland' after "Watcher" finishes. Also the "Moonlit Knight" story ties in with others from this part of the tour being different to the one found on the tape that had been masquerading as this show.

"Moonlit Knight" is laboured and not very inspiring, although the end sequence is very long and gets quite hypnotic. "Cinema Show" suffers because of the recording quality, as does "The Musical Box" which loses all its atmosphere.

An edit between "I Know What I Like" and "The Musical Box" accounts for the absence of "Firth Of Fifth" and of course "Supper's Ready" is missing altogether.

An incomplete tape which sounds like it was recorded outside the venue.

MAY 2nd, 1974

MASSEY HALL, TORONTO, CANADA. (Early Show)

Personnel: PG, TB, MR, PC, SH.

Set List: Watcher of the Skies, Dancing With The Moonlit Knight, The Cinema Show, I Know What I Like, Firth Of Fifth, The Musical Box, Supper's Ready.

Two gigs in one day was not the way Gabriel liked to play it, but as with the December '73 shows at the Roxy Theatre in Los Angeles, sometimes the band had no choice. It meant two shorter sets with "Epping Forest" and "More Fool Me" being the casualties and the singer hoping his voice would hold out.

The opening number is forceful and the stunning sound quality conjures up the ambience in the hall. "Moonlit Knight" is played at a measured but majestic pace with the tension slowly rising until the choirs rise up and nearly swamp everything else.

Gabriel uses his sleazy salesman voice for the Romeo story, and then puts on his best Noel Coward for the start of "The Cinema Show". Rutherford's rhythm guitar is prominent throughout this piece as he backs Banks during a spellbinding synth solo instrumental section. The lawnmower comes, gets funky and goes, only managing polite applause in the process.

The story for "Firth of Fifth" is told in another strange voice:

'On our way here we saw a field of death by the river, and it was wet and green and yellow and covered with moss the field was with death. And in the middle were these stumps, stumps sticking right up, up and up and up, but they had moss crawling all over the bottom and they were crumbling at the top all these stumps with death. And in the middle of this field was a very pretty sight, very pretty because it was blue in the green and the yellow, there was some blue little blob of blue, a little blob. And the green was crawling up from the bottom, and yellow too was a dead human body and the human body looked very pretty because it was beginning to rot in the field, and all it would have done was to make the ground a little more rich, a little more dark, a little more fertile, and seeing how we were thirsty and in greater need we pulled the body from out of the field and laid it down in a horizontal position to facilitate us jumping upon it. (Gabriel jumps) That was a jump to give you an idea as to what we were doing to the body. (applause) Thank you. Anyway we began after several hours to get a small puddle of water out of the left-hand side, and a heap of dust on the right. And the pool of water was clear and we drank the water of course, and it tasted good, the fifth body we found they were hard to find these bodies in that field, the fifth body we found the water was very dirty around where the mouth had been, and seeing as how it was a Scottish gentleman that we were jumping upon, we used to affectionately refer to his mouth as the firth the dirty source; it was the firth of the fifth that we started off this one (more applause)

After a sublime Hackett solo the Mellotron ushers Gabriel in for the last verse and a superb performance comes to a close. Some shouts for "Epping Forest" and one for "The Knife" cut no ice with Gabriel as he begins the Henry story.

A slightly hurried "The Musical Box" is still full of tension and lots of manic tambourine shaking, and even with a small edit near the end is a mighty piece of work.

A long-winded 'Old Michael' story leads to a near-perfect "Supper's Ready", no words needed for this one.

MAY 2nd, 1974
MASSEY HALL, TORONTO, CANADA. (Late Show)

Personnel: PG, TB, MR, PC, SH.

Set List: Watcher of the Skies, Dancing With The Moonlit Knight, The Cinema Show, I Know What I Like, Firth of Fifth, The Musical Box, Supper's Ready.

Same day, same venue, same set list. Another excellent recording, though not as clear as the early show. "Watcher" is less aggressive than usual – except Hackett who gets a cheer each time he slides up the fret board.

Gabriel greets the audience with 'Welcome to the late night show with Genesis'. He then mentions the Knights of the Green Shield who leap up to defend their queen Britannia. As per usual "Moonlit Knight" is all about Collins and Hackett, who liven up a slowish performance with some red-hot finger work.

The taper and his friends obviously intend to enjoy themselves, as one asks the other if he has any roaches! Romeo has fungus problems and Banks get stuck on the solo again; it seems to be causing him all sorts of problems during this part of the tour. It almost sounds as if he is trying too hard.

Lots of comments from the surrounding crowd with 'far out' being quite popular. "I Know What I Like" is short and sweet, with some nice up-front bass lines from Rutherford and a very silly voice from the singer. The 'lady on the tube train' story is wheeled out for "Firth of Fifth" which cuts in during the first verse. Hackett's "Firth" solo is one of the best yet, with lots of sustained notes and several fiddly bits. Banks weighs in with some fine Mellotron backing, then Gabriel brings things home again.

With no "Epping Forest" or "More Fool Me" in the set, it's straight into Henry and Cynthia and some dangerous outdoor games, and of course "The Musical Box". The talkative taper and his friends are silent for the opening verses, obviously transfixed by this masterpiece. The power chord section is a bit hurried, then Hackett revs up his guitar and takes control of proceedings once again. The audience let off steam at the end of this song with all sorts of strange exclamations.

'Old Michael' has now acquired a taste for lettuce as well as worms – and not a pet shop in sight. It takes Gabriel ages to get Collins to join in for a 'little song'.

Then "Supper's Ready" jumps in with the first few bars missing. The song rattles along in a competent but not inspiring fashion, perhaps playing it twice in one day had taken the sting out of it. '666' is still scary and the Mellotron does sound fantastic and Collins does throw in some classic drum rolls. Not that bad then.

MAY 4th, 1974

ACADEMY OF MUSIC, NEW YORK, USA.

Personnel: PG, TB, MR, PC, SH.

Set List: Watcher of the Skies, Dancing With The Moonlit Knight, The Cinema Show (cut), I Know What I Like, Firth Of Fifth, The Musical Box, Horizons, The Battle Of Epping Forest (cut), Supper's Ready.

A very good audience recording and another show plagued by technical problems, also it is the last complete gig from the *Selling England* tour.

"Watcher" is spot on, lots of nice harmonies from Collins and some serious riffing from Hackett. More 'What has happened to my fucking lead' antics next as Rutherford's equipment breaks down yet again, so Collins does his solo with one hand while Gabriel does the Russian spastic joke.

Unfortunately there is a cut in "The Cinema Show" which is a great shame as it was shaping up to be one of the best yet. Just as Banks gets going, there are a couple of annoying edits, but at least the rest of the piece is faultlessly played with Banks flying across the ARP, and Collins making his snare drum burn.

Someone forgets to switch the lawnmower off during the first few lines of "I Know What I Like" which is played in a very laid-back style, drum-powered of course.

'It's hard up here tonight I can assure you,' says a somewhat stressed sounding Collins before Gabriel tells his human bodies story without a care in the world. Banks launches into the piano solo and recklessly adds a few extra flourishes, but pulls it off without a bum note in sight.

Hackett gets some well-deserved cheers after his "Firth" solo which is full of invention and is backed up by some sumptuous Mellotron. A superb performance all round.

After the streaking Henry story, Collins asks if anyone wants to buy some equipment. Gabriel asks for some 'in-betweens', then Collins and Hackett, with Gabriel on tambourine, launch into a funky jam that adds some fusion to the technical confusion.

"The Musical Box" suffers from sound problems with the guitar and Hackett plays his first solo at a different speed to everyone else. Having said that, everyone else is playing at breakneck speed, and Hackett's second solo is even faster than the first, but at least he has caught up this time. The 'Old Man' is somewhat unnerving and the organ all-powerful, this is vintage Genesis at their very best.

After "Horizons" and a badly cut "Epping Forest" comes the last recorded "Supper's Ready", Gabriel has to shout to get the 'Old Michael' story started, Collins adds some Latin percussion to a brief Jerusalem boogie, before this most epic of epics finally begins.

This is one of the best "Supper's" ever, with Gabriel in complete control of his cast of thousands, Banks deliverers a mesmerizing organ solo, Collins fills in wherever he can, while Hackett and Rutherford are note-perfect. The climax is breathtaking, with '666' sending shivers up the spine, the flash pots explode, Gabriel takes off and Hackett solos for all he's worth.

A truly great show even with the technical problems, which must have galvanised the band into some classic performances.

MAY 6th, 1974

ACADEMY OF MUSIC, NEW YORK, USA.

Personnel: PG, TB, MR, PC, SH.

Set List: Watcher of the Skies, Dancing With The Moonlit Knight, The Cinema Show (cut), I Know What I Like, Firth of Fifth, The Musical Box, The Battle of Epping Forest.

The final show of the tour and once again the sound gremlins are at work. The opening of "Watcher" is plagued by keyboard problems, as Banks does his best to hurry through the intro so the hideous oscillating sound is not so noticeable.

The sound quality is excellent and so is "Watcher" itself. Gabriel then explains how six of their guitars were stolen after the gig on the fourth, and then how they had to buy them back so they could play tonight's show. The knights of the Green Shield appear and an average "Moonlit Knight" is played, although the coda is full of classical Mellotron and some nice Hackett touches.

The story for "Cinema Show" is missing and the there are a few hiccups in the opening verses, but once the solo kicks in Collins takes charge with some astonishing drumming. Sadly both his glory and the song are cut short by one of the most mistimed edits I have ever heard.

"Firth of Fifth" is good if not quite great, whereas "The Musical Box" and "Epping Forest" are both good examples of the well-oiled Genesis machine in motion. "Epping Forest" is so good that all the vocals are perfectly audible, and all the characters perfectly believable. Gabriel is in his element here and it's a credit to him that he could remember all the voices. Hackett adds some mean guitar to the fight section before Banks skips in with that delicate synth line.

No "Supper's Ready" on this recording, which is a shame as this is the last time it would have been played by this line up, and judging by the rest of the show it would have been a classic.

Some silent footage of this show has some nice clips of Gabriel in various guises, including the "Epping Forest" hard man complete with stocking mask and pick axe handle, the flower, and a nice shot of him flying up into the air at the climax of "Supper's Ready".

5. THE LAMB LIES DOWN, GABRIEL JUMPS SHIP, AND NO SUPPER!

With a double-album concept-thingy to promote, the band followed in the footsteps of Jethro Tull, Yes and, of course, The Who, and played the whole thing from start to finish. Unlike Tull with *A Passion Play* and Yes with *Topographic Oceans* they did not drop whole sections of it, or insert more familiar songs half-way through to stop any mass exodus to the bar. They stuck to their guns and played the album 102 times with only a rotating selection of 3 oldies for the encores.

A slide show was developed, and the stage filled with fake rocks and a horrible spotty man with a speech impediment.

The first batch of UK dates were cancelled when Hackett had a squeezing competition with a wine glass, although this was probably just as well, as the early USA shows were pretty ropey and not quite with it. By the time the tour finally hit the UK, the band were cooking with gas and playing as well as they ever had.

Hindsight says a tour without "Supper's Ready" was a mad idea, it would have made a great encore.

The last few French shows were not even sold out, some were cancelled and the tour spluttered to a halt and Gabriel was gone.

What they needed, of course, was a singing drummer.

LAMB'S TALES

The *Lamb Lies Down on Broadway* tour was new ground for Genesis, a whole double concept album was to be played to an unsuspecting crowd with only a couple of old chestnuts thrown in to ease the tension, and if that wasn't enough "Supper's Ready" didn't get a look in.

To shed some light on the ever-so-slightly mad storyline Gabriel decided to try and explain things as they went along. Of course this meant another series of ever-so-slightly strange tales, told as only he could.

The opening section is from the Indianapolis show on the 22nd November, 1974. A slightly stilted Gabriel sets the scene:

'The thing is a story concerning a guy off the streets of New York by the name of Rael. A large wall is lowered into Times Square and sinks across 47th street until it eventually wipes off the entire Manhattan Island, the wall hits our hero and knocks him unconscious. He regains consciousness in a cocoon-like situation, which in turn becomes a rock-like cave which causes a claustrophobic fear.

He removes himself from this at the sight of his brother John, and is taken into a place called The Grand Parade of Lifeless Packaging which is an inanimate building filled with motionless bodies.

We have divided it up roughly as we have on the record, which is four sides and this is the first section of the story of Rael, thank you.'

As the tour progressed, Gabriel began adding to the story. This second part of the story comes from 1975, with the February 4th show at the Arie Crown Theatre in Chicago:

'And at this point our hero is moving into an almost perfect reconstruction of the streets of New York, and he begins to recollect his childhood adventures particularly his romantic adventures. He purchased a discount book titled Erogenous Zones and overcoming the difficulties in finding them (applause). I understand there are few fanatics of the book in here tonight.

He spent many months studying this miraculous piece of literary accomplishment, until he mastered his sexual motions by numbers. The day of judgement arrived, and complete performance from initial arousal to completion, he came to the end, was a mere 78 seconds. This miraculous feat of masculine achievement failed to even remotely titillate his opposite number.

He was left cuddling a rather large prickly porcupine, which he took onto a soft carpeted corridor with thousands of other people, small people, little people crawling obsessively towards a large wooden door, which in turn led them up a spiral staircase into a chamber with 32 other doors, only one of which was capable of getting any of them out.'

The final section of ramblings is from the Manchester Palace Theatre on April 27th, 1975.

By these later shows Gabriel had turned from nervous-sounding storyteller into multi-voiced comic and often went on way past the five-minute mark:

'This chamber with hundreds of doors and a woman who was as pink and pale as all the little beetles and creatures that I had seen crawling around the floor of the caves, approached me and she said, 'Can you help me?' 'How could I resist a proposition like that? So we held sweaty hands and she led me through one of the doors down a passageway that I hadn't seen before, into a series of tunnels entering a large dark cave, and she left me on a cold wet stone throne.

This wasn't comfortable and being on my own I begin to hear funny things and there was this strange noise on my left, a whirring sound and these two golden globes hovered in filling the cave with this amazingly bright, white, light, (adopts high pitched voice). 'I was amazed at the whiteness,' Mrs JH of Bournemouth, (audience laughter & applause) 'It was the whitest I've ever seen'. Mrs PW of Bognor Regis (more applause). I know this is getting boring but I too was astonished at the whiteness so I picked up this little pebble, hurtled it at the centre of it and smashed it, I hit it right in the middle in fact, and the whole ceiling collapsed on my head. This was a little painful, I escaped like all good heroes and went into the small rescue area, where the delightful shattering, shimmering, spectre (bizarre Kenneth Williams voice) your friend and mine better known to all of us here tonight as Death that's D E A T H. (even more cheers)

Mmm this lovely man is wearing one of his delightful costumes he designed so painfully himself, this particular number is his snuff puff outfit, one little puff and you snuff it, mm love it, get it. I escaped again, like all good heroes, only to be sensually and erotically assaulted by three half-woman, half-snake creatures with very long tongues beginning to coil on my body, licking the strange blue liquid that was emanating from my pores. This had the effect of giving these creatures indigestion.

All of a sudden I heard a huge roar to my right (section of the crowd attempt a roar) thank you. Shall we try it again? A roar (much louder noise). A huge express train hurtled in carrying a packet of R E N N *I E S but alas it was too late as they had shrivelled up and died. I ate all that was left of their horrible bodies, lovely bodies and this turned me, changed me, into a ugly, lumpy, humpy, – wait for it – bumpy species of humanity not totally dissimilar to Mr Philip Collins on my left (several bouts of applause).*

The only way of getting rid of all these horrible lumps and bumps was the severing of the sexual organs, (cheers). Rael (that's me) and John's organs were placed in a fully sterilised yellow plastic tubes, by Doktor Dyper notorious sniper, who for a very small fee is guaranteed to cut off very neatly our very own windscreen wipers. The tubes, the yellow plastic tubes. But all of a sudden a huge black bird called Raven, zoomed out of the air – zoom zoom zoom – grabbed the yellow plastic tube with my deceased sexual organ in it an flew off. "Christ," (very high voice) I said. (cheers and applause) So I hurtled off in hot pursuit, and just as I was about to catch the tail of this Raven, it dropped it into a huge area of gushing water with R *A V I N* E *in blue watery letters. "A ravine," I thought.*

I watched the yellow tube disappearing, bobbing away, bob bob bob, and I saw my drowning brother John also in the water, Oh dear.

With an imagination like that a screenplay must have been just around the corner.

NOVEMBER 22nd, 1974
INDIANA CONVENTION CENTRE, INDIANAPOLIS, USA.

Personnel: PG, TB, MR, PC, SH.

Set List: The Lamb Lies Down on Broadway, Fly on a Windshield, Broadway Melody of 1974, Cuckoo Cocoon, In The Cage, The Grand Parade of Lifeless Packaging, Back in N.Y.C, Hairless Heart, Counting Out Time, Carpet Crawl, The Chamber of 32 Doors, Lilywhite Lilith, The Waiting Room, Anyway, Here Comes the Supernatural Anaesthetist, The Lamia, Silent Sorrow in Empty Boats, The Colony of Slippermen, Ravine, The Light Dies Down on Broadway, Riding the Scree, In the Rapids, It, The Musical Box.

This excellent audience recording is the third show from the *Lamb* tour and while that elusive first tape from the opening night in Chicago still remains hidden, this is a pretty good place to start.

With the album not yet released, Gabriel wisely takes some time to explain to the audience what is about to happen, he fails to mention that they won't know any of the material but instead opts for a brief summary of the story, or 'This is the story of Rael'.

Hackett must still be suffering from the effects of his hand injury so he is quite down in the mix for the first part of the show. Things get underway after a brief pause and progress as per the album until "In The Cage" when a loud bass noise threatens, then vanishes, before any serious interruption.

Banks cruises through his solo on "Cage" and Gabriel gets down and dirty for "Back in N.Y.C". Gus the roadie and Rutherford almost cause a delay before "N.Y.C", but the song does contain a brief edit and loses some vocals on the last chorus.

"Hairless Heart", one of several instrumentals at last brings Hackett to the fore with some nice volume pedal work, Banks oozes Mellotron, which sounds unusually smooth. The delicate intro to "Carpet Crawl" is totally ruined by some loud bass notes, then Gabriel's vocals disappear completely and the band almost lose it. The vocals return, albeit quite low, and the song keeps going with some classic harmonies from Collins. The lyrics to "Crawl" confuse the singer who gets stuck and repeats a few of the lines.

More pieces of the story are added after the first two sides of the album are played. What the US fans made of Gabriel and his surreal ramblings is anybody's guess, but his joke about Death looking dandy falls on deaf ears.

"Lilywhite Lillith" is counted in and rocks along with that great bass riff from Rutherford, things go weird for "The Waiting Room" which at this early stage of the tour is actually shorter than the album version. "Anyway" goes from gentle piano to dramatic chords and some speedy synth work, with the keyboards sounding very up-front. Hackett gets stuck during his "Anaesthetist" solo but that's allowed as he is still recovering from his run-in with the wine glass.

'Oh God' is how one fan greets the spectacle that is "The Lamia", Gabriel enveloped in the swirling multicoloured contraption whilst being accompanied by Banks on shimmering electric piano and Collins on cool vibes. Hackett's solo is almost drowned-out by the bass, and the atmosphere of the song is lost as Rutherford booms his way to the end.

More vocal loss during the "Slipperman" but no surprises there, the applause is polite when "It" brings the main show to a close, but is very enthusiastic after a rousing "Musical Box" that suffers no vocal problems at all.

NOV 25th, 1974

ALLEN THEATRE, CLEVELAND, OHIO, USA.

Personnel: PG, TB, MR, PC, SH.

Set List: The Lamb Lies Down on Broadway, Fly on a Windshield, Broadway Melody of 1974, Cuckoo Cocoon, In The Cage, The Grand Parade of Lifeless Packaging, Back in N.Y.C, Hairless Heart, Counting Out Time, Carpet Crawl, The Chamber of 32 Doors, Lilywhite Lilith, The Waiting Room, Anyway, Here Comes the Supernatural Anaesthetist, The Lamia, Silent Sorrow in Empty Boats, The Colony of Slippermen, Ravine, The Light Dies Down on Broadway, Riding the Scree, In the Rapids, It, The Musical Box.

Nice atmospheric recording for the first of two shows at the Allen Theatre. Just seven months after they presented *Selling England by the Pound,* the band are back with *The Lamb.* Lucky old Cleveland – four shows in the same year.

The opening story is missing from this tape but the first few songs proceed without incident until "In The Cage" when Gabriel comes in a bit too soon and Banks fluffs the first part of his solo. The vocals are well down in the mix which is a shame as everyone seems to be on form for this first rockier number of the show. "The Grand Parade" gradually gets louder, but the vocals do not, so it all ends up as a bit of a mess.

The singing on "Back in N.Y.C." is full of anger and makes the hairs rise on the back of your neck, the rhythm is aggressive and unrelenting, but it shows the band could rock when they really wanted to. In contrast the gentle instrumental that is "Hairless Heart" is very Genesis and even features an out-of-tune Mellotron.

A couple of cuts during "Carpet Crawl" and "Chamber of 32 Doors" are annoying but not too disruptive, some idiots heckle Gabriel during his next story until one fan yells at them to 'Shut up'. As if in response the beginning of "The Waiting Room" is incredibly loud and full of disturbing noises which soon shuts everybody up.

The whole show changes gear when "The Waiting Room" ends and the shorter songs begin to merge together as the story enters its most surreal phase. Gabriel has vocal problems on both"The Lamia" and especially "The Colony of Slippermen" where his costume was obviously getting in the way of the microphone. Banks even comes in late for his solo, not the best "Slipperman" to ever grace a stage.

Several hesitations and hiccups during the last few tracks indicate a band still not totally familiar with the set, the vocals drift in and out and there are several keyboard moments when things just don't go right.

The story for "The Musical Box" earns more applause than the *Lamb* did in its entirety, Rutherford's absence from the stage is blamed on guitar tuning, and is even accompanied by some 'sleazy night club music' before the only familiar song of the show makes its subdued entrance. A somewhat hurried version doesn't do this most important of all Genesis songs justice, but it still steals the show.

NOV 26th, 1974

ALLEN THEATRE, CLEVELAND, OHIO, USA.

Personnel: PG, TB, MR, PC, SH.

Set List: The Lamb Lies Down on Broadway, Fly on a Windshield, Broadway Melody of 1974, Cuckoo Cocoon, In The Cage, The Grand Parade of Lifeless Packaging, Back in N.Y.C, Hairless Heart, Counting Out Time, Carpet Crawl, The Chamber of 32 Doors, Lilywhite Lilith, The Waiting Room, Anyway, Here Comes the Supernatural Anaesthetist, The Lamia, Silent Sorrow in Empty Boats, The Colony of Slippermen, Ravine, The Light Dies Down on Broadway, Riding the Scree, In the Rapids, It, The Musical Box, Watcher of the Skies.

An enthusiastic performance, but a lousy recording is the best way of describing the second night at the Allen Theatre. Gabriel gives it his all but the poor sound quality takes away all the subtleties of the show.

The crowd get a brief story about what is going on before the *Lamb* finally kicks in, there is some nice jamming on "Windshield", while Gabriel gets suitably aggressive during a raucous "In The Cage".

The recording has several cuts and splices that, combined with a very noisy audience, make it pretty hard going at times. "Counting Out Time" features a very strange-sounding guitar solo, and "32 Doors" still sounds great with the singer coming over all sincere.

"The Waiting Room" is short but full-on, lots of flute and guitar before Rutherford brings that riff in from the cold and Collins picks up the baton and runs with it.

"Anyway" is cut in half and there is a small spoken interlude between "Scree" and "Rapids". The one redeeming feature from this show is that it features both usually played encores with "Watcher of the Skies" being added to the almost compulsory "The Musical Box".

NOV 28th, 1974

MASONIC TEMPLE, DETROIT, MICHIGAN, USA.

Personnel: PG, TB, MR, PC, SH.

Set List: The Grand Parade of Lifeless Packaging (cut), Back in N.Y.C, Hairless Heart, Counting Out Time, Carpet Crawl, The Chamber of 32 Doors, Lilywhite Lilith, The Waiting Room, Anyway, Here Comes the Supernatural Anaesthetist, The Lamia, Silent Sorrow in Empty Boats, The Colony of Slippermen (cut), Ravine, The Light Dies Down on Broadway, Riding the Scree, In the Rapids, It, The Musical Box, Watcher of the Skies.

An excellent recording which misses out the first few songs due to someone forgetting to press record or maybe the microphone was switched off. Whatever the reason, it's a shame as the group finally seem to be getting to grips with this epic production.

Hackett plays some nice lines during "Hairless Heart" and is backed by the classic Mellotron string sound that is perfect for this short piece. "Carpet Crawl" is a bit laboured, but "32 Doors" is getting better and better and is already a great showcase for Gabriel's emotive vocals.

During the next section of the story an enthusiastic heckler is put down by Gabriel, but is promised the five dollars after the show. The "Slipperman" is compared to Collins who then leads a powerful "Lilith" straight into another shortish, but noise-laden "Waiting Room", which apart from some great guitar effects is still very similar to the album version. Gabriel fluffs the intro to "Anyway" and seems to struggle on some of the high notes, Banks throws in the odd bum note on the piano but handles the synth with ease.

"The Lamia" takes an age to emerge from the dreamy vibes that Collins is playing, Banks plays some totally different chords during "Silent Sorrow" as if he's forgotten how this piece goes.

The "Slipperman" intro sounds very oriental and you can hear the crowd's reaction as the rubberised vocalist appears, the vocals are a bit muffled but still discernible but a nasty edit in the middle does somewhat spoil the song.

There are some nice harmonies during "The Light Dies Down" this follows a very spooky "Ravine" which manages to keep the audience in its spell without even one single call for "rock 'n' roll", and at one point sounds like it features a distant sax – very strange indeed.

Collins duels with Banks during a lively "Scree" with honours even on the speed stakes. "It" rocks along with a really forceful vocal, Banks adds some Mellotron strings in a most unsubtle fashion before a desperate-sounding Gabriel finally has enough 'knock and know all' to keep him happy.

The first encore of "The Musical Box" is an absolute beauty and one of the best versions I have yet heard. The applause starts with the final chord still playing and lasts for a long time, playing something familiar was obviously a good idea.

The appearance of Gabriel in cloak and batwings, coupled with the Mellotron, sets pulses racing again, and a very punchy "Watcher" takes to the sky. A classic end to a show still full of hiccups but one that is quickly falling into place.

NOVEMBER 30th, 1974

SYRIA MOSQUE, PITTSBURG, USA.

Personnel: PG, TB, MR, PC, SH.

Set List: The Lamb Lies Down on Broadway, Fly on a Windshield, Broadway Melody of 1974, Cuckoo Cocoon, In The Cage, The Grand Parade of Lifeless Packaging, Back in N.Y.C, Hairless Heart, Counting Out Time, Carpet Crawl, The Chamber of 32 Doors, Lilywhite Lilith, The Waiting Room, Anyway, Here Comes the Supernatural Anaesthetist, The Lamia, Silent Sorrow in Empty Boats, The Colony of Slippermen, Ravine, The Light Dies Down on Broadway, Riding the Scree, In the Rapids, It, The Musical Box (cut).

A nice clear recording which has some volume changes early on and is a bit on the thin side, but at least the taper switched on the machine at the start of the show this time.

"The Lamb" appears out of nowhere with Banks hunched over the electric piano, not the most convincing of opening numbers but it passes without incident and leads into the Mellotron-laden doom march that is "Fly on a Windshield". This version lacks the bass power of the album version but is still an early highlight.

Banks stutters the opening of the "In the Cage" solo and also cocks up some of the chords in "Grand Parade". Collins is on fire here, playing as fast as he can all the time and has obviously got to grips with playing the whole album quicker than his synth-worrying colleague.

"Hairless Heart" glides by on a wash of Mellotron with Rutherford adding some powerful bass lines, Hackett plays all the way through "Carpet Crawl" and adds to the gradual build-up of the song. As individual songs go "Chamber of 32 Doors" is as good as any and gives Gabriel a chance to shine, although he does struggle with the very high notes at the end.

"The Waiting Room" is very precise and is still lacking any spirit of adventure, Collins sings some great harmonies during "Anyway" before the lounge lizard guitar solo on "Supernatural" takes centre stage.

Gabriel gets a bit lost during "Slipperman" not just with the microphone but also staying in the right key, his appearance in the ultimate costume earns some gasps from the crowd and probably a few 'What the hell is that?' exclamations.

Several songs are played slower than usual, which in the case of "The

Lamia" makes things drag a bit, Collins adds some Caribbean touches to "Riding the Scree" with an impressive display of tom tom work. "It" is very lively and lets Collins do his stuff, although Hackett's repetitive riffing does grate after a while.

The tape runs out on "The Musical Box" just as the second heavy section kicks in. Why didn't these people take more blank tapes with them?

DECEMBER 1st, 1974

LYRIC THEATRE, BALTIMORE, USA.

Personnel: PG, TB, MR, PC, SH.

Set List: The Lamb Lies Down on Broadway, Fly on a Windshield, Broadway Melody of 1974, Cuckoo Cocoon, In The Cage, The Grand Parade of Lifeless Packaging, Back in N.Y.C, Hairless Heart, Counting Out Time, Carpet Crawl, The Chamber of 32 Doors, Lilywhite Lilith, The Waiting Room, Anyway, Here Comes the Supernatural Anaesthetist, The Lamia, Silent Sorrow in Empty Boats, The Colony of Slippermen, Ravine, The Light Dies Down on Broadway, Riding the Scree, In the Rapids, It, The Musical Box.

A nice balanced recording that has improved greatly with some studio tinkering, Gabriel starts things off with the first part of the story and informs the crowd that they are about to hear the new album in its entirety. Talk about sowing the seeds of doubt...

Hackett has fun during a very heavy "Windshield" wailing away over the stabbing bass chords and that glorious Mellotron. Gabriel gets his vocal cue slightly wrong on "Cage" but makes up for it with a great gutsy performance.

After another longwinded storytelling session and a very angry Rael spits his way through "Back in NYC" – surely the heaviest of all Genesis tracks and an obvious pointer for Gabriel's solo career. It has quickly become one of the show's highlights and is the perfect foil to the tranquillity of "Hairless Heart".

Gabriel sings the first half of "Carpet Crawl" with an almost reverential feel before becoming Rael again for the last two verses, Collins almost takes over the vocals on the fade-out – no surprises that this would be one of the songs carried on into the post-Gabriel era.

There is a cut in the middle of "The Waiting Room" and the volume changes, then settles down again. Hackett delivers a nice solo on "The Lamia" and has plenty of support from an enthusiastic percussionist who then goes onto his tubular bells for "Silent Sorrow".

Plenty of laughs and applause as the "Slipperman" appears, the vocals start off well but soon odd words start disappearing as the ridiculous costume restricts Gabriel's mic use. Another powerful encore shows how the audience appreciate the more familiar numbers and if "Watcher" was played I am sure it would have gone down just as well.

DECEMBER 4th, 1974
MOSQUE THEATRE, RICHMOND, VIRGINIA, USA.

Personnel: PG, TB, MR, PC, SH.

Set List: The Lamb Lies Down on Broadway, Fly on a Windshield, Broadway Melody of 1974, Cuckoo Cocoon, In The Cage, The Grand Parade of Lifeless Packaging, Back in N.Y.C, Hairless Heart, Counting Out Time, Carpet Crawl, The Chamber of 32 Doors, Lilywhite Lilith, The Waiting Room (cut), The Lamia (cut), Silent Sorrow in Empty Boats, The Colony of Slippermen, Ravine, The Light Dies Down on Broadway, Riding the Scree, In the Rapids, It, The Musical Box (story).

A seriously good recording from yet another not very rock 'n' roll venue. The beginning of the title track is lost as the sound levels are adjusted, but things pick up for "Windshield" where Hackett pours out his heart with a delicious solo – without "Firth of Fifth" he has to slip his trademark sustained notes in where he can.

"Back in NYC" is getting better as the tour progresses, Gabriel is getting seriously into character during this song, often spitting out the lyrics in a very convincing impression of an angry young man. In complete contrast, "Hairless Heart" is quietly powerful and gives Hackett more precious time in the limelight.

The Mellotron intro to "32 Doors" is perfect, everything is in tune and no other keyboard would sound this good, the organ replaces the mighty strings and shadows the despairing vocals – a great Genesis song that gave another good indication as to where the singer was heading.

After a rather disjointed "Waiting Room", a lapse in concentration by the taper means we join the show again halfway through "The Lamia" so "Anyway" and "Supernatural Anaesthetist" are lost. Hackett is all-at-sea for the "Lamia" solo; he recovers briefly, but on the whole makes a right pig's ear of it.

Banks plays a great "Slipperman", the organ is bubbling away under the rubbery vocals and the ARP sounds spot-on for the solo. The vocals are very clear despite the costume, if just a little out of breath. Collins can be heard humming a little tune just as "Ravine" starts. He then drums like a demon at the end of "Riding the Scree". Then things mellow out for "In the Rapids" before the anti-climax that is "It" brings the show to an end.

The encores are missing from the recording with only part of the "Musical Box" story surviving. The band are gradually getting the hang of this mammoth performance, with only the solo or vocal drop-out causing any major problems. Shame about the edits though.

DECEMBER 5th, 1974
TOWER THEATRE, PHILADELPHIA, PA, USA.

Personnel: PG, TB, MR, PC, SH.

Set List: The Lamb Lies Down on Broadway, Fly on a Windshield, Broadway Melody of 1974, Cuckoo Cocoon, In The Cage, The Grand Parade of Lifeless Packaging, Back in N.Y.C, Hairless Heart, Counting Out Time, Carpet Crawl, The Chamber of 32 Doors, Lilywhite Lilith, The Waiting Room, Anyway, The Lamia, Silent Sorrow in Empty Boats, The Colony of Slippermen, Ravine, The Light Dies Down on Broadway, Riding the Scree, In the Rapids, It, The Musical Box.

It takes a while to sort out the sound balance, but things soon settle down for another really good recording. Lots of calling out for people to sit down during the beginning of "Windshield" then the band pile in for a slightly longer jam than usual, with Hackett sounding a little lost in places.

A hint of feedback threatens "Cocoon" but luckily does not get any louder. Banks has mastered the solo during "In the Cage" and flies through it with ease. Gabriel, however, is having mic problems and some of the "Grand Parade" vocals are missing in action.

"Carpet Crawl" earns polite applause, maybe because the song never really takes off and lacks the dynamic that is present in "32 Doors" which is also becoming a crowd favourite.

Collins is again compared to the "Slipperman" – Gabriel would get around to the other members of the group in due course, but for now the percussionist is the chosen one. "The Waiting Room" gets off to a good start with everyone going crazy at the same time, Hackett throws in some cat sounds then Rutherford starts up the bass riff, Banks joins in on organ and Collins stops ringing his bells to lay down a steady beat. It sounds like a flash pot goes off as the audience respond to something happening on stage. Collins turns up the heat with some frantic drum work before the whole thing settles down again.

There is a nasty cut at the end of "Anyway" and the sound quality dips slightly for "The Lamia", but things are back to normal by the time "The Slipperman" takes to the stage.

Two firecrackers go off before the encore starts, it annoys most of the crowd but doesn't put the band off as they play another dramatic version of one of the two regular show closers.

DECEMBER 6th, 1974
ACADEMY OF MUSIC, NEW YORK, USA.

Personnel: PG, TB, MR, PC, SH.

Set List: The Lamb Lies Down on Broadway, Fly on a Windshield, Broadway Melody of 1974, Cuckoo Cocoon, In The Cage, The Grand Parade of Lifeless Packaging, Back in N.Y.C, Hairless Heart, Counting Out Time, Carpet Crawl, The Chamber of 32 Doors, Lilywhite Lilith, The Waiting Room, Anyway, Here Comes the Supernatural Anaesthetist, The Lamia, Silent Sorrow in Empty Boats, The Colony of Slippermen, Ravine, The Light Dies Down on Broadway, Riding the Scree, In the Rapids, It, The Musical Box.

A nice audience recording and a soundboard with some buzzing noises at the start from the New York Academy. Last time they were there Gabriel flew through the air, this time around he sings about being underground in the strange New York landscape that exists inside his head and the three big screens behind him.

The performance almost seems hurried and lacks some of the power of previous shows, "Windshield" makes its usual entrance but Hackett seems to have run out of ideas as to where to take it. The vocals vanish at the start of "Back in NYC" and even when things are sorted, Gabriel lacks that edge that elevates this piece to one of the show's highlights.

During Gabriel's second instalment of the story, he blames the delay on Hackett doing his nails. Some dodgy vibes almost spoil "Hairless Heart", then Hackett and the Mellotron appear and all is well. "Counting Out Time" benefits from the increased tempo although the switch to "Carpet Crawl" is rather clumsy.

They lose the plot completely during "Carpet Crawl" with vocal and melody lines very rarely meeting, but at least they keep going. Things improve for "32 Doors" until an edit in the tape spoils things. A blistering "Waiting Room" is full of strange guitar and bubbling synth, Collins makes as much noise as he can, and as ever Rutherford brings things back to earth with that bass riff. Then a power failure results in a enforced drum solo that Collins delivers without missing a beat, the juice comes back on and they get away with it. Another edit means we lose the last few bars of the most interesting 'Evil Jam' yet.

Some excitable fans call out for "Supper's Ready" and "The Knife" during the prelude to "The Lamia". Whether that's because they can't get into the *Lamb,* or they just want to call something out is anyone's guess. The song itself is full of emotion and Hackett does the business as usual, the vocals are a little suspect during the "Slipperman" but that is no surprise considering the costume.

The applause for the *Lamb* is long, but not as intense as is usually generated by "The Musical Box", for instance. Luckily for the audience this is the encore but the taper forgot to press record until the first heavy section, luckily for us the sound crew were on the case and the "Box" is complete. The song is classic Genesis and rightly brings the house down, a nice way to end this unconvincing performance.

DECEMBER 7th, 1974
ACADEMY OF MUSIC, NEW YORK, NY, USA.

Personnel: PG, TB, MR, PC, SH.

Set List: The Lamb Lies Down on Broadway, Fly on a Windshield, Broadway Melody of 1974, Cuckoo Cocoon, In The Cage, The Grand Parade of Lifeless Packaging, Back in N.Y.C, Hairless Heart, Counting Out Time, Carpet Crawl, The Chamber of 32 Doors, Lilywhite Lilith, The Waiting Room, Anyway (cut), Here Comes the Supernatural Anaesthetist, The Lamia, Silent Sorrow in Empty Boats, The Colony of Slippermen, Ravine, The Light Dies Down on Broadway, Riding the Scree (cut).

The noisy audience is greeted by Gabriel who announces that they will be playing the entire *Lamb Lies Down on Broadway* tonight, and that this particular dose of cosmic excretion concerns the streets of New York and a character called Rael. The crowd respond by calling for an encore, and a cry of 'play all night' is plainly heard.

This excellent recording, which actually improves as the show progresses, has a more controlled feeling than the previous night's performance, and the audience are most definitely in the mood to be entertained.

The title track is full-on rock, with Collins driving everyone along, as well as contributing some nifty backing vocals. The change to "Windshield" is seamless, then Hackett takes control and his guitar wails into the New York night.

The underwater vocal effects transform "Cuckoo Cocoon" into a strange, almost '80s sounding piece, then some excellent harmonies from Collins add even more bite to an in-your-face "Back in NYC". The Mellotron dominates "Hairless Heart", maybe Banks wanted to put Hackett back in his box for a few minutes.

The guitar break in "Counting Out Time" is possibly the worst thing Hackett has ever played, so we won't dwell on it. "Carpet Crawl" bustles along nicely then almost ends too soon with Gabriel and Collins still singing after the music has stopped.

Gabriel identifies some of the audience as being Lamia, the audience reply with a few cries of 'Yeah', so the story carries on without most of them being the slightest bit interested. "The Waiting Room" is one of the best yet, everyone is being inventive and lots of weird and wonderful sounds merge in a melting pot of organised chaos.

A couple of tape edits during "Anyway" spoil the continuity, then a couple of idiots during "Silent Sorrow" ruin the atmosphere as they call out for an encore again just as Banks floats the ghostly choirs into the ether. There is plenty of reaction as "The Slipperman" emerges, accompanied by plenty of feedback, no doubt from Gabriel's microphone.

Unfortunately the tape cuts off just as "Riding the Scree" gets going so we don't know how the crowd react when an encore is played. But at least the band are starting to fit the pieces together in a convincing manner.

DECEMBER 8th, 1974
PALACE THEATRE, PROVIDENCE, RI, USA.

Personnel: PG, TB, MR, PC, SH.

Set List: The Lamb Lies Down on Broadway, Fly on a Windshield, Broadway Melody of 1974, Cuckoo Cocoon, In The Cage, The Grand Parade of Lifeless Packaging, Back in N.Y.C, Hairless Heart, Counting Out Time, Carpet Crawl, The Chamber of 32 Doors, Lilywhite Lilith, The Waiting Room, Anyway, Here Comes the Supernatural Anaesthetist, The Lamia, Silent Sorrow in Empty Boats, The Colony of Slippermen, Ravine, The Light Dies Down on Broadway, Riding the Scree, In the Rapids, It, The Musical Box, Watcher of the Skies.

As audience recordings go this is very much top-drawer, excellent sound balance and plenty of kick, plus this copy has been cleaned up in a studio, so now has even more depth. It's a complete show, with both encores and only a couple of tiny edits, so if you don't have a copy already, you should get one and not bother with the doctored 'Shrine' recording on the first Genesis box set. There is also a very good soundboard/ambience recording, but it is touch-and-go as to which is the better tape.

'This is the story of Rael,' announces Gabriel, there is then a lengthy pause and a few shouts from the audience, which only raises the tension. Banks eventually arrives and the title track flutters into life, with his shimmering piano and bombastic power chords.

Collins batters his way through "In the Cage" and assaults "The Grand Parade" with a barrage of percussive brilliance. As Gabriel tells the next part of the story, he sounds well out-of-breath, which considering his output during the last ten minutes is not at all surprising.

Some hideous crackling and feedback threatens the storytelling, but Gabriel makes light of it and things are sorted in time for a classic "Back in NYC". Collins is everywhere on this song, throwing in extra fills whenever and wherever he can, the emotive vocals are full of anger and most definitely in character.

"Hairless Heart" is almost perfect from the bubbling organ and the volume pedal guitar, to the sea of Mellotron and that oh-so subtle slide into "Counting Out Time". A bit more crackle at the close of a slowly building "Carpet Crawl" which has a tiny cut at the end, and then "32 Doors" jumps straight in and puts the spotlight back onto the singer.

After a slightly restrained, but still excellent "Waiting Room", Banks leads everyone through an emotional "Anyway". He utilizes his entire keyboard rig for this simple song, piano and synth lead the way then some heavy Hammond during the instrumental section, before the Mellotron announces the arrival of the "Supernatural Anaesthetist".

The audience do bird whistling impressions while waiting for "The Lamia" to begin. They have also started calling out, indicating the collective attention span is starting to wane. Hackett gets a little stuck in the closing solo, so Collins tries to drown him out. A well-played duel ends in a well-played tie. Some masterful Mellotron and ghostly flute complement the Fripp-esque guitar in an exquisite "Silent Sorrow" – one of the best yet.

Banks is on top form for this show, with no bum notes to his credit he flies through the "Scree" super-solo with smoking fingers, the Mellotron makes an unobtrusive entrance at the fade out of "It", instead of the usual heavy chords. The applause is long but not deafening, that is always saved for the encore.

Collins thanks everyone for staying up so late, and gets a loud cheer when he informs the audience that they've still got a way to go yet, now at last some songs they will know.

Both encores are well-played and gratefully received, "Watcher" is one of the best I have yet heard and is so clear you can hear the organ keys being pressed down during the fanfare. Collins makes this the jazziest version yet, with some fancy hi-hat work. Hackett's guitar is also very clear and sounds fantastic as he fires off his razor sharp riffs.

This is an excellent *Lamb* show ending on two absolute highs.

DECEMBER 12th, 1974
PALACE THEATRE, WATERBURY, CT, USA.

Personnel: PG, TB, MR, PC, SH.

Set List: The Lamb Lies Down on Broadway, Fly on a Windshield, Broadway Melody of 1974, Cuckoo Cocoon, In The Cage, The Grand Parade of Lifeless Packaging, Back in N.Y.C, Hairless Heart (cut), Counting Out Time, Carpet Crawl, The Chamber of 32 Doors, Lilywhite Lilith, The Waiting Room (cut), Anyway, Here Comes the Supernatural Anaesthetist, The Lamia, Silent Sorrow in Empty Boats, The Colony of Slippermen, Ravine, The Light Dies Down on Broadway, Riding the Scree, In the Rapids, It, The Musical Box,

Another good audience show captures the atmosphere of the whole theatre and not just the stage. At this stage of the tour, Gabriel still continues informing the audience of the band's intention to play the whole of their new album, before setting the scene with a few words about Rael.

After an excellent title track, the temporary lull in "Windshield" is blasted into the balcony seats as the band pile in for the heavy section. This is easily one of the show's live highlights and gives Hackett an early chance to shine, which he does with a seriously good solo, as Collins pounds away behind him.

Some hillbilly-like heckling spoils the tranquillity of "Cuckoo Cocoon" as some of the fans are already demanding some rock 'n' roll. No calls for "The Knife" yet, but they can't be far away. "In the Cage" settles everyone down as Gabriel and Banks take the spotlight for a thunderous version. Some of the vocals almost vanish during "The Grand Parade" but as Hackett is playing at full volume it's hardly surprising.

The second part of the story concerning Rael's first sexual encounter, his prickly porcupine, and the 32 doors makes absolutely no sense at all and seems to fall on deaf ears. Even Gabriel sounds like he doesn't believe it himself – no wonder some of the audiences found it heavy going.

"Back in NYC", like "Fly on a Windshield", has become one of the live highlights as the entire group get a chance to crank it up and rock out for six minutes. The very last bar of "NYC" is cut and "Hairless Heart" starts halfway though the first quiet passage, but the Mellotron sounds great, so such a small edit can be overlooked. A dreamy, almost mesmeric "Carpet Crawl" gradually builds in volume and power, only slightly spoiled by a drop in the vocals.

When Gabriel attempts to tell more of the story, the yelling and general bad manners of the crowd obviously gets to him, as he gives up near the end and waits for Collins to count in a heavy "Lilywhite Lilith". An excellent "Waiting Room" is spoiled by being cut at the end, just as things were coming to a climax.

The vocals are missing completely from the start of "The Lamia" but the band play on and Rael eventually makes himself heard. Hackett is a bit heavy-handed during his solo, or is it a hint of frustration at the continual technical problems that seem to plague this tour? The entrance of the Slipperman causes mass hysteria in the audience as if they need an excuse to yell out. The vocals of course are barely audible.

The main part of the concert ends with a spirited run through of "It", Hackett churns out that repetitive riff, while Rutherford thrashes away on the twin-neck. Gabriel gives his all as Rael ends his strange journey.

Before the encore the audience are asked to refrain from lighting matches and cigarettes. They then get another story, but as this one ends with the words "Musical Box" nobody seems to mind. The song is a breath of fresh air to the noisy crowd who greet the Old Man's arrival with their usual exuberance.

DECEMBER 13th, 1974

CAPITOL THEATRE, PASSAIC, NJ, USA.

Personnel: PG, TB, MR, PC, SH.

Set List: The Grand Parade of Lifeless Packaging (cut), Back in N.Y.C, Hairless Heart, Counting Out Time, Carpet Crawl, The Chamber of 32 Doors, Lilywhite Lilith, The Waiting Room, Anyway, Here Comes the Supernatural Anaesthetist, The Lamia, Silent Sorrow in Empty Boats, The Colony of Slippermen (cut), Ravine, The Light Dies Down on Broadway, Riding the Scree, In the Rapids, It, The Musical Box (cut), Watcher of the Skies.

The show arrives in New Jersey and once again someone forgets to press record until the "Grand Parade" has almost finished. As this is a soundboard recording, the blame must lie with a forgetful crew member who was possibly more concerned with who was rolling the next joint.

The sound on most 'boards' is generally on the flat side and lacking in atmosphere, but in this case a couple of ambience mics were also used, so there is a bit more depth than usual, although the audience do sound like they are next door. There is some variation of sound quality during "Counting Out Time" and things are pretty dull for "Carpet Crawl".

Collins is once again on top form, his drumming is so much more inventive live than on the album versions, plus his backing vocals perfectly complement Gabriel's deeper, rougher voice. The drum/Mellotron intro to "32 Doors" is suitably dramatic, then the singer turns on the emotion and makes the song his own.

The next section of the story again compares Collins to the "Slipperman" and the audience is told that the only reason he played the drums was so that you couldn't see his distorted legs, and as he is wearing headphones he won't be able to hear any of this.

A lazy sounding "Lilywhite Lilith" rather swings its way into the "Waiting Room", which is full of cat-like guitars, manic percussion and even some ghostly flute, before the reassuring rhythm gradually builds – into a power cut. Collins, of course, goes into drum solo mode and things eventually get back to normal despite an edit in the tape.

Gabriel has trouble remembering the lyrics to "The Lamia", he also gets attacked by some vicious feedback. The sound goes very woolly during Hackett's solo and he is almost drowned out by the organ, another downside to the soundboard recording. "Silent Sorrow" has the sound suddenly crystal clear again just in time for the swirling choirs and some dodgy flute.

We jump into "The Musical Box" just as Old King Cole gets jolly but at least the rest of the song is in intact. The "Watcher" fanfare, and indeed the whole piece, sounds stunning, with the keyboards benefiting from the desk recording, a great way to end another troubled concert.

DECEMBER 14th, 1974
MARKET SQUARE ARENA, KANSAS CITY, KANSAS, USA.

Personnel: PG, TB, MR, PC, SH.

Set List: The Lamb Lies Down on Broadway, Fly on a Windshield, Broadway Melody of 1974, Cuckoo Cocoon, In The Cage, The Grand Parade of Lifeless Packaging, Back in N.Y.C, Hairless Heart, Counting Out Time, Carpet Crawl, The Chamber of 32 Doors, Lilywhite Lilith, The Waiting Room (cut), Anyway, Here Comes the Supernatural Anaesthetist, The Lamia, Silent Sorrow in Empty Boats, The Colony of Slippermen, Ravine, The Light Dies Down on Broadway, Riding the Scree, In the Rapids, It, The Musical Box (cut), Watcher of the Skies (cut).

An excellent recording, very clear and sharp, but with some volume fluctuation during the opening track. After a sluggish start things pick up with a seriously heavy "Windshield", which earns itself an enthusiastic cheer before "Cocoon", which is perfectly balanced and keeps the audience quiet.

Gabriel has a battle with Hackett as "In The Cage" pumps up the volume, Hackett riffing away just gets the better of Gabriel whose vocals are way-too-low in the mix. Banks plays a note-perfect solo, and brings in the organ as brother John makes his hair-raising appearance. "The Grand Parade" is one of the best yet, with Collins adding a silly whistle to his massed percussive onslaught.

Hackett plays some really nice lines during "Carpet Crawl", although they sound a little distant. Along with Collins, he is the only member of the group willing to improvise something other than the album version, which does add some interest to such a rigid set-list.

There's a nasty edit in "The Waiting Room" and also a few dodgy tape noises, which most likely happened during the transfer to CD; the first half of the jam is very similar to the album version with only the last couple of minutes straying from the path.

Gabriel has trouble with the words to "Anyway", either he has forgotten them and is singing low on purpose or his mic is being problematic. The opening words to "The Lamia" are missing, and Hackett once again makes a meal of the closing solo.

A long and spooky "Silent Sorrow" is punctuated with some whistles and a cry of 'Yeah', then a rubber-clad Gabriel crawls into view and delivers a mic-perfect version.

Both the encores are cut. A case of someone forgetting to press a certain button, but the applause indicates what part of the show was the most appreciated.

DECEMBER 15th, 1974

THE FORUM, MONTREAL, CANADA.

Personnel: PG, TB, MR, PC, SH.

Set List: The Lamb Lies Down on Broadway, Fly on a Windshield, Broadway Melody of 1974, Cuckoo Cocoon, In The Cage, The Grand Parade of Lifeless Packaging, Back in N.Y.C, Hairless Heart, Counting Out Time, Carpet Crawl, The Chamber of 32 Doors, Lilywhite Lilith, The Waiting Room (cut), Anyway, Here Comes the Supernatural Anaesthetist, The Lamia, Silent Sorrow in Empty Boats, The Colony of Slippermen, Ravine, The Light Dies Down on Broadway, Riding the Scree, In the Rapids, It, The Musical Box, Watcher of the Skies.

A reasonable audience recording that is sometimes listed as being from the 10th of December, but I am sure the 15th is the right date, especially as they played Toronto the next day.

Hackett obviously wants to stretch out more as each "Windshield" gets a little wilder and a little longer. This one is a real beauty with lots of wailing guitar and plenty of power Mellotron. "The Grand Parade" is as chaotic as usual but is really starting to gel into a live favourite.

A more restrained "Hairless Heart" is run by Hackett and Banks, and works really well as a link between the aggression of "Back in NYC" and the music hall of "Counting Out Time", which this time features a good guitar solo for a change.

Gabriel's storytelling is still less than convincing and doesn't really help anyone understand what is going on. An ordinary "Lilywhite Lilith" leads us into "The Waiting Room", full of drum fills and weird sounding guitars. Not the most inspired version, but still a break from the norm. Hackett fluffs some of the "Supernatural" solo which does tend to go on a bit too long.

The arrival of Gabriel in "The Lamia" is greeted by a surge of applause from the audience who are obviously impressed by the swirling multi-coloured contraption. The guitar solo takes a while to get going but builds nicely as Rael enjoys his supper.

Lots more cheering as "The Slipperman" crawls out of its hole, the vocals are generally fine with only the odd drop-out as Mr Lumpy waddles across the stage and loses control of his microphone. The show ends with a great version of "It" which earns the band one of the loudest receptions yet, at least the Canadians liked the *Lamb*, two very loud fire crackers explode to more cheering.

The sound briefly changes to an inferior somewhat distant quality before returning to normal, the audience go crazy when they realise "The Musical Box" is next. This is the song they have been waiting for and most sections are applauded. Gabriel makes a hash of his flute line but his vocals are full of menace and seem to spur everyone along; a passionate if not technically brilliant performance.

More excitement as "Watcher" starts up, Gabriel's headgear gets its own cheer, and he delivers a fine vocal as Collins and Rutherford keep up the tempo. One of the most appreciative audiences so far on this tour which has resulted in a good all-round show.

DECEMBER 16th, 1974
MAPLE LEAF GARDENS, TORONTO, CANADA.

Personnel: PG, TB, MR, PC, SH.

Set List: The Lamb Lies Down on Broadway, Fly on a Windshield, Broadway Melody of 1974, Cuckoo Cocoon, In The Cage, The Grand Parade of Lifeless Packaging, Back in N.Y.C, Hairless Heart, Counting Out Time, Carpet Crawl, The Chamber of 32 Doors, Lilywhite Lilith, The Waiting Room, Anyway (cut), The Lamia (cut), Silent Sorrow in Empty Boats, The Colony of Slippermen, Ravine, The Light Dies Down on Broadway, Riding the Scree, In the Rapids, It, The Musical Box (cut), Watcher of the Skies.

Very clear soundboard/ambience recording with the balance of power being with the keyboards that are loud throughout, but at least the vocals are up there as well. The title track is very sluggish and Hackett continues his Robert Fripp impressions during a potent "Windshield".

Gabriel is a bit hesitant during "Cuckoo Cocoon" and Banks fluffs his solo in a very strong "Cage". Collins finally wakes up and adds his magic to "The Grand Parade" which is the first number of the night where everyone is spot-on.

An out-of-breath singer tells the story with Hackett tuning up behind him, "Back in NYC" is not as convincing as usual and even "Hairless Heart" is only going through the motions, but the Mellotron does sound so good. Collins vocals on "Carpet Crawl" perfectly complement Gabriel's deep, slightly non-melodic voice. He also plays some seriously good drums while Hackett is being very inventive in the background.

The Mellotron washes all over "32 Doors", while once more Hackett adds some subtle touches that often get lost on some audience recordings. The silences in this song fill it with atmosphere and leave the vocals to take all the glory. One of the band (not sure who) asks to be whipped whilst Gabriel is continuing the story, Collins is of course compared to the "Slipperman" as the last part of the narrative comes to an end.

Two cuts in the tape mean "Anyway" is reduced to less than a minute, the "Supernatural Anaesthetist" is missing altogether, and "The Lamia" is down to the last verse and guitar solo. Well, at least "Silent Sorrow" is complete, although it did acquire a couple of skips during the transfer to CDR.

A rather flat-sounding "Slipperman" and an emotive "Light Dies Down" lead to a Banks-dominated "Scree" where he really puts the ARP synth through its paces. Collins gets in on the act with some frantic phased tom rolls.

Only a fraction of "The Musical Box" remains but a near perfect run through of "Watcher of the Skies" more than makes up for it. Collins and Rutherford push Gabriel along as Hackett and Banks embellish the powerful and relentless rhythm.

DECEMBER 17th, 1974

THE DOME, ROCHESTER, NY, USA.

Personnel: PG, TB, MR, PC, SH.

Set List: The Lamb Lies Down on Broadway, Fly on a Windshield, Broadway Melody of 1974, Cuckoo Cocoon, In The Cage, The Grand Parade of Lifeless Packaging, Back in N.Y.C, Hairless Heart, Counting Out Time, Carpet Crawl, The Chamber of 32 Doors, Lilywhite Lilith, The Waiting Room, Anyway (cut), Here Comes the Supernatural Anaesthetist, The Lamia, Silent Sorrow in Empty Boats, The Colony of Slippermen, Ravine, The Light Dies Down on Broadway, Riding the Scree, In the Rapids, It, The Musical Box.

Excellent soundboard/ambience recording that catches Banks and his piano intro, but no opening story. The choir sounds a bit wobbly during the "Windshield" vocals, but then Hackett piles in with some killer guitar and has a lot of fun before leading the band into "Melody 74".

Right from the heartbeat start "In the Cage" sounds a bit special, Collins and Banks are as tight as usual and Gabriel is right on top of the vocals. The guitar grinds out that fuzzy riff then Banks makes a monkey out of the first part of the solo and Gabriel is nowhere when the vocals come back in. Well it did start well.

The backing vocals don't get such a good deal in the overall sound and some of the excellent harmonies Collins provides get a little lost, "Back In NYC" is finally becoming the show's outstanding rocker with Gabriel really in the mood for a fight, while Collins comes up with the goods yet again.

The beginning of "Carpet Crawl" gets a bit lost as Banks and Gabriel can't work out where they are, they keep going and the drums pull them together. Hackett is lost in the mix, and the song never really gets past chaotic.

'Anyone here from England?' asks Collins before the next story begins. The story, or as Gabriel calls it Cosmic Excretion, features the usual Collins comparisons and a comment about grapes.

From "32 Doors" onwards, the recording experiences some sound problems with the tape playing a bit slow for a while – well it is twenty-seven years old. During the "Waiting Room" this is barely noticeable, although things do sound a bit strange towards the end of this gradually lengthening piece.

A savagely cut "Anyway" is at least at the right speed and a brief snatch of guitar suggests Hackett played a blinder. The first two words of vocals are missing from "The Lamia" – whether it's timing or something technical, it's such a shame when this happens as it really takes the sting out of the piece and it must have pissed off the rest of the band.

There's an air of sadness about "The Light Lies Down" as it always seems to signal the last section of the album, "In The Rapids" and "It" flow smoothly and this above average performance comes to an end.

Hackett reigns supreme for a storming "Musical Box" – lots heavy chords and that great screaming riff when he first takes flight, Banks blasts the black notes for his solo then it's back to Gabriel to do his old dying swan routine. Once again this song is classic Genesis.

JANUARY 10th, 1975
CONVENTION HALL, WEST PALM BEACH, FLORIDA, USA.

Personnel: PG, TB, MR, PC, SH.

Set List: The Lamb Lies Down on Broadway, Fly on a Windshield, Broadway Melody of 1974, Cuckoo Cocoon, In The Cage, The Grand Parade of Lifeless Packaging, Back in N.Y.C, Hairless Heart, Counting Out Time, Carpet Crawl, The Chamber of 32 Doors, Lilywhite Lilith, The Waiting Room, Anyway, Here Comes the Supernatural Anaesthetist, The Lamia, Silent Sorrow in Empty Boats, The Colony of Slippermen, Ravine, The Light Dies Down on Broadway, Riding the Scree, In the Rapids, It, The Musical Box (cut).

The first shows of 1975 see the band down in Florida where they play two well-received dates at West Palm Beach and Lakeland respectively. Both these shows exist as soundboard and audience recordings. The soundboards are the infamous Rutherford 'boards' that allegedly originated from the bassist and soon got into circulation.

There has also been some confusion as to which show is which, with various collectors not always agreeing about the venue for the slew of bootlegs that soon appeared on the scene. Luckily the audience recordings, although not as clear answer the location question, add the atmosphere lacking in the flat-sounding desk versions.

The taper at this show is surrounded by some seriously happy fans who just love to call out song titles and such original cries as 'Alright' and 'Yeah'. By the time the title track gets underway they are on the planet 'Far Out' and having plenty of fun.

"Windshield" fills the hall with its sheer power and Hackett and Banks make the most of the chance to stretch out, this is a great example of audience over soundboard if you want the real feel of the show, even though it's not as sharp. "In the Cage" is much anticipated and causes more excitement when the band join Gabriel as he sets the scene, the solo is spot-on and Collins blitzes his way to the fade at the end.

"32 Doors" sounds fantastic in the vastness of the auditorium with the wash of Mellotron and echoed drums adding a dramatic feel to the song. The second story prompts so many calls of 'Alright', you begin to wonder if the residents of West Palm Beach can actually say anything else at all. When "The Waiting Room" begins you half-expect endless calls of 'Far out', instead everyone is rendered speechless by the cacophony coming from the stage.

This is another excellent full-on "Waiting Room", Collins makes a meal out of joining Rutherford as the bass riff bounces along, when he does the pieces all fit together and things make sense. It gets a round of applause as Banks gently ushers in "Anyway", in case he'd forgotten the song's name, a member of the crowd shouts it out for him.

The crowd flip out completely when "The Slipperman" appears, the taper asks his friend what he thinks, his reply of 'very good' seems a bit reserved considering the excitement it has caused. This is one time when the vocals do get a bit obscured by the lumpy bumpy costume Gabriel was trapped in.

The audience recording ends at the story for "The Musical Box" but that is available on the board version, needless to say it was very well received.

JANUARY 11th, 1975
CIVIC CENTRE, LAKELAND, FLORIDA, USA.

Personnel: PG, TB, MR, PC, SH.

Set List: *The Lamb Lies Down on Broadway, Fly on a Windshield, Broadway Melody of 1974, Cuckoo Cocoon, In The Cage, The Grand Parade of Lifeless Packaging, Back in N.Y.C, Hairless Heart, Counting Out Time, Carpet Crawl, The Chamber of 32 Doors, Lilywhite Lilith, The Waiting Room, Anyway, Here Comes the Supernatural Anaesthetist, The Lamia, Silent Sorrow in Empty Boats, The Colony of Slippermen, Ravine, The Light Dies Down on Broadway, Riding the Scree, In the Rapids, It, The Musical Box.*

The second of the so-called Rutherford soundboards of which this is the more infamous, due to the fact that some of the bootleg versions have pieces added from the Providence show from December '74. As with all *Lamb* boards they were recorded on 120-minute cassette tapes which meant the turn around always happened during "The Waiting Room" or "Anyway", this recording lost the latter and some of the former so sections were added to complete the show.

The audience recording is distant but complete, and like the West Palm Beach tape gives a better idea of the atmosphere generated at this show. The opening story is brief but gets the Florida crowd revved up and ready to go. What they get is a band on form if not quite at the dizzy heights they would later reach in Europe.

Collins adds his now customary swing to "Grand Parade" and the track sounds better for it. "Back in NYC" is rapidly becoming the Gabriel showstopper, with his bare-chested macho aggression all over the almost pre-punk backing. "Hairless Heart" is short and sweet with the Mellotron just about holding on until "Counting Out Time" comes in.

Hackett plays a fine solo in "The Supernatural Anaesthetist", but a real stinker at the end of "The Lamia", where he seems very stilted and the whole thing just fizzles out. In contrast "Silent Sorrow" is almost restful in its simplicity and is handled with the utmost care.

The synth solo that dominates "Scree" is best listened to from the desk recording, where the incredible dexterity of Banks is prominent. The way the solo and the rhythm section knit together is amazing, Collins is so tight with the beat that even when Banks occasionally strays he is always there to tidy up.

The *Lamb* reaches its frantic conclusion and it's back to the audience tape for the encore. Once the crowd realise what song is going to be played they become a lot more excited and keep applauding and yelling out as Gabriel relates the Henry and Cynthia story. The "Box" raises the roof and brings to an end an entertaining, if not quite classic, show.

JANUARY 12th, 1975
MUNICIPAL AUDITORIUM, ATLANTA, GA, USA.

Personnel: PG, TB, MR, PC, SH.

Set List: The Lamb Lies Down on Broadway, Fly on a Windshield, Broadway Melody of 1974, Cuckoo Cocoon, In The Cage, The Grand Parade of Lifeless Packaging, Back in N.Y.C, Hairless Heart, Counting Out Time, Carpet Crawl, The Chamber of 32 Doors, Lilywhite Lilith, The Waiting Room (cut), Anyway (cut), Here Comes the Supernatural Anaesthetist, The Lamia, Silent Sorrow in Empty Boats, The Colony of Slippermen, Ravine, The Light Dies Down on Broadway, Riding the Scree, In the Rapids, It, The Musical Box (cut).

A soundboard recording in the true sense of the word. The quality is superb but the sound is quite flat with not much atmosphere, hardly any crowd noise and the keyboards are very high in the mix. After all that, it is still a good show with some stand-out moments and very few breakdowns.

After a bass-heavy "Lamb" Hackett leads them through a nice driving "Windshield" with some great guitar work, Gabriel and Collins harmonise with an underwater flavour on "Cuckoo" which acts as the calm before the storm with "In the Cage" really setting the show alight, Hackett is again at the wheel but this is wrestled from his grasp by a stunning solo from Banks.

A seriously heavy metal "NYC" has Gabriel's voice almost breaking as he screams out his defiance. This is one of the most passionate performances of the whole tour but things seem a bit unsure during "32 Doors" with Hackett stumbling around and Gabriel opting for the low notes at the end, perhaps he was suffering from the exertion of the previous track.

The second story features Lilywhite Lilith in a cave full of wet pebbles, Gabriel in several different accents saying how nice it is that there are several Golden Globes here tonight. Collins is the Slipperman and is apparently very shy. "The Waiting Room" is very scary with plenty of echo on just about everyone, lots of bubbling synths and mad oboe. Hackett even goes all classical for a few bars before Rutherford gets things moving. A brief power cut is handled with ease as Collins keeps going until normal service is resumed.

A touch of Latin drumming livens up "Supernatural Anaesthetist" but things go astray during a fine "Lamia" solo when the keyboards cut out and the rest of the band have to struggle on for a while. More problems in "It", this time with vocals, but they get there in the end.

We join "The Musical Box" in the first verse and make it all the way to the end, which is just as well as the Old Man section is breathtaking and at last the crowd can be heard.

JANUARY 15th, 1975

MUSIC HALL, NEW ORLEANS, LA, USA.

Personnel: PG, TB, MR, PC, SH.

Set List: The Lamb Lies Down on Broadway, Fly on a Windshield, Broadway Melody of 1974, Cuckoo Cocoon, In The Cage, The Grand Parade of Lifeless Packaging, Back in N.Y.C, Hairless Heart, Counting Out Time, Carpet Crawl, The Chamber of 32 Doors, Lilywhite Lilith, The Waiting Room (cut), Anyway, Here Comes the Supernatural Anaesthetist, The Lamia, Silent Sorrow in Empty Boats, The Colony of Slippermen, Ravine, The Light Dies Down on Broadway, Riding the Scree, In the Rapids, It, The Musical Box.

Another of the excellent soundboard/ambience shows that is a touch light on atmosphere but top-drawer when it comes to sound quality. The bass comes through a bit loud on most tracks, but it's nice to hear Rutherford in such detail and is a great example of his supreme musicianship.

The Mellotron dominates "Windshield" which is great for all the 'Tron' freaks out there, but not too good for Hackett who gets swamped in strings and never really gets going. The aforementioned bass is high in the mix and there is some excellent picking going on which helps make up for the low-key guitar.

The vocal mix on "Cuckoo" is almost reversed with Collins coming through stronger than Gabriel, this makes for an interesting and highly enjoyable performance and highlights Collins considerable vocal prowess. The mix also causes the flute to all-but-vanish so the ending seems a bit empty.

'That was the first chunk of a larger bit,' is how Gabriel starts the first story. He keeps it short and they plough into "NYC" and a truly stunning "Hairless Heart" with the Mellotron and guitar in perfect balance. The second story includes a north of England accent for the Death character and a demand for more appreciation for Collins as he his once more given the Slipperman honour.

The sound of "The Waiting Room" is very similar to the Atlanta show with masses of echo on the guitar and Mellotron choirs and several bursts of free-form oboe before the rhythm gets going. The bass almost disappears in a lightweight "Light Dies Down" although the harmonies are excellent, the fade out to "It" is full of Collins singing 'I like it' in a kind of Rolling Stones way.

Collins counts in "The Musical Box", which is very odd considering how it starts! It seems like they are playing in slow motion but it is very powerful and slightly disturbing and always a fine way to end a show.

JANUARY 19th, 1975

MUSIC HALL, OKLAHOMA CITY, OK, USA.

Personnel: PG, TB, MR, PC, SH.

Set List: The Lamb Lies Down on Broadway, Fly on a Windshield, Broadway Melody of 1974, Cuckoo Cocoon, In The Cage, The Grand Parade of Lifeless Packaging, Back in N.Y.C, Hairless Heart, Counting Out Time, Carpet Crawl, The Chamber of 32 Doors, Lilywhite Lilith, The Waiting Room, Anyway, Here Comes The Supernatural Anaesthetist, The Lamia, Silent Sorrow In Empty Boats, The Colony of Slippermen, Ravine, The Light Dies Down On Broadway, Riding The Scree, In the Rapids, It, The Musical Box (cut).

The band is on good form for this show, which is just as well as it is one of the best quality soundboard/ambience tapes I have yet heard. The sound is crystal clear and although the audience noise is pretty low in the mix it is a perfectly well-balanced recording and very enjoyable to listen to. The audience tape only features the first half of the show and suffers from speed problems, but it is the only source available to collectors at this time.

"Windshield" is very heavy and a perfect balance of light and shade before Gabriel runs through his list of infamous Americans during "Broadway Melody of 74". Lots of bubbly underwater vocals for "Cuckoo Cocoon" and a really frantic "In the Cage", complete with a blistering solo from Banks and some fiery vocals from Gabriel and Collins, making this one of the best versions yet.

"Back in NYC" is aggressive and very much the style of rock 'n' roll that American audiences were used to. No vocals at the start of "Carpet Crawl" means Banks has to keep playing until the problem is sorted. Eventually Gabriel almost apologetically starts singing.

An excellent "Lamia" features a stirring solo from Hackett, who then superbly elects to stray from the recorded version of "Silent Sorrow" to great effect. He was obviously on form that night. A very slow "Light Dies Down" has some excellent drumming, which returns for a super-fast "It" where Collins is right on the button and just about every drum in his possession.

"The Musical Box" cuts in at about the halfway point, but we do get to hear a seriously heavy finale with Gabriel screaming himself hoarse as he pleads to be touched, if only the soundman had been on the ball.

JANUARY 22nd, 1975

COMMUNITY THEATRE, BERKLEY, CA, USA.

Personnel: PG, TB, MR, PC, SH.

Set List: The Lamb Lies Down on Broadway, Fly on a Windshield, Broadway Melody of 1974, Cuckoo Cocoon, In The Cage, The Grand Parade of Lifeless Packaging, Back in N.Y.C, Hairless Heart, Counting Out Time, Carpet Crawl, The Chamber of 32 Doors, Lilywhite Lilith, The Waiting Room (cut), Anyway (cut), Here Comes the Supernatural Anaesthetist, The Lamia, Silent Sorrow in Empty Boats, The Colony of Slippermen, Ravine, The Light Dies Down on Broadway, Riding the Scree, In the Rapids, It, The Musical Box (cut), Watcher of the Skies.

The Lamb rolls into Berkley for the first of four shows in the sunshine state of California, a long way from the streets of New York City, but at least the audience seem more receptive. This excellent soundboard recording captures a band playing with a lot more confidence than at recent shows.

The opening track which was always one of the less-inspired numbers competently leads into another Hackett dominated "Windshield", his powerful solo gets longer each time and the band have to wait for him to have his freedom before bringing Gabriel back in for the next piece.

Someone calls out 'New York City' as the heartbeat intro to "In the Cage" gets underway; a slight hiccup at the start of the keyboard solo is the only mistake in an otherwise classic performance. Collins goes berserk with the whistles during "Grand Parade" blowing them all through the song, he was obviously enjoying himself.

"Back in NYC" builds on the growing momentum and is a suitably muscular performance, with lots of pounding basslines and almost frantic vocals. After Collins kicks some life into a lazy "Carpet Crawl" they almost fall into "32 Doors" which is so laidback it sounds like Little Feat.

During a long-winded second story, Collins is of course compared to the "Slipperman" and gets introduced three times. A member of the audience does a Raven impression when said bird is mentioned, so at least somebody was paying attention. Gabriel adds his flute and possibly an oboe to the controlled wackiness that is "The Waiting Room". A small

Above: Gabriel monitors the skies.
Photo: Janet Macoska

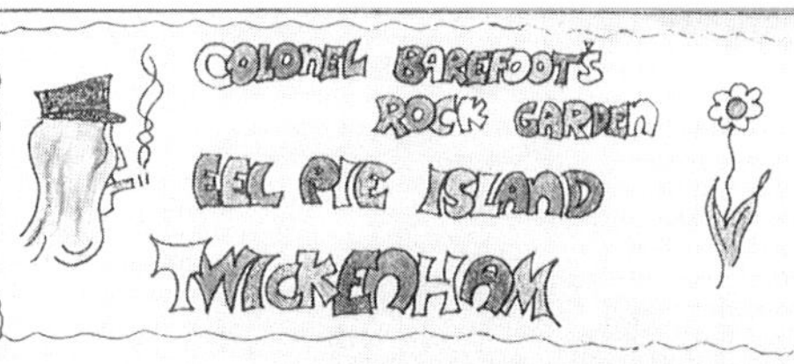

APRIL

FRIDAYS		SATURDAYS	
3	LITTLE FREE ROCK plus EASY LEAF	4	MOTT THE HOOPLE plus WHITE LIGHTNING
10	JAN DUKES DE GREY plus GENESIS	11	EAST OF EDEN plus CRACIOUS
17	**TASTE** plus WHITE LIGHTNING	18	STRAY
24	(Back by demand) CLIMAX CHICAGO BLUES BAND	25	SHADES

FREE DRAUGHT BITTER & COLONEL BAREFOOT KILLER PUNCH
VERY CHEAP HOT SNACKS
SOFT DRINKS FAGS ETC.
INCREDIBLE LIGHT SHOW BY AURAL PLASMA
FREAKY SOUNDS - INCENSE
DOORS OPEN 7.30p.m. CLOSE 11.30 p.m.

ASGARD ENTERPRISES present — in Concert
DE MONTFORT HALL, Granville Road, Leicester
Monday, 13th April 7.30 p.m.

FAIRPORT CONVENTION

plus MANDRAGON Licensed Bar
Tickets from Municipal Office, Charles Street, Leicester, or at door on night. Please send s.a.e. Prices: Balcony 20/-, 15/-, Tier 15/-, Gallery 11/-, 8/-. Stalls 17/-, 15/-, 11/-, 8/-. Box Office Tel. Leics. 27632.

CENTRAL HALL - CHATHAM HIGH STREET

Saturday, April 4th
LIVERPOOL SCENE with MR. CHARLEY

Saturday, April 11th
DEEP PURPLE with GENESIS

Tickets 10/-, 14/-, 17/-, 20/- (send S.A.E.) from Central Hall Box Office, High Street, Chatham, Kent, Medway 43930, or at door on night. Doors open 7 p.m.

Nº 0092 **Imperial College**

Saturday November 18th.

GENESIS

Ticket 60p. Adv. 70p. Door

(Not Returnable)

Nov 25 Stackridge 50p
Dec 2 Amon Duul 60p.
Dec 9 Kinks £1

ronnie scott's
3 floors of entertainment

Now appearing
LEON THOMAS
NUCLEUS
JOE HENDERSON

Commencing June 15 for 2 weeks — SALENA JONES, HENRY LOWTHER BAND

upstairs AT RONNIE'S

Thursday, June 11th	AFFINITY
Friday, June 12th	FLARE
Saturday, June 13th	FLARE
Tuesday, June 16th	GENESIS
Wednesday, June 17th	AFFINITY

(Ladies' Free Night every Wednesday)

Ronnie Scott's are now exclusively booking—
NUCLEUS

Left: Paul Russell's autographed copy of *Zigzag* magazine.
Opposite top: Peter Gabriel and Anthony Phillips reunited backstage in Cleveland '74. *Photo: Janet Macosk*
Opposite bottom: Mr Banks and Mr Hackett. *Photo: Paul Russell archive*

"The festival which has traditionally been an almost perfect event" (THE GUARDIAN)

READING

is less than 40 miles west of London on Motorway M4 or 30 minutes by train from Paddington. Just 10 minutes walk from the Station will bring you to the beautiful Thames-side Arena and Camp Site of the—

12th NATIONAL JAZZ BLUES and ROCK

FESTIVAL

24 AUGUST Friday from 4 p.m.	RORY GALLAGHER GREENSLADE • CAPABILITY BROWN JO'BURG HAWK • ALQUIN (Holland) EMBRYO (Germany) • STRAY DOG Special Guest Stars COMMANDER CODY (USA)	LINKS BY Jerry Floyd
25 AUGUST Saturday from noon	THE FACES LINDISFARNE ALEX HARVEY • FUMBLE • ANDY DOWN TASAVALLAN PRESIDENTTI (Finland) • MAGMA (France) STRIDER • CLAIRE HAMILL • RIFF-RAFF QUADRILLE • DAVE ELLIS and ... ★ THE CHRIS BARBER BAND *Special guest stars* STATUS QUO	LINKS Bill Barclay
26 AUGUST Sunday from noon	GENESIS JON HISEMAN'S TEMPEST MEDICINE HEAD • STACKRIDGE • SPENCER DAVIS JACK THE LAD • MAHATMA • P.F.M. (Italy) TIM HARDIN • LESLEY DUNCAN • ANGE (France)	LINKS BY Bob Harris

GREAT WESTERN EXPRESS
SPRING BANK HOLIDAY FESTIVAL
LINCOLN
Official Programme 10p

Far left top: The fox's head and that dress.
eft: Supper's Ready. *Photos: Paul Russell archive*
Far left bottom: 'Ol Blue Eyes' Phil Collins.
Above: Gabriel and Banks in Cleveland '74.
Photos: Janet Macoska
ight: The gig cancelled due to Hackett's injury.
Below: *Circus* magazine, March '75, asks the question, "Will America swallow *The Lamb*?"
elow right: Epping Forest. *Photo: Janet Macoska*

EMPIRE POOL, WEMBLEY

JOHN SMITH ENTERTAINMENTS
presents
GENESIS IN CONCERT
MONDAY, NOVEMBER 4th, 1974
at 8 p.m.

ARENA
£2.00

TO BE RETAINED. See conditions on back

NOVEMBER 4
ENTER AT SOUTH DOOR
BLOCK C
ROW 18
SEAT 33

NO. 106
GREAT BRITAIN 35p
MARCH 1975/$1.00
CIRCUS
MARK FARNER
INTERVIEW – Confessions Of A Rock Farmer
ENESIS–
ONI
ITCHELL–
INGO–
HE GUESS
VHO
ISS–
EKTAR
HE KINKS'
N ANDERSON
LANCE LOUD On The Death Of A Fan
SPECIAL REPORT!
THE YOUNG DRUNKS– A NEW NATION OF ALCOHOLICS?
CONCERT GUIDE–
FUNK
ZEPPELIN
& More
PETER GABRIEL

GENESIS
I KNOW WHAT I LIKE
and by public demand
c/w TWILIGHT ALEHOUSE
CB 224

ar left: Guaranteed Eternal Sanctuary Man.
ft: Gabriel with tambourine and Rutherford with trademark twin-neck.
Right: Gabriel and Rutherford.
elow left: Queues outside the Allen Theater, Cleveland, Ohio, April 1974.
Below right: Gabriel with *Lamb* backdrop.
Opposite bottom:
The Battle of Epping Forest.
Photos: Janet Macoska

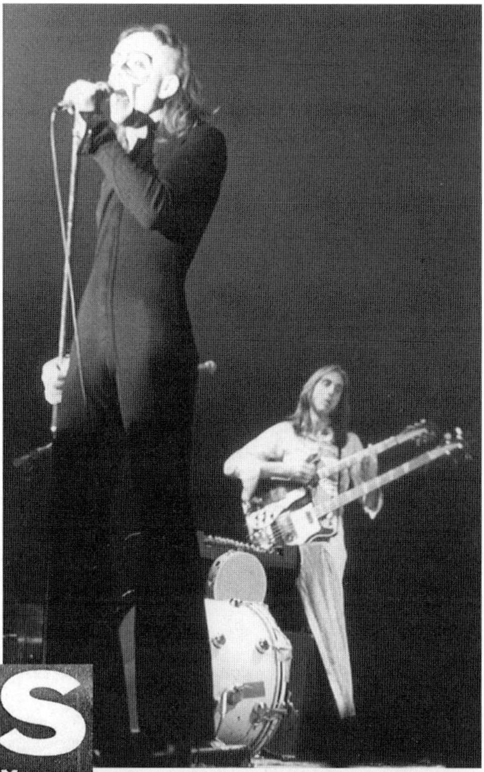

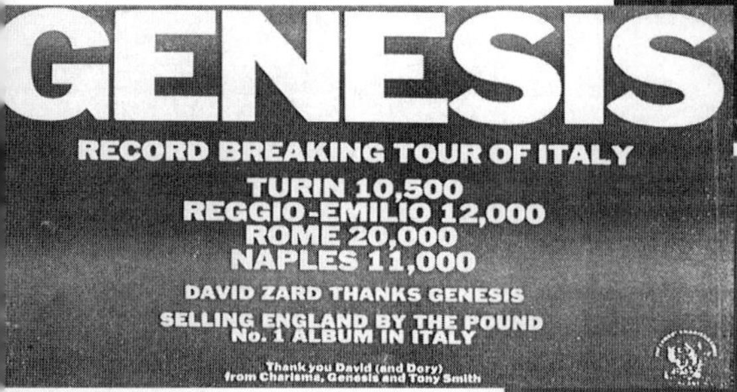

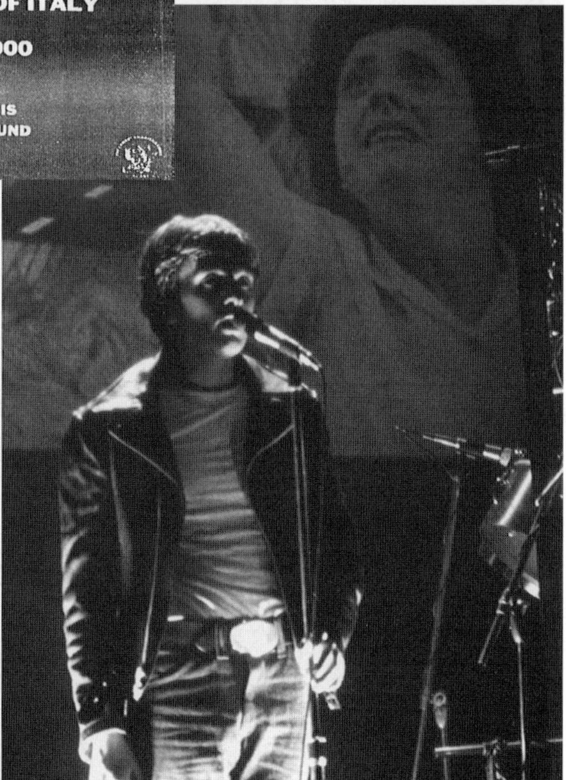

GENESIS

RECORD BREAKING TOUR OF ITALY

TURIN 10,500
REGGIO-EMILIO 12,000
ROME 20,000
NAPLES 11,000

DAVID ZARD THANKS GENESIS

SELLING ENGLAND BY THE POUND
No. 1 ALBUM IN ITALY

Thank you David (and Dory)
from Charisma, Genesis and Tony Smith

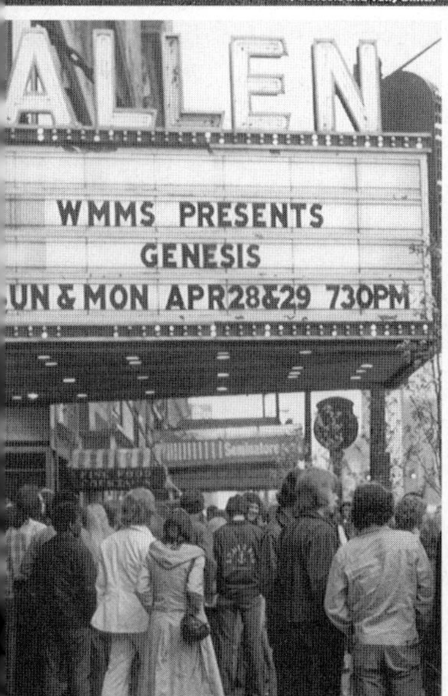

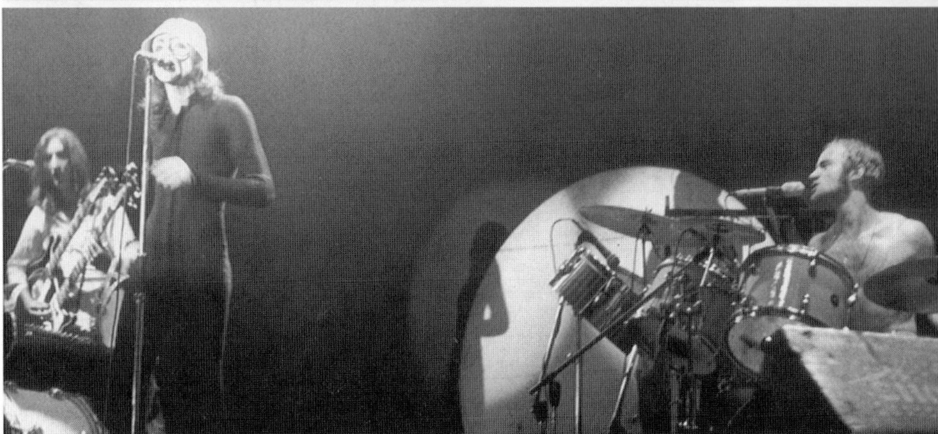

Top: Cuckoo Cocoon. Above: I Know What I Like. *Photos: Janet Macoska*
Below: Genesis reformed at Heathrow airport, 1997. (l-r) Tony Banks, Steve Hackett, Pet
Gabriel, Anthony Phillips, Mike Rutherford, John Silver and Phil Collins. *Photo: Paul Russe*

edit at the end where the tape was turned over spoils the feel but when Hackett skips his way through the "Anaesthetist" solo the mood changes for the better again.

Birds are obviously the order of the day because the first few notes of Hackett's "Lamia" solo sound like a sick goose. He pulls himself together and with the aid of some funky drumming, delivers a very mediocre performance. "Silent Sorrow" gets a laugh when Rutherford plays a chord that is so wrong it is funny.

Gabriel and his blow up genitalia slobber their way through a convincing "Slipperman" with no microphone problems at all, in fact he comes out well on the technical front leaving it to the others to bum those notes.

We join "The Musical Box" a few minutes in but get a complete "Watcher". Both are top drawer versions, which seem to be the norm at this stage of the tour.

JANUARY 24th, 1975
SHRINE AUDITORIUM, LOS ANGELES, CA, USA.

Personnel: PG, TB, MR, PC, SH.

Set List: The Lamb Lies Down on Broadway, Fly on a Windshield, Broadway Melody of 1974, Cuckoo Cocoon, In The Cage, The Grand Parade of Lifeless Packaging, Back in N.Y.C, Hairless Heart, Counting Out Time, Carpet Crawl, The Chamber of 32 Doors, Lilywhite Lilith, The Waiting Room, Anyway, Here Comes the Supernatural Anaesthetist, The Lamia, Silent Sorrow in Empty Boats, The Colony of Slippermen, Ravine, The Light Dies Down on Broadway, Riding the Scree, In the Rapids, It, The Musical Box, Watcher of the Skies.

The most famous *Lamb* of all and easily the most controversial, firstly because of the fabulous professionally filmed footage that gave us that tantalising view of the spectacle that was the live show, and more recently as the doctored, late-nineties offering, that seemed to contradict itself when issued under the archive banner.

There also exists several incomplete bootlegs from various radio shows and audience recordings, which at least include both encores, sadly missing from the Box-set version. The first Genesis *Archive* set featured the Shrine gig in what was a much anticipated release, as it turned out the multi-track tapes used ran out before "It" so the studio version was used with Gabriel singing over the top, it also meant both encores were missing.

Then Gabriel decided to re-do most of the vocals, as he felt there were too many mistakes. Over twenty years after the original, his voice has obviously changed and sounds very "Sledgehammer". Songs like "In The Cage" and "Back In NYC" don't sound anywhere near the Gabriel of

1975. To these ears this devalues the show and the whole idea of a live archive performance.

Then to cap it all Hackett jumped on the 're-do it again' bandwagon with several fresh attempts at perfection. His solo on "Windshield" is full of fine riffs and typical Hackett-sounding sustained notes. Trouble is, he did not play like that in 1975 and it sounds like it. Maybe Banks had some fun as well as some of the organ on "In the Cage" which sounds very un-Hammond like to these ears and has sample written all over it.

The radio show discs include great versions of both encores and could have easily been used as part of the Archive release, here Gabriel sounds like a man in his mid-twenties and if he misses the odd note or his microphone cuts out that's what happened, that was the real live Shrine.

The video footage is a total revelation, and its all too brief images give a great indication as to what really happened in LA. The film was made about the late Bill Graham, the legendary concert promoter, so the live footage is mixed up with Graham being accosted by a journalist whilst he is trying to catch a plane somewhere. The first image is Gabriel as The Slipperman emerging from a pink tunnel franticly tugging at his microphone lead, he finally stands and inflates his balloon-like genitalia. This is a truly surreal image and still amazes me all these years later.

The prime shots are the ones from "In the Cage", where Gabriel stripped to the waist and wrapped himself around the mic stand spitting out the lyrics. Rutherford stands behind him dressed in white, sporting the twin-neck. The camera pans around to Collins just as he throws in a typical fill; great stuff indeed. The stage set is typically very dark with just spots on the performers; this of course put a greater emphasis on the slide show behind them.

At the end of the film we get the old man sequence from "The Musical Box" only brief snatches, but enough to know that it is still the greatest of all Genesis songs, and the film ends with Gabriel falling backwards as the final chord dies down.

The big 'what if' about this footage is, 'Was the whole gig filmed?' As it spans "Cage" to encore, the answer could be 'Yes'. Where then, is the rest? Who knows? Locked in a vault, wiped, or just lost? The fact that it has not surfaced yet, when so much other stuff has, does not bode well. But we live in hope.

JANUARY 25th, 1975

FOX THEATRE, SAN DIEGO, CA, USA.

Personnel: PG, TB, MR, PC, SH.

Set List: The Lamb Lies Down on Broadway, Fly on a Windshield, Broadway Melody of 1974, Cuckoo Cocoon, In The Cage, The Grand Parade of Lifeless Packaging, Back in N.Y.C, Hairless Heart, Counting Out Time, Carpet Crawl, The Chamber of 32 Doors, Lilywhite Lilith, The Waiting Room, Anyway, Here Comes the Supernatural Anaesthetist, The Lamia, Silent Sorrow in Empty Boats, The Colony of Slippermen, Ravine, The Light Dies Down on Broadway, Riding the Scree, In the Rapids, It, The Musical Box, Watcher of the Skies (cut).

Good soundboard recording that starts out sounding like mono but it is most likely that only one mic was working, anyway by "Cuckoo" everything sounds fine.

Hackett piles into "Windshield", and with the aid of an 'on-the-case' Collins, draws first blood. First mistake goes to Gabriel who misses the opening words to "In the Cage", but otherwise does a good job. The band seem to toil through "Back in NYC", even though Collins is trying his best to get things moving.

Things seem to slow down even more for "Counting Out Time" but at least the guitar break is suitably quirky and in tune. During the second story Gabriel informs the audience that "Lilywhite Lilith" is here tonight with some of her family, this draws a modicum of applause and most likely had a few people looking over their shoulders for a strange looking woman.

A heavy dose of cat noises invades "The Waiting Room", not very inspired but still interesting. Even less thrilling is the squeal of feedback that precedes "The Lamia". It seems to put Gabriel off as he barely murmurs the words.

The rest of *The Lamb* passes without much inspiration but at least the encores get the fans going. "The Musical Box" is very powerful and gets the biggest cheer of the night. A beefy sounding "Watcher" just gets going when it is cut during the first verse, the Mellotron sounded awful, but that was better than none at all.

JANUARY 28th, 1975

CIVIC CENTRE, PHOENIX, AZ, USA.

Personnel: PG, TB, MR, PC, SH.

Set List: The Lamb Lies Down on Broadway, Fly on a Windshield, Broadway Melody of 1974, Cuckoo Cocoon, In The Cage, The Grand Parade of Lifeless Packaging, Back in N.Y.C, Hairless Heart, Counting Out Time, Carpet Crawl, The Chamber of 32 Doors, Lilywhite Lilith, The Waiting Room (cut), Anyway, Here Comes the Supernatural Anaesthetist, The Lamia, Silent Sorrow in Empty Boats, The Colony of Slippermen, Ravine, The Light Dies Down on Broadway, Riding the Scree, In the Rapids, It, The Musical Box.

After some first-verse bass distortion, the recording levels are adjusted and this excellent audience recording settles down. Hackett is keeping himself sparse during the first half of his "Windshield" solo, he then turns up the heat and burns his way into "Melody of 74". Gabriel takes the vocal volume right down and Banks obliges with some delicate Mellotron. This is appreciated by the audience who offer up some early applause and a few whistles of approval.

"In the Cage" is almost note-perfect and is full of attacking organ and pounding drums, Rael is desperate and convincing and Hackett is his usual understated but spot-on self. A rather tame "Back in NYC" almost loses the momentum, but the madness that is "The Grand Parade" soon puts things back on track.

Gabriel keeps the crowd relatively quiet as they try and grasp the next part of the story; "Lilywhite Lilith" is a touch slow but very heavy and Collins throws in some excellent fills that add an certain swing. "The Waiting Room" starts off with lots of strange percussive noises, Hackett finally throws in the fiddly guitar part from "Dance With the Moonlit Knight", something he had been hinting at for several shows. Rutherford then starts his riff and the rest of the band soon fall back in line and carry on as usual. An edit in the tape spoils the ending but an emotional "Anyway" soon makes up for that.

A large chunk of the "Slipperman" vocals go missing which is a shame as the song was doing rather well. Then the gremlins really get to work as Gabriel screws up the lyrics to "Light Dies Down" and the microphone twice cuts out during "Scree". Collins of course plays like a man possessed, or should that be a man pissed off.

The Lamb ends to not much more than polite applause and once again it is left to "The Musical Box" to save the day. It does of course, and the audience respond accordingly. Seems they only want to hear stuff they already know.

FEBRUARY 2nd, 1975
GRAND VALLEY STATE COLLEGE, GRAND RAPIDS, MI, USA.

Personnel: PG, TB, MR, PC, SH.

Set List: The Lamb Lies Down on Broadway, Fly on a Windshield, Broadway Melody of 1974, Cuckoo Cocoon, In The Cage, The Grand Parade of Lifeless Packaging, Back in N.Y.C (cut), Hairless Heart, Counting Out Time, Carpet Crawl, The Chamber of 32 Doors, Lilywhite Lilith, The Waiting Room (cut), Anyway (cut), Here Comes the Supernatural Anaesthetist, The Colony of Slippermen, The Light Dies Down on Broadway (cut).

An enthusiastic taper and his friends are obviously in the mood for a Genesis concert, as their exclamations are loud and frequent when this good, but variable audience recording gets going. As the house lights go up a confused fan says, 'Wow, "Watcher of the Skies".' Of course they don't get it, but instead Gabriel relays the first part of the story about a black cloud descending into Times Square. This goes down well with the taper and his friends, as they mention the album title several times, which means at least a few people had bought it before they saw the show.

The band deliver a good opening number, but as usual, things kick in during "Windshield" as Hackett gets down to business. "In the Cage" is again quite restrained, so Collins shifts up a gear for "The Grand Parade" which is full of chaotic aggression and some very hot drumming.

The sound quality varies a bit as the recording volume is adjusted, plus there is an edit at the end of "Back in NYC" and a sudden fade in "Counting Out Time". Something strange happens during the first verse of a ragged "Carpet Crawl" – Banks is all over the place and there is a jump in the recording as if a second or two was lost. The song recovers once the band come in, although Collins is a bit heavy-handed this time around.

The initial excitement seems to have worn off by the time the next section of story is told; maybe they had only listened to some of the album, as there are no more shouts of recognition.

Collins is perfecting the double-beat he now uses on "Lilywhite Lilith". It almost sounds too clever, but it does spice things up a bit. A large dose of cat noises is how Hackett enters "The Waiting Room", which is starting to sound like a haunted house, it rocks along nicely until a savage edit takes us to the last few seconds of "Anyway".

With only the "Slipperman" and "The Light Dies Down" left, the whole thing comes to a rather deflating conclusion, so we'll never find out how the taper and his friends reacted to "The Musical Box".

FEBRUARY 4th, 1975

ARIE CROWN THEATRE, CHICAGO, IL, USA.

Personnel: PG, TB, MR, PC, SH.

Set List: Fly on a Windshield (cut), Broadway Melody of 1974, Cuckoo Cocoon, In The Cage, The Grand Parade of Lifeless Packaging, Back in N.Y.C, Hairless Heart, Counting Out Time, Carpet Crawl, The Chamber of 32 Doors, Lilywhite Lilith, The Waiting Room, Anyway (cut), Here Comes the Supernatural Anaesthetist, The Lamia, Silent Sorrow in Empty Boats, The Colony of Slippermen, Ravine, The Light Dies Down on Broadway, Riding the Scree, In the Rapids, It, The Musical Box, Watcher of the Skies.

Someone forgot to press record at the start of this soundboard recording so we join things at the end of "Windshield". There is an urgency about "In the Cage" which gives the song that extra edge. This spills over into "Back in NYC" which sees Gabriel turn in a great vocal performance. Several cries of 'Oh yeah' before an almost perfect "Hairless Heart" shows audience approval of the rockier numbers at least.

The ambience mics pick up enough of the general atmosphere to give this recording an excellent sound balance with the clarity of the desk being complemented by the full overall sound.

The gradual build-up during "Carpet Crawl" is due to Collins being totally on the case and adding that bit extra for each verse, he seems to draw Rutherford and Banks along with him as Gabriel tells his surreal tale. There is warm applause for "32 Doors" and the 'Oh yeah' man is at it again.

Gabriel's next story promises that Hackett will shave off his beard and finally compares the "Slipperman" to someone other than Collins. Banks is the lucky recipient and duly gets a round of applause. Gabriel seems a lot more at ease than usual and is obviously in a good mood.

A superb "Waiting Room" is one of the longest yet and the audience appreciates its controlled, improvised chaos, everyone has a good workout but as usual Collins steals the show. Some annoying tape noise interrupts "Anyway" which loses a small section near the end. The same problem affects the start of "The Supernatural Anaesthetist" but then things settle down for a very good "Lamia" which Gabriel manages to spoil at the end by getting his words mixed up. This throws Hackett who stutters through his solo.

The "Slipperman" is greeted by applause and by Mr 'Oh yeah' who was also having a good evening, which is more than can be said of the "Slipperman" who gets into a tangle with his lyrics and loses some altogether.

The shorter link pieces like "Silent Sorrow" and "Ravine" are very effective at creating an atmosphere of their own, as well as giving Gabriel time to change, and at this show they hold the audience spellbound until Rael is ready to continue.

More tape noises during "It" but all is quiet for the beginning of the first encore. When the band kick in all Hell breaks loose and this soon becomes one of the great versions. Gabriel's old man is creepy, Banks is solid at the organ, Collins is Collins, while Rutherford and Hackett take the song to a new level.

More applause as the batwings appear, with everyone still buzzing from "The Musical Box". They are totally blown away by an incredibly tight and powerful "Watcher of the Skies". Collins sounds like three drummers and Gabriel is spot-on with all his cues.

A very strong way to end a very good concert, but however strong *The Lamb* is, it just can't match the old classics.

FEBRUARY 19th, 1975

EKERBERGHALLEN, OSLO, NORWAY.

Personnel: PG, TB, MR, PC, SH.

Set List: The Lamb Lies Down On Broadway, Fly on a Windshield, Broadway Melody of 1974, Cuckoo Cocoon, In The Cage, The Grand Parade of Lifeless Packaging, Back in N.Y.C, Hairless Heart, Counting Out Time, Carpet Crawl, The Chamber of 32 Doors, Lilywhite Lilith, The Waiting Room, Anyway (cut), The Lamia (cut), Silent Sorrow in Empty Boats, The Colony of Slippermen, Ravine, The Light Dies Down on Broadway, Riding the Scree, In the Rapids, It.

The tour hits Europe and kicks off in the rock 'n' roll city of Oslo. This excellent soundboard recording gets off to a bad start because the man on the sound desk is a bit slow with the record button so we join the title track near the end.

"Windshield" is very heavy with Banks and Hackett battling it out but they end up sharing the honours. A very mellow "Cuckoo" and a nicely manic "Cage" are surpassed by an enthusiastic and Collins-led "Grand Parade" that ends with Gabriel and the drummer trying to out-scream each other.

The first story has a welcome return for Nick the roadie who once again is mentioned in the 'What's happened to my fucking lead?' story, and once again Rutherford is the culprit as Gabriel introduces him as being straight from Hollywood.

The original tape was obviously turned over just as "Anyway" was getting going, so we rejoin the show in the middle of "The Lamia". This means "Supernatural Anaesthetist" is snuffed out altogether. To make up for it, "Silent Sorrow" is one of the spookiest yet and is dominated by some heavenly choirs.

The "Slipperman" eventually appears after what seems like an age of oriental sounding improvisation, no mic problems this time, but there is some annoying tape noise, which has more to do with the age of the tape than anything else.

Like "Silent Sorrow", "Ravine" is also very atmospheric and fades into silence before "The Light Dies Down" comes in. As "Scree" finishes there is a lengthy silence before Rutherford strokes the chords for "Rapids", and Gabriel delivers an emotional performance.

The biggest surprise of the evening comes right at the end of "It". The pyrotechnic finale to the show suddenly becomes very dangerous after too much explosive is put into the flash bomb and a massive explosion stuns the audience into silence.

Collins remembers large splinters of wood shooting across the stage and telling a sheepish-looking roadie that he was fired. As long as his name wasn't Nick.

FEBRUARY 21st, 1975
FALKONERTEATRET, COPENHAGEN, DENMARK.

Personnel: PG, TB, MR, PC, SH.

Set List: The Lamb Lies Down on Broadway, Fly on a Windshield, Broadway Melody of 1974, Cuckoo Cocoon, In The Cage, The Grand Parade of Lifeless Packaging, Back in N.Y.C (cut), Hairless Heart, Counting Out Time, Carpet Crawl, The Chamber of 32 Doors, Lilywhite Lilith, The Waiting Room, Anyway, Here Comes the Supernatural Anaesthetist, The Lamia, Silent Sorrow in Empty Boats, The Colony of Slippermen (cut), Ravine, The Light Dies Down on Broadway, Riding the Scree, In the Rapids, It, The Musical Box, Watcher of the Skies.

An audience recording of reasonable quality that is a bit distant but still very listenable and it does contain both encores.

For once the opening story is included, although it is mostly lost due to the less-than-perfect sound quality. The first few songs pass without problem and things start to get into gear for "In the Cage" and "Back in NYC". Both carry a lot more punch than some of the earlier versions on the tour.

"Carpet Crawl" builds nicely, but it is hard to enjoy it on such an average recording. On audence tapes this song often suffers by comparison to some of the great soundboards that tend to highlight subtleties of the quieter songs.

Collins and his exaggerated drumbeat almost slows "Lilywhite Lilith" down, but Rutherford and Hackett are tuned in and the song makes its way into "The Waiting Room". This version has Gabriel playing his flute a lot more than usual, although what he plays is not that inspiring. But when the band arrive to take up Rutherford's offer of a jam, the tempo changes and a serious rock band having a blow emerges from the abstract noises that start the thing off.

There is a small edit near the end of the "Slippermen" not quite the edit the good Doktor was talking about, but still quite annoying, as is the sudden fluctuation in volume as the taper moves the microphone around.

Banks positively tears his way through the "Scree" solo, leaving everyone trailing in his wake. Collins does his best to catch up, but the rest of the band always seem a fraction behind the smoking-fingered keyboard player.

The end of *The Lamb* brings one of the best receptions yet, with loud sustained clapping until the band return. Calls for the "The Giant Hogweed" and "The Knife" go unheeded and Gabriel begins the story about the two little Victorian children.

A touch of confusion as the vocals start in "Watcher" but everyone keeps going and a somewhat hurried performance gains as much applause as its illustrious predecessor. The audience leave the hall to the somewhat bizarre strains of 'Ole Man River' – must be that good old English humour.

FEBRUARY 22nd, 1975
NIEDERSACHSENHALLE, HANNOVER, GERMANY.

Personnel: PG, TB, MR, PC, SH.

Set List: The Lamb Lies Down on Broadway, Fly on a Windshield, Broadway Melody of 1974, Cuckoo Cocoon, In The Cage, The Grand Parade of Lifeless Packaging, Back in N.Y.C, Hairless Heart, Counting Out Time, Carpet Crawl, The Chamber of 32 Doors, Lilywhite Lilith, The Waiting Room (cut), Anyway (cut), Here Comes the Supernatural Anaesthetist, The Lamia, Silent Sorrow in Empty Boats, The Colony of Slippermen, Ravine, The Light Dies Down on Broadway, Riding the Scree, In the Rapids, It, The Musical Box.

The first of the German shows starts off as an excellent soundboard/ambience recording, but ends up as a soundboard recording with lots of annoying tape noise. It might be possible to remove it in a studio environment, but it's unfortunately present during this review.

The band cruise through "Windshield" while Hackett plays a restrained, but interesting solo, before finally cueing them back in for "Melody 74". Gabriel sounds confident during an almost casual "Cuckoo Cocoon" and positively magnificent for a top-drawer "Cage", where Banks is perfection on the solo and Collins, of course, is everywhere.

As the cage dissolves the audience greet "The Grand Parade" with applause and seem very on the ball as far as the album goes. Collins makes things go with a swing and adds the odd silly whistle for a laugh, Hackett is soloing away for all his worth in the background as the first of the tape noise starts.

Lots of noisy tuning from Banks and Rutherford undermines the first story, and lots of noise undermines a powerful "Back in NYC". A very slow but compelling "Hairless Heart" is like an oasis in a desert of interference as the next three songs all suffer from an infernal squeaking.

Gabriel and Collins pull out all the vocal stops for a classic "32 Doors" – lots of dramatic silences and powerful drumming with Gabriel pleading for help, all very moving stuff.

The audience applaud the story when Gabriel talks about the severing of the sexual organ. No "Slipperman" comparisons this time, in fact the story is much shorter, and in no time at all Collins counts in one of the best "Lilywhite Lilith's" yet. Lots of heavy drums, that incessant riff and plenty of Mellotron lead us into a manic, but superb "Waiting Room".

Rutherford loses the plot halfway through the "Supernatural Anaesthetist" but they just manage to hold it together. Gabriel leads them through a stunning "Lamia" where he seems genuinely emotional; it must have affected Hackett as he makes a complete mess of his solo.

Lots of applause as Mr Lumpy Bumpy arrives, he takes a while to sort himself out but then gets overwhelmed with tape noise, which becomes more noticeable as the show reaches its conclusion.

An excellent "Scree" bounces along with Collins and Banks in the driving seat, Gabriel sings his part then the synth and some heavily treated drums battle it out again with Banks having the last word. More interference spoils the end of the show and ruins a fine "Musical Box".

FEBRUARY 23rd, 1975

EISSPORTHALLE, BERLIN, GERMANY.

Personnel: PG, TB, MR, PC, SH.

Set List: The Grand Parade of Lifeless Packaging, Back in N.Y.C, Hairless Heart, Counting Out Time, Carpet Crawl, The Chamber of 32 Doors, Lilywhite Lilith, The Waiting Room, Anyway, Here Comes the Supernatural Anaesthetist, The Lamia, Silent Sorrow in Empty Boats, The Colony of Slippermen,The Musical Box, Watcher of the Skies.

A crystal-clear audience recording that starts late and finishes early – which is a shame because the band are mostly on top form.

The quality of the show had definitely shifted up a gear by the time the European leg started. There is an air of confidence about the whole group as they steamroller the heavier numbers like "Back in NYC" and then glide through the likes of "Hairless Heart" and "Carpet Crawl" with ease. At the centre of this resurgence is Collins who has been on the case from the very first show, now it seems like the others have caught up with him and are turning in some classic performances.

Hackett plays the most delicate lines throughout "Carpet Crawl" and Collins backs Gabriel to perfection whilst keeping the whole thing ticking over with some slick hi-hat work. A very laidback but emotional "32 Doors" is very well-received and brings Gabriel back to the spotlight.

Lots of silly voices during the next section of story, which again is quite short and never really explains how things end, but the audience find the part about Rael's part being grabbed by a raven very funny.

"Lilywhite Lilith" is simply stunning, Collins and his staggered off-beat, the repetitive guitar riff and a tidal wave of Mellotron – shame it was so short. "The Waiting Room" is a nightmare in a haunted house, lots of everything all at once and then silence. Then the riff from "Moonlit Knight", lots of percussion and bubbling synth. Eventually Rutherford's bass emerges, accompanied by Gabriel attempting a little jig on his flute.

Gabriel comes over all deep-voiced for "Anyway" and then keeps everyone waiting at the start of "The Lamia". When he does finally arrive, he delivers a surprisingly lacklustre performance and even Collins sounds a bit heavy-handed. Hackett is also wide of the mark with his solo – it's as if he could not think of anything new to play.

Someone near the mic coughs their way through "Silent Sorrow" which now includes some weird seagull noises near the beginning. The "Slipperman" takes almost two-and-a-half minutes to appear, and when he does, the sound becomes very bass-heavy. To make matters worse the tape cuts out and we join the applause as the audience wait for the encore.

A lengthy, though not thoroughly convincing "Musical Box" is given a long round of applause with much foot-stamping thrown in, so the band finish them off with a gutsy "Watcher of the Skies".

FEBRUARY 24th, 1975

CARRE THEATRE, AMSTERDAM, HOLLAND.

Personnel: PG, TB, MR, PC, SH.

Set List: The Lamb Lies Down on Broadway, Fly on a Windshield, Broadway Melody of 1974, Cuckoo Cocoon, In The Cage, The Grand Parade of Lifeless Packaging (cut), Back in N.Y.C, Hairless Heart, Counting Out Time, Carpet Crawl, The Chamber of 32 Doors (cut), Lilywhite Lilith, The Waiting Room, Anyway, Here Comes the Supernatural Anaesthetist, The Lamia (cut), Silent Sorrow in Empty Boats, The Colony of Slippermen, Ravine, The Light Dies Down on Broadway, Riding the Scree, In the Rapids (cut), It, The Musical Box.

A nice audience recording that suffers a few edits in several unusual places, and sometimes the vocals do sound a bit distant.

Things don't really take off until "In the Cage" when the whole band suddenly wake up, step on the gas and kick proverbial butt. The first of the dodgy edits leaves us with just under a minute of "The Grand Parade".

Some of the vocals for "Back in NYC" are very distant, which indicates Gabriel getting too energetic with the mic stand, when he does get going he sounds a bit like a angry drunk at closing time. The start of "Hairless Heart" goes a bit astray but soon settles down with Banks at the helm.

The next cut comes near the end of "32 Doors" and ruins the atmosphere this song always creates. Collins is right on top of "Lilith" and adds even more fiddly stuff than usual; perhaps he was pleased at being compared to "The Slipperman" again, as Gabriel reverts to some past themes for his storytelling.

Hackett and Collins pull the strings in "The Waiting Room" with all sorts of weird and wonderful noises, many of them sounding just like the ones on the album. More Hackett gold stars during a fluent "Supernatural Anaesthetist" which he sounds like he really enjoys playing, unlike the solo at the end of "The Lamia" which still sounds stiff with the odd note getting stuck here and there. A good chunk is missing from the middle of this female snake-fest in another one of the strange edits.

Inconsistent vocals spoil "The Slipperman", followed by a very long and spooky "Ravine" (the band fiddle about while Gabriel gets out of his costume). Collins and Rutherford get all-syncopated and jazzy for "The Light Dies Down", then they extend the intro to "Scree" – or was it that Banks just missed his cue? Either way they all get very loud and stay with the swing.

Only the very end of "Rapids" is left before the band pile into "It" but again Gabriel's antics mean we lose a lot of the vocals. He then almost talks the lyrics for the first part of "The Musical Box" which sounds rather odd. The "Old Man River" tape starts playing, so no second encore this night.

FEBRUARY 26th, 1975
PALAIS DES GROTTES, CAMBRAI, FRANCE.

Personnel: PG, TB, MR, PC, SH.

Set List: Fly on a Windshield (cut), Broadway Melody of 1974, Cuckoo Cocoon, In The Cage, The Grand Parade of Lifeless Packaging, Back in N.Y.C, Hairless Heart, Counting Out Time, Carpet Crawl, The Chamber of 32 Doors, Lilywhite Lilith, The Waiting Room, Anyway (cut), Here Comes the Supernatural Anaesthetist (cut), The Lamia, Silent Sorrow in Empty Boats, The Colony of Slippermen, Ravine, The Light Dies Down on Broadway, Riding the Scree, In the Rapids, It, The Musical Box (cut), Watcher of the Skies.

There is more than one recording of this show. There's an audience tape the correct date of which is open for discussion, comprising of a full *Lamb* but no second encore. There's also an excellent soundboard that misses the opening track but includes "Watcher". No prizes for which show is featured here.

A somewhat casual "Windshield" and a very lightweight "Cocoon" pave the way for a classic run-through of "In the Cage". The rhythm section is on fire and Banks blitzes the solo with consummate ease, Gabriel has to work hard just to keep up with his inspired band-mates. The audience are well up for this show and "Cage" gets its own round of applause.

A French greeting goes down well with the audience, so Gabriel goes the whole hog and attempts some of the story in French as well.

Even during the tightly structured beat of "Back in NYC" Collins manages to fit in a whole host of lightning-quick fills, his inventiveness and desire to push things further seem to get stronger at every gig. He plays it straight for the Mellotron moment that is "Hairless Heart" but soon picks up the tempo and runs with it for "Counting Out Time".

Hackett plays a sublime intro to "32 Doors" with those trademark sustained notes, he adds some perfect backing and gives a classic demonstration of 'it's what you don't play that counts'. It's the complete opposite to Collins, yet both complement each other every time.

More applause, but this time no attempt at continuing the story in French. The crowd respond to the narration, especially the Collins/ Slipperman routine where they even break into a fast handclap, so Gabriel brings on "Lilywhite Lilith" without getting anywhere near the end of his speech.

Seven-and-a-half minutes of stunning Genesis later, and the best "Waiting Room" so far ends – all five members contribute to this most un-Genesis sounding track. Hackett explodes in a fury of screeching guitar, Collins bashes everything he can but holds back on the main beat a bit longer than usual so that the tension can build, Banks detunes the Mellotron choirs to great effect and Gabriel adds some flute as Rutherford starts up the bass riff that signals the engine room to start pumping.

The rhythm-out-of-chaos effect the "Waiting Room" creates is reminiscent of 1973-74 King Crimson, who put several of these 'jams' on record (*Larks Tongues in Aspic* and *Starless and Bible Black*) then took the whole thing to another level in a live situation. Hackett, being a big Robert Fripp fan, must have had a good deal to do with this break from the structured way that the band normally wrote their songs.

"The Lamia" guitar solo is still very stiff and all the glory goes to Collins who spices up the ending in a particularly creative manner. The emergence of the "Slipperman" earns him applause, it's almost as if no one had ever seen inflatable testicles before. Some of the vocals are missing in action and Hackett almost seems unsure of what he is playing. Banks of course blasts out his solo at full volume without breaking sweat.

"Scree" is executed with the kind of frightening precision of which Banks is a master, even "It" seems more organised than usual. We join "The Musical Box" for the heavy Rutherford chords, which is a shame as it is a killer performance. "Watcher" brings the house down and lots of French fans go home very happy indeed.

FEBRUARY 28th, 1975
SALLE DES EXPOSTIONS, COLMAR, FRANCE.

Personnel: PG, TB, MR, PC, SH.

Set List: The Lamb Lies Down on Broadway, Fly on a Windshield, Broadway Melody of 1974, Cuckoo Cocoon, In The Cage, The Grand Parade of Lifeless Packaging, Back in N.Y.C, Hairless Heart, Counting Out Time, Carpet Crawl, The Chamber of 32 Doors, Lilywhite Lilith (cut), The Waiting Room, Anyway, Here Comes the Supernatural Anaesthetist, The Lamia, Silent Sorrow in Empty Boats, The Colony of Slippermen, Ravine, The Light Dies Down on Broadway, Riding the Scree, In the Rapids, It, The Musical Box (cut).

Perfectly balanced soundboard/ambience recording that gives everyone a fair crack of the whip from the word go. The title track has the slightly aggressive bounce missing on many of the earlier versions; some nice harmonies from Collins complement Gabriel's leather-clad bravado.

Hackett takes his time over "Windshield" and the band indulge him for nearly three minutes, he never really gets going but it still sounds good. They take a while to open "In The Cage" and it lacks a lot of its usual bite, but "Grand Parade" is as mad as ever and Gabriel and Collins push it along as it becomes more and more frantic.

Some low-key but beautifully played guitar decorates a slowly building "Carpet Crawl", Collins' vocals are very up in the mix, but he keeps just behind Gabriel to create a subtle combination. A laidback "32 Doors" with some slightly different phrasing from the singer is a perfect way to end the second section of the show.

Rutherford's loud tuning threatens to disrupt the story but at least he escapes the "Slipperman" comparison, which of course is bestowed upon Collins. A keyboard breakdown is explained by Gabriel in his usual, 'What has happened to my fucking Mellotron?' way. The sound engineer must have pressed pause at this point so we don't know how long this latest time-out lasted for. "Lilywhite Lilith" is almost entirely missing as the tape is being turned over but we are treated to another lively and inventive "Waiting Room".

At last Hackett gets to grips with the "Supernatural Anaesthetist" solo and picks his way to the big closing chords in style; his playing at this gig is full of confidence and the solos flow rather than stutter. The elegant offering at the close of "The Lamia" is a choice example.

Lots of lyrics get forgotten near the end of the "Slipperman" and the band almost sound like they might stop. But things carry on, and *The Lamb* concludes without further incident. We join "The Musical Box" as Collins sings 'Here it comes again'. The mellow section sounds a lot like early King Crimson, especially the guitars. The loud section is pure Genesis and as ever, earns the song the best reception of the evening.

MARCH 1st, 1975

PALAIS DES SPORTS, DIJON, FRANCE.

Personnel: PG, TB, MR, PC, SH.

Set List: The Lamb Lies Down on Broadway, Fly on a Windshield, Broadway Melody of 1974, Cuckoo Cocoon, In The Cage, The Grand Parade of Lifeless Packaging, Back in N.Y.C, Hairless Heart, Counting Out Time, Carpet Crawl, The Chamber of 32 Doors, Lilywhite Lilith, The Waiting Room (cut), Anyway, Here Comes the Supernatural Anaesthetist, The Lamia, Silent Sorrow in Empty Boats, The Colony of Slippermen, Ravine, The Light Dies Down on Broadway, Riding the Scree, In the Rapids, It, The Musical Box (cut), Watcher of the Skies (cut).

Another soundboard/ambience recording with a nice sound-balance settling down after the title track has faded, to become a very laboured "Windshield". Hackett seems uninspired and the Mellotron is quite low in the mix. Gabriel kicks some life into "The Cage" and Collins adds his spot-on harmonies. Banks is the dominant figure here, his solo is precise and loud and you can see why this song appeared in the live set for many years after Gabriel had left.

Some nice smooth Mellotron and synth on "Hairless Heart" and those fabulous chords that introduce "32 Doors" show that the temperamental tape machine-cum-sideboard can stay in tune if handled with care.

"The Waiting Room" is cut in half as the tape is turned over, the first half is very low key with lots of disjointed noises, and it is not until the rhythm gets going that things really take off. Collins plays like a demon filling the hall with a mass of drums, and the bass and guitar finally cut loose with some heavy stuff.

Hackett makes a reasonable job of the "Supernatural Anaesthetist" solo; still not fluent, but at least he keeps going. The dreamy sequence before "The Lamia" seems to last for an age, as Gabriel keeps everybody waiting, when Banks finally strokes those delicate piano chords there is a cheer as Gabriel appears and takes on the watery sirens.

Some of the words go astray in the "Slipperman" costume – no surprise there then. The crowd find the big yellow rubber man amusing and give him a big cheer when he staggers to his feet and starts singing about castration.

The final release of "It" adds a touch of rock 'n' roll to the surreal last half of the show and also brings the audience back to some kind of reality, before they are taken away again by the encores

The soundman was obviously carried away, as he forgets to press record until the old man has shuffled onto the stage, we also lose the last few minutes of "Watcher" but I am sure they both went down a storm.

MARCH 2nd, 1975

PALAIS DES SPORTS, ST ETIENNE, FRANCE.

Personnel: PG, TB, MR, PC, SH.

Set List: The Lamb Lies Down on Broadway, Fly on a Windshield, Broadway Melody of 1974, Cuckoo Cocoon, In The Cage, The Grand Parade of Lifeless Packaging, Back in N.Y.C, Hairless Heart, Counting Out Time, Carpet Crawl, The Chamber of 32 Doors, Lilywhite Lilith, The Waiting Room (cut), Anyway, Here Comes the Supernatural Anaesthetist, The Lamia, Silent Sorrow in Empty Boats, The Colony of Slippermen, Ravine, The Light Dies Down on Broadway, Riding the Scree, In the Rapids, It, The Musical Box, Watcher of the Skies (cut).

One of the shows that always causes confusion to a lot of collectors as to whether it is genuine or not. Is it the Dijon show from the 1st March or even the Paris show from the 3rd? Well this is a very good soundboard/ ambience recording and it is most definitely from St Etienne.

The overall sound is toward the ambient side and includes lots of crowd noise as the enthusiastic French fans welcome another *Lamb* performance. Gabriel gives his all from the start and is full of character during "Melody of 74", and very creepy in an effects laden "Cuckoo". Banks copes with a squeal of feedback at the start of his "Cage" solo, it fails to put him off and he delivers the goods as usual. Some relentless riffing from Hackett drives "The Grand Parade" to its madhouse conclusion.

The audience appreciate Gabriel's attempt at the native tongue for the first story, albeit a very short one, it still gets a very generous round of applause. "Counting Out Time" is almost jolly in its tempo and very music hall in its style, its one of those tracks that sounds a bit strange on its own, but slots perfectly into the grand scheme of things and still sounds like Genesis.

The second story is in English, as if Gabriel realised there was no adequate translation for the stuff he was about to come up with. Hackett is "The Slipperman", a complement that must have woken him up as he dominates the first half of "The Waiting Room" with some crunching echo-heavy guitar. Then Collins comes in and batters down at least 32 doors with a hectic percussive assault.

The 'live' feel to this tape shines through on "Anyway", with the drums echoing around the hall and the big ending sounding even bigger than usual. An inspired Hackett shines once more with a blissful solo on "The Lamia", without missing a note he plays with a confidence that was all-too-often lacking earlier in the tour.

Some serious shuffle-style percussion and a super-fast synth solo takes the "Scree" into another league. Playing of this stature could only be topped by a couple of songs, one of those is the first encore – a truly great rendition of "The Musical Box" with Gabriel earning the longest applause of the night for the old man routine. "Watcher of the Skies" gets about halfway through before the tape runs out.

MARCH 3rd, 1975
PALAIS DES SPORTS, PORTE DE VERSAILLES, PARIS, FRANCE.

Personnel: PG, TB, MR, PC, SH.

Set List: The Lamb Lies Down on Broadway, Fly on a Windshield, Broadway Melody of 1974, Cuckoo Cocoon, In The Cage, The Grand Parade of Lifeless Packaging, Back in N.Y.C, Hairless Heart, Counting Out Time, Carpet Crawl, The Chamber of 32 Doors, Lilywhite Lilith, The Waiting Room (cut), Anyway, Here Comes the Supernatural Anaesthetist, The Lamia, Silent Sorrow in Empty Boats, The Colony of Slippermen, Ravine, The Light Dies Down on Broadway, Riding the Scree, In the Rapids, It, The Musical Box (cut).

Fairly clear audience tape that suffers a bit from the recording level being up too high so we do get some distortion. This one actually includes Gabriel's spoken intro before the music starts. Great audience reaction they cheer long and hard after most songs. Must have been heartening for the band to play to such an appreciative crowd.

There are several versions of this show, some claim to be Dijon and some St Etienne, but as those two shows are soundboards, we know this to be the real thing and definitely not one of the May shows some collectors hope for.

As with most audience tapes the quiet numbers tend to suffer and this show is no exception. "Windshield" thuds along with Collins hammering out that 'one two' beat, during a very slow "Grand Parade" which starts off with some mic problems. Then he suddenly wakes up, kicks the rest of the band into next week, the difference in volume and tempo is quite astonishing.

Gabriel wins many fans by telling the story in both French and English, and then explodes into a raucous "Back in NYC". Collins adds some heavy double beats after the 'don't care who I hit' line and again at the corresponding places in the next verses. It's only a small change but it works and shows that he will never just play what's expected of him.

Either the echo in the hall is giving the impression that there is a tempo problem with "Counting Out Time", or Gabriel is singing several beats in front of everyone else, it sounds odd and something similar happens again during "Riding the Scree" and "It".

Gabriel whips the crowd into a frenzy during the next story with a call and response session, he then compares Rutherford to the "Slipperman" and gets lots more applause. "Lilywhite Lilith" follows with an even more complicated drum pattern than usual.

An unfortunate cut at the start of "The Waiting Room" spoils the flow but things soon get going as Collins makes a spectacular entrance with several energetic rolls around his kit. Everyone joins in, even Gabriel, who gives it some serious, if low-key flute.

A somewhat fuzzy but very atmospheric "Lamia" finally features a decent Hackett solo and surprisingly some rather heavy-handed drumming. "Silent Sorrow" even has a few bird noises to accompany the slightly distorted choirs. The "Slipperman" is all over the place and the sound quality deteriorates for this song.

The show ends and the French audience show their appreciation with some heavy applause, Collins teases by telling them the next song is an old one from *Nursery Cryme*' but the song in question gets cut so we miss the reaction to that one, which undoubtedly would have raised the roof.

MARCH 7th, 1975
PAVIHAO DOS DESPORTOS, CASCAIS, PORTUGAL.

Personnel: PG, TB, MR, PC, SH.

Set List: The Lamb Lies Down on Broadway, Fly on a Windshield, Broadway Melody of 1974, Cuckoo Cocoon, In The Cage, The Grand Parade of Lifeless Packaging, Back in N.Y.C, Hairless Heart, Counting Out Time, Carpet Crawl, The Chamber of 32 Doors, Lilywhite Lilith, The Waiting Room, Anyway, Here Comes the Supernatural Anaesthetist, The Lamia, Silent Sorrow in Empty Boats, The Colony of Slippermen, Ravine, The Light Dies Down on Broadway, Riding the Scree, In the Rapids, It, The Musical Box (cut).

One of the better soundboard recordings, not only do you get the clarity from the desk, the ambience mics have picked up a lot of the atmosphere, so the instruments have a nice round sound and the excitable crowd is easily heard.

A confident "Lamb Lies Down" leads to a lengthy-guitar driven "Windshield", Hackett is on form for this one and, without being fancy, lays down a fine understated solo. "In The Cage" is one of the best versions yet, Gabriel decides to greet the audience in Portuguese just as the song starts so misses his first few words. Collins is a man possessed and delivers an almost impossible drum fill before the Banks solo then throws in several more during it. Banks must have been shocked by the ferocity of the Collins attack as he stutters halfway through.

The desk picks out Hackett's fabulous guitar work in "Grand Parade". He begins with the vocal line harmony then goes into that manic strumming riff, Collins continually blows his whistle and Gabriel shouts a lot, such magnificent chaos.

The soundman pauses the tape at the end of "Grand Parade" so we have to listen to the story, "Back in NYC" and "Hairless Heart" from the inferior audience recording. Why can't these guys just leave things alone? Lots of calling out during this show sounds like the band have a big following in Portugal.

An aggressive beginning to "The Waiting Room" is mostly Collins and Hackett trying to out-noise each other; the second half is simply stunning as the whole band shift into overdrive conjuring up some spine-tingling improvisation. Easily the highlight of the entire show, this is something they should have definitely tried more often.

"Scree", "Rapids" and "It" are all expertly performed with Hackett and Banks flying through the "It" lead lines, lots of funky hi-hat and complicated fills bring *The Lamb* to a close. Lots of cheering and applause but only a minute or two of "The Musical Box".

MARCH 9th, 1975

PABELLON NUEVO, BARCELONA, SPAIN.

Personnel: PG, TB, MR, PC, SH.

Set List: The Lamb Lies Down on Broadway, Fly on a Windshield, Broadway Melody of 1974, Cuckoo Cocoon, In The Cage, The Grand Parade of Lifeless Packaging, Back in N.Y.C, Hairless Heart, Counting Out Time, Carpet Crawl, The Chamber of 32 Doors, Lilywhite Lilith, The Waiting Room, Anyway, Here Comes the Supernatural Anaesthetist, The Lamia, Silent Sorrow in Empty Boats, The Colony of Slippermen, Ravine, The Light Dies Down on Broadway, Riding the Scree, In the Rapids, It, Watcher of the Skies.

An audience recording that has improved as lower generation tapes have been found, the stories have mysteriously been added from one of the Birmingham UK shows, which is most annoying, but presumably as the original taper pressed the pause button to save tape so the bootlegger added the stories to present a complete show. Either way the joins are quite obvious.

There is a touch of distortion with some of the bass notes and this is most noticeable at the start of "In the Cage". The song itself just keeps getting better with the Rutherford, Banks and Collins triumvirate speeding their way through the keyboard solo. Gabriel's vocals are almost an intrusion as Banks starts another keyboard smoking run.

"Back in NYC" and "Lilywhite Lilith" both suffer from distortion but "Carpet Crawl" and a very good "32 Doors" emerge unscathed, the taper was also guilty of pausing between some of the songs so there are some tiny jumps which do nothing for the continuity of the show.

"The Waiting Room" kicks off with Hackett adding some echo to his guitar and coming over all Jimmy Page for a few seconds, a much wilder beginning than usual, with the "Moonlit Knight" solo making a welcome return. Rutherford is left alone with the bass riff for a while before Gabriel joins in on abstract flute and then those Hammond chords smooth their way in as a signal for Collins to pick up the beat and take it to another level.

The quality of the recording starts to go downhill during a fuzzy "Lamia" but at least the costume gets a cheer and Hackett plays one of his best solos for ages. Lots of choirs in "Sorrow" and some fine synth work in "Scree".

The breaks in the recording and the bogus stories spoil this show. We're not even sure if "The Musical Box" was played, as there is another edit before "Watcher" starts.

MARCH 17th, 1975
PALAIS DES SPORTS, PORTE DE VERSAILLES, PARIS, FRANCE.

Personnel: PG, TB, MR, PC, SH.

Set List: The Lamb Lies Down on Broadway (cut), Fly on a Windshield, Broadway Melody of 1974, Cuckoo Cocoon, In The Cage, The Grand Parade of Lifeless Packaging, Back in N.Y.C, Hairless Heart, Counting Out Time, Carpet Crawl, The Chamber of 32 Doors, Lilywhite Lilith, The Waiting Room (cut), Anyway, Here Comes the Supernatural Anaesthetist, The Lamia, Silent Sorrow in Empty Boats, The Colony of Slippermen, Ravine, The Light Dies Down on Broadway, Riding the Scree, In the Rapids, It, The Musical Box (cut).

The reception at the start of this excellent recording is one of the best yet, with the very excitable fans giving the band the type of applause normally reserved for the end of a show, even more cheers when Gabriel tries out his French again.

Rutherford is very prominent from the start with is some excellent bass on the "Lamb Lies Down", his trademark Rickenbacker sound continuing through a stunning "Windshield". Hackett is the business here, with a continuous solo that weaves its way around the Mellotron and moves into "Broadway Melody" with consummate ease, the crowd respond well and it looks like we're in for a good show.

"In the Cage" keeps the pace going with Gabriel having to try his hardest to remain the centre of attention as Banks and Collins strut their stuff This really is a band at the top of their game and it seems that playing the same songs every night is at last paying off.

The second story is a mixture of French and English but still entertains the taper and his friends. The band then deliver a nice attacking "Back in NYC", the Mellotron threatens to swamp "Hairless Heart" and it sounds just great. "32 Doors" is almost perfect with Gabriel hitting the emotion button just at the right moment.

After a gentle start to "The Waiting Room" things soon go mad with Hackett and Collins the main culprits, the bass riff has an almost military march feel to it, especially when Gabriel adds his flute. Banks plays some sombre organ then the drums kick in as Collins gets impatient.

Hackett again nails the "Lamia" solo and gets applauded for his work, he also adds some nice guitar to "Silent Sorrow", the mood of which is spoiled by some silly bird noises.

The flow from "Light dies Down" to "It" is now as seamless as it is on the album, Banks dominates this last section of the show and his keyboard work is faultless, with the solo on "Riding the Scree" as unbelievable as ever.

The last section is missing from the "Musical Box" on this recording but the whole song appears on a poorer quality tape.

MARCH 22nd, 1975
SALLE DES EXPOSITIONS, ANNECY, FRANCE.

Personnel: PG, TB, MR, PC, SH.

Set List: The Lamb Lies Down on Broadway, Fly on a Windshield, Broadway Melody of 1974, Cuckoo Cocoon, In The Cage, The Grand Parade of Lifeless Packaging, Back in N.Y.C, Hairless Heart, Counting Out Time, Carpet Crawl, The Chamber of 32 Doors, Lilywhite Lilith, The Waiting Room, Anyway, Here Comes the Supernatural Anaesthetist, The Lamia, Silent Sorrow in Empty Boats (cut), The Colony of Slippermen (cut), Ravine, The Light Dies Down on Broadway, Riding the Scree, In the Rapids, It, Watcher of the Skies.

A good audience recording that took a while to surface, but was a nice surprise when it did. For some strange reason the tape that first appeared started with "Watcher" but even the casual listener can identify the edit in the tape at 7.37 minutes, so I'll stick it at the end where it belongs.

The first major highlight is "In the Cage" which, like some of the more recent versions is now the Banks, Collins and Rutherford show. Their casual brilliance during the synth solo keeps getting better and Hackett has to take a back seat as they stray into the world of the Mahavishnu Orchestra and create a heavy jazz-fusion feel.

In contrast "Back in NYC" is all stop-start aggressive rock and still sounds like a Gabriel solo track, the lack of acoustic guitars and the fact that Rutherford is almost welded to his twin-neck has given the overall sound a much harder edge, another reason "The Musical Box" is always so well received.

Several squeals of feedback interfere with "Counting Out Time" but have been sorted out in time for the silly *Monty Python* style shouting at the end. Hackett's presence is felt again with some beautiful playing during a mellow "Carpet Crawl" and a very atmospheric "32 Doors" – his simple lines perfectly complement the vocals and are generally a little different from what you would expect him to play.

Gabriel thanks someone in German at the start of the next story and compares Rutherford to the "Slipperman". Collins seems to have returned to a more conventional style for "Lilywhite Lilith" and opts to restrict his double-beats to one near the end, in fact the song itself lacks some of its usual clout.

The opening of the "Waiting Room" is a lot more manic than at recent shows with everyone getting stuck-in from the start. Hackett is sounding more and more like Robert Fripp, and Collins obviously wants to play in some John Coltrane free-form jazz tribute band. It all makes for very exciting listening with Rutherford's pounding fuzzy bass gradually rising then falling as the whole thing slows down.

Gabriel has a memory lapse in the middle of a rather low-key "Lamia". "Silent Sorrow" is drastically cut short by a nasty edit. Another cut in "The Slippermen" spoils the good work the band had built up but Hackett makes amends by some tasteful work in a heart-wrenching "In the Rapids".

Having moved "Watcher" to the encore slot, I'm not even sure it's from the same show; something about the overall sound is not the same as the *Lamb* section. But on the other hand…

MARCH 24th, 1975

PALASPORT PARCO RUFINO, TURIN, ITALY.

Personnel: PG, TB, MR, PC, SH.

Set List: The Lamb Lies Down on Broadway, Fly on a Windshield, Broadway Melody of 1974, Cuckoo Cocoon, In The Cage, The Grand Parade of Lifeless Packaging, Back in N.Y.C, Hairless Heart, Counting Out Time, Carpet Crawl, The Chamber of 32 Doors, Lilywhite Lilith, The Waiting Room, Anyway, Here Comes the Supernatural Anaesthetist, The Lamia, Silent Sorrow in Empty Boats, The Colony of Slippermen, Ravine, The Light Dies Down on Broadway, Riding the Scree, In the Rapids, It, The Musical Box, Watcher of the Skies.

At least two different audience recordings exist from this show, both have a complete *Lamb* with two encores. One is a bit clearer than the other but it is also recorded a bit further away so it's a matter of personal choice as to the best version. This review is taken after listening to them both.

Unfortunately at this show, fans and police clashed, tear gas was used and general mayhem ensued as people tried to enter the building. The trouble left several injured and a nasty feeling all round. Not surprisingly, this would be the band's only Italian show.

Fellow labelmates Van der Graaf Generator would encounter similar problems when they toured the country later that year, they actually had to leave one show in a hurry and had a lot of their equipment stolen. For a country that initially welcomed both bands in 1972 it seems a strange way to welcome them back.

Gabriel immediately wins over the large, excitable audience by speaking in Italian as he explains what will happen over the next hour-and-a-half. As Italian audiences have always worshipped Genesis he could have been spouting any old surreal nonsense and they'd have lapped it up.

"Windshield" and "Melody 74" are not quite as powerful as usual but they set the mood for the evening and are greeted with loud applause. Banks has some kind of synth problem during "In the Cage" with the solo sounding most strange. Things finally catch fire with a very energetic "Grand Parade" which even features a few seconds of the 'Old Man River' tape the band use for clearing the arena at the end of the show. Someone lent on the wrong switch there then...

An out-of-breath Rael resorts to mostly English for the next story and then soon gets stuck into a particularly rhythmic "Back in NYC". The sound balance does not favour the backing vocals, so a lot of excellent work from Collins is barely audible.

A couple of small edits in "32 Doors" are the first of the night, but are soon forgotten when Collins gets loose in an extremely percussive "Waiting Room". He gives the kit what-for, while Hackett and Banks work on the strange-noise front. There's an excellent solo from Hackett in "Supernatural Anaesthetist" which he improves upon in "The Lamia" and then goes all moody during a spooky "Silent Sorrow".

Wild applause as "Sorrow" ends and Collins persists with some annoying Rolf Harris-style metallic noises. The "Slipperman" must get stuck in his tunnel as he takes ages to arrive, when he does several people cry out and lots more just cheer. More vocal drop-out problems as the singer struggles to get the microphone near his mouth.

More cuts appear in "Ravine" and "Light Dies Down" and more dynamic drumming from Collins during an almost out-of-control "It". Lots of cheering and deafening whistling before they return for the encores, which of course cause thousands of progressive-rock crazed Italians to erupt in a kind of Genesis mania.

MARCH 26th, 1975

STADHALLE, OFFENBURG, GERMANY.

Personnel: PG, TB, MR, PC, SH.

Set List: The Lamb Lies Down on Broadway (cut), Fly on a Windshield, Broadway Melody of 1974, Cuckoo Cocoon, In The Cage, The Grand Parade of Lifeless Packaging, Back in N.Y.C, Hairless Heart, Counting Out Time, Carpet Crawl, The Chamber of 32 Doors, The Waiting Room (cut), Anyway, Here Comes the Supernatural Anaesthetist, The Lamia, Silent Sorrow in Empty Boats, The Colony of Slippermen, Ravine, The Light Dies Down on Broadway, Riding the Scree, In the Rapids, It.

Someone is late with the record button yet again so we lose most of the title track this time. "Windshield" is a bit wayward on the guitar front but is still very heavy when the band kick in and holds its position as one of the set's highlights.

Overall it's another very good desk/ambience recording, the date of which could possibly be the 28th but is more likely to be the 26th. Like Nurnburg it was one of the last-minute additions to make up for the lack of Italian shows.

Gabriel is a bit early with the 'sunshine' vocals on "Cage" so he has to slow down the words so the band can catch up, once they are all in synch everything is fine and another powerful version can be logged. Lots of whistles in "The Grand Parade" as Collins gets into his seemingly inexhaustible fairground mood. The sound for "Back in NYC" suffers from aged tape syndrome with several brief dropouts and a few wobbly bits but these soon settle down. Gabriel seems to be struggling a bit on the 'No time for romantic escape' lines as if he can't quite reach the high notes.

More tape problems in "Hairless Heart" which get worse as the piece progresses, it almost sounds like someone covering up the mic for a few seconds, most annoying.

The tape is turned over after a classic "32 Doors" but "Lilywhite Lilith" and the first few minutes of "The Waiting Room" get cut out, the heavy section is quite controlled and almost sounds like it was rehearsed. Hackett does well in "Supernatural Anaethetist" then adds some nice touches to "Silent Sorrow" which is a lot quieter than some recent versions.

The arrival section of "The Slipperman" is almost three minutes long – maybe he got stuck again or something? Or couldn't work out where to put the mic? The rest of the show passes quite smoothly with only the odd drop in sound. The stop button is hit at the end of "It" so no encores or audience reaction at this gig.

MARCH 27th, 1975
MESSEZENTRUM, NURNBURG, GERMANY.

Personnel: PG, TB, MR, PC, SH.

Set List: The Lamb Lies Down on Broadway (cut), Fly on a Windshield, Broadway Melody of 1974, Cuckoo Cocoon, In The Cage, The Grand Parade of Lifeless Packaging, Back in N.Y.C, Hairless Heart, Counting Out Time, Carpet Crawl, The Chamber of 32 Doors, Lilywhite Lilith, The Waiting Room, Anyway, Here Comes the Supernatural Anaesthetist, The Lamia, Silent Sorrow in Empty Boats, The Colony of Slippermen, Ravine, The Light Dies Down on Broadway, Riding the Scree, In the Rapids, It, The Musical Box (cut).

Another excellent recording with plenty of live ambience, in what sounds like a pretty large concert hall. The button isn't pressed until well into the title track, but we are soon lost in yet another Hackett dominated "Windshield". His guitar soars above the Mellotron and twists and turns until he plays that familiar set of notes that cue in the intro to "Melody 74". One riff he constantly slips in would later be used in "All in a Mouse's Night" (the end section) from 1977's *Wind And Wuthering* album.

Gabriel plays some interesting flute during "Cuckoo" with that mellow, early King Crimson sound never far away. The sound of the hall adds to the power of "In The Cage". Collins is busy, Banks is note-perfect, and Rutherford thumps out that fuzzed bass line, Hackett always seems to vanish when the three of them get going.

"The Grand Parade" works its way from a slightly quirky number into a full blown, raise-the-roof epic in the space of three minutes which is some feat if you can do it. The band manage it with ease and Gabriel just keeps that manic edge to his vocals that makes you wonder how far he could go.

The story is edited out so it's straight into "Back in NYC" with lots of great bass lines and that great bass pedal slide in the last verse threatening to blow the speakers. A Mellotron-packed "Hairless Heart" bears a passing resemblance to "Shadow of the Hierophant" from Hackett's first solo album *Voyage of the Acolyte* that appeared in 1975 and also featured the current rhythm section.

A barrage of drums and a good Bill Bruford impression all feature in one of the best "Waiting Rooms" yet. It rolls along for a breathtaking eight minutes, getting louder as it goes and is then rewarded with some generous and well-earned applause.

The mic fails on that crucial last line of "The Lamia", it comes back on for the last few words but the damage has been done. At least Hackett manages a very fluent solo. Some kind of power failure almost threatens the "Slipperman" but they manage to keep going although Gabriel does get some of the lyrics mixed up.

Collins plays so fast at the end of "Scree", he almost sounds as if he has been speeded up, but set against Banks and his precise synth work it sounds exactly right. The echo in the hall makes "Rapids" sound even sadder than usual and then it all kicks off for a rockin' "It".

We get the story for "The Musical Box" but hardly any of the song itself which is a great pity, as it would have sounded fantastic here.

MARCH 30th, 1975
SAARLANDHALLE, SAARBRUCKEN, GERMANY.

Personnel: PG, TB, MR, PC, SH.

Set List: The Lamb Lies Down on Broadway (cut), Fly on a Windshield, Broadway Melody of 1974, Cuckoo Cocoon, In The Cage, The Grand Parade of Lifeless Packaging, Back in N.Y.C, Hairless Heart, Counting Out Time, Carpet Crawl, The Chamber of 32 Doors, Lilywhite Lilith, The Waiting Room, Anyway, Here Comes the Supernatural Anaesthetist, The Lamia, Silent Sorrow in Empty Boats, The Colony of Slippermen, Ravine, The Light Dies Down on Broadway, Riding the Scree, In the Rapids, It, The Musical Box (cut).

Good desk recording, although not quite as clear as some of the others, there is a reasonable all-round sound with the rhythm section coming out slightly louder than the rest. For the third time in a row we join the title track halfway through. Maybe someone else was operating the deck on this part of the tour, and pressing record was not a top priority.

"Windshield" has Collins playing a heavy pattern, but still keeping it very rhythmical while a slightly distant Hackett plays a three-minute solo. Some beautiful vocal harmonies in "Cuckoo" from Collins are somewhat offset by some primary school flute from Gabriel.

The stories are edited out again so "Back in NYC" follows the Pete and Phil silly shouting contest that ends "Grand Parade". The crowd love it, so they make it as loud as possible. Hackett is very low in the mix for "NYC" but is back up for "Hairless Heart", which is nice and laidback and not too full of Mellotron.

Collins actually sounds a bit hurried on "Carpet Crawl", which is strange for such a simple track, perhaps he was concentrating on his vocals. There is some applause before the song ends – whether something happened or everyone was getting a bit over-excited is anybody's guess.

A groovy vibes solo from Collins, a sound like a crashing plane and then a quirky riff from Hackett which Collins picks up on gives "The Waiting Room" an altogether different feel. In fact it's totally new and sounds fantastic. No sign of Rutherford's bass riff here, just some fine improvisation that ends rather sheepishly to appreciative applause, before Banks can bring "Anyway" in.

The vocals for "The Lamia" are a bit on the quiet side but at least Hackett unleashes a fine fluent closing solo, lots of choirs for "Silent Sorrow" plus the odd tubular bell and some strange metallic percussion.

As the band shuffle into "Riding the Scree", Collins adds some lightning-quick snare rolls and some slick hi-hat work as Banks plays that impossible solo, whilst Gabriel gets wet. "Rapids" is slow and dramatic and Gabriel turns up the emotion levels with that classic cry of 'It's mine' as the story reaches its improbable conclusion.

We join "The Musical Box" at the 'Play me my song' line just in time for Hackett to deliver a vintage solo and the whole band steam through the heavy section in style. The old man is a little low in the mix until he starts shouting and then the tape cuts off, definitely the worst tape cut yet.

APRIL 1st, 1975
FREDRICH EBERT HALLE, LUDWIGSHAFEN, GERMANY.

Personnel: PG, TB, MR, PC, SH.

Set List: The Lamb Lies Down on Broadway, Fly on a Windshield, Broadway Melody of 1974, Cuckoo Cocoon, In The Cage, The Grand Parade of Lifeless Packaging, Back in N.Y.C, Hairless Heart, Counting Out Time, Carpet Crawl, The Chamber of 32 Doors, Lilywhite Lilith, The Waiting Room, Anyway, Here Comes the Supernatural Anaesthetist, The Lamia, Silent Sorrow in Empty Boats, The Colony of Slippermen, Ravine, The Light Dies Down on Broadway, Riding the Scree, In the Rapids, It, The Musical Box (cut).

April Fool's Day yeilds an above-average soundboard/ambience recording and a pretty grim and distant audience tape. The board show is one of the best I have yet heard, but the audience tape has the taper and his friends clearly enjoying the show as they talk enthusiastically throughout.

The stories are intact and the sound balance is almost perfect, the atmosphere is pretty good, especially as the crowd is seemingly well acquainted with the album and in the case of "Counting Out Time" they can actually be heard singing along.

"Windshield" is again very heavy and workmanlike with Hackett blasting out an almost-metal solo over its slow, driving drumbeat and waves of Mellotron. This is Genesis playing the heavy rock game and winning. "Back in NYC" boasts an angry Rael and lots of bass, while the quiet numbers sound so clear they could almost be in the studio.

During the next story it is Banks who is at last compared to "The Slipperman" which merits a cheer or two and lots more talking from the general vicinity of the taper and his friends. Show-by-show "Lilywhite Lilith" is rapidly evolving back towards the album version. Collins' extra drum fills from the American tour have all-but vanished with only one now remaining, which is a shame as it definitely sounded better before.

Some spooky Theramin-type noises in "The Waiting Room" most likely emanating from Hackett's box of tricks are mixed in with lots of low generator-type noises lending an early Tangerine Dream feel to the song. The band opts for the jagged guitar riff/marching rhythm again, as opposed to the standard Rutherford bass riff approach.

Some dodgy fan singing at the start of "The Musical Box" at least gives us a pointer to where we are in the song amongst all the bass notes and hiss. Things pick up when Hackett plies his trade with another exemplary solo, although when things quieten down half-a-dozen German 'Old King Cole's' start singing, until they are mercifully cut off in their prime.

APRIL 2nd, 1975
KILLESBERGHALLE, STUTTGART, GERMANY.

Personnel: PG, TB, MR, PC, SH.

Set List: Broadway Melody of 1974 (cut), Cuckoo Cocoon, In The Cage, The Grand Parade of Lifeless Packaging, Back in N.Y.C, Hairless Heart, Counting Out Time, Carpet Crawl, The Chamber of 32 Doors, Lilywhite Lilith, The Waiting Room, Anyway, Here Comes the Supernatural Anaesthetist, The Lamia (cut), Silent Sorrow in Empty Boats, The Colony of Slippermen, Ravine, The Light Dies Down on Broadway, Riding the Scree, In the Rapids, It, The Musical Box.

Good audience recording, with lots of atmosphere and a nice sound balance. Like Ludwigshafen, it shows the Germans are really behind the album and are a lot more receptive than the poor old Americans, who hadn't had a chance to digest four sides of new material leaving them generally pretty hard-going on the acceptance front.

The tape starts at "Melody 74", progresses through a frantic "In The Cage" and a fairly restrained "Grand Parade", through to the first story which is relatively short, but still gets a few laughs. Halfway into "Back in NYC" a sudden injection of bass threatens to swamp the song but it is soon adjusted and everything sounds better for it. Hackett is reserved, but sublime, as "Hairless Heart" slides its way past. The guitar is controlled *par excellence* and backed by the lush Mellotron. It's as good as anything in the entire show.

The end of "Counting Out Time" has Gabriel and Collins acting like a couple of old lecherous drunks as they imitate the song's 78-second act in slightly less time, but make a startling amount of noise doing so. Story two gets cut after a minute, then it's straight into "Lilith" with Collins propelling the Mellotron into the back of the hall. A wonderful sound.

A mammoth nine-and-a-half minute visit to "The Waiting Room" is rather a let-down compared to some recent eye-openers. Not a lot happens, they get to the disjointed riff section then just cruise along with out any spine-tingling moments. The end of "The Lamia" is all that survives the tape-turning procedure, Hackett's solo is one of his best yet and Collins is really forceful as the sustained notes sail out into the audience.

A rather messy start to "Scree" is soon erased by Collins with a multi-speed phased drum roll that comes out of nowhere but brings everyone back in line. Lots of audience chatter in "Rapids" – in fact the talk has got louder as the show has got longer, perhaps the taper has moved nearer the bar.

"It" is Collins giving a drum class. He is everywhere but not overpowering, his across-the-kit rolls outdo each other at the end of every verse, until the Mellotron brings in those "Watcher" style chords and it's all over.

Sighs of recognition at the start of "The Musical Box" turn to wild applause at the end of an epic performance, Gabriel screams the house down, and the band play their collective socks off and end the show on a high.

APRIL 3rd, 1975
JAHRHUNDERTHALLE, FRANKFURT, GERMANY.

Personnel: PG, TB, MR, PC, SH.

Set List: The Lamb Lies Down on Broadway, Fly on a Windshield, Broadway Melody of 1974, Cuckoo Cocoon, In The Cage, The Grand Parade of Lifeless Packaging, Back in N.Y.C, Hairless Heart, Counting Out Time, Carpet Crawl, The Chamber of 32 Doors, Lilywhite Lilith, The Waiting Room, Anyway, Here Comes the Supernatural Anaesthetist, The Lamia, Silent Sorrow in Empty Boats, The Colony of Slippermen (cut), Ravine, The Light Dies Down on Broadway, Riding the Scree, In the Rapids, It, The Musical Box.

Superior audience recording that has recently been upgraded and unlike many of the soundboard tapes, it includes the stories and an uncut encore, which, due to the length of the show didn't always fit on the regulation 120-minute tape the sound crew usually used.

After a short introduction in German "The Lamb" kicks off this highly entertaining performance, Gabriel states his claim to the streets of New York, then the rest of the band grind out a heavy rock "Windshield". The guitar and Mellotron duel with each other but the drums steal the honours.

After a loud, but reasonably controlled "Grand Parade", Gabriel tickles the German sense of humour with his translation of the words prickly porcupine, he manages it and even mimics the Tarzan impression that rings out from the crowd.

The sound has a couple of funny turns halfway through "Back in NYC" but soon reverts to normal, Hackett does the business in "Hairless Heart" which is a perfect vehicle for his trademark sound. The tape again does funny things during "32 Doors" where it slows down for a while but soon returns to its original speed.

'Far out brothers, Woodstock less than ten years ago, how soon we forget,' is Gabriel's response to a cry from a happy-sounding member of the crowd. Collins reverts to "Slipperman" duties once more and a mixture of pidgin German and English finishes the story.

Another very long "Waiting Room" is a bit more experimental than some of the more recent versions with lots of strange electronic effects, some frantic vibes and some positively crazed oboe from Gabriel. The fast section again comes out of the new-style bubbling bass riff that the band jam over until the whole thing simply fizzles out. The piano on "Anyway" sounds terrible – definitely one of the tracks not originally meant to be played live with limited electric keyboard sounds.

The instrumental at the start of "The Lamia" is almost a song in itself – two minutes of delicate guitar and synth with a soothing violin effect. There is applause as the snake-covered costume first envelops Gabriel, it must have been a spectacular sight to see the multicoloured 'cone' spinning round bathed in ultra-violet light.

Some more tape glitches during the "Slipperman" and Gabriel has his usual microphone-nowhere-near-his-mouth-problem, so this is not a version for the archives. "The Musical Box" is another victim of the change in sound quality but at least it's complete and well-played.

APRIL 4th, 1975

CIRCUS KRONE, MUNICH, GERMANY.

Personnel: PG, TB, MR, PC, SH.

Set List: The Lamb Lies Down on Broadway, Fly on a Windshield, Broadway Melody of 1974, Cuckoo Cocoon, In The Cage, The Grand Parade of Lifeless Packaging, Back in N.Y.C, Hairless Heart, Counting Out Time, Carpet Crawl, The Chamber of 32 Doors, Lilywhite Lilith, The Waiting Room (cut), Anyway, Here Comes the Supernatural Anaesthetist, The Lamia, Silent Sorrow in Empty Boats, The Colony of Slippermen, Ravine, The Light Dies Down on Broadway, Riding the Scree, In the Rapids, It.

Good soundboard/ambience recording that is plagued by a loud buzz from either the PA system or possibly the Mellotron. The buzz is offputting and constant through most of the first three numbers and it causes lots of whistling from the audience, who seem to have a low tolerance level. Some frantic lead-changing sorts things out, only for it to return during "Melody 74".

By the time they launch "In the Cage" things are behaving themselves again. It is a classic in-your-face performance – almost as if the band wants to make up for the early interference – there's that bit more edge to their playing with the keyboard solo being even faster than usual. Gabriel is the star of "Back in NYC", his vocals are some of the strongest yet as he spits out his defiance, most of which is probably aimed at the road crew.

The buzz is back in "32 Doors" and almost scuppers the ending but Banks manages the last few chords even though Gabriel does not. More trouble in "Lilith" and the crowd start whistling again, if only they had listened they would have heard another top-grade version. Banks makes some strange synth noises in "The Waiting Room", Gabriel tortures his oboe and sounds like an Indian snake-charmer.

This new-sounding "Waiting Room" may not have the improvised shock impact the earlier versions did, but it is still very different for Genesis and they are obviously enjoying themselves as it keeps getting longer and longer. There is a slight edit around the seven-minute mark but we don't miss much and Collins leads the charge, which as per the last few nights has eventually slowed down to a crawl.

The performances at this show are easily some of the best from the tour which makes the technical problems even more infuriating, at least a stunning "Silent Sorrow" is unaffected, its ethereal choirs and mysterious riff holding the audience spellbound.

Things go slightly astray as Banks gets behind with his ARP work in "Scree", the rhythm playing sounds fabulous, but the synth is always a fraction late, this only lasts a while and Banks is soon leading from the front again with Collins snapping at his heels as always.

The tape stops before any encore is played but it wouldn't surprise me that after all the evening's problems that was it.

APRIL 6th, 1975

PHILIPSHALLE, DUSSELDORF, GERMANY.

Personnel: PG, TB, MR, PC, SH.

Set List: The Lamb Lies Down on Broadway, Fly on a Windshield, Broadway Melody of 1974, Cuckoo Cocoon, In The Cage, The Grand Parade of Lifeless Packaging, Back in N.Y.C, Hairless Heart, Counting Out Time, Carpet Crawl, The Chamber of 32 Doors, Lilywhite Lilith, The Waiting Room, Anyway, Here Comes the Supernatural Anaesthetist, The Lamia, Silent Sorrow in Empty Boats, The Colony of Slippermen, The Light Dies Down on Broadway, Riding the Scree, In the Rapids, It, The Musical Box, Watcher of The Skies.

The German leg of the tour continues and is captured on a very good audience recording including all the stories and very few cuts – and most important of all, no gig-spoiling buzzing noise.

The Gabriel/Collins vocal combination is perfectly illustrated during a delicate "Cuckoo Cocoon", Collins shadows the lead vocals with some telling harmonies that shine almost as much as Gabriel himself. The very King Crimson-sounding flute lulls the listener into the story, which still doesn't make any sense.

Gabriel is again in a most aggressive mood that adds more power to an already heavy "Back in NYC" and gives an extra edge to the show every time he sings. A few members of the audience attempt to clap along to "Carpet Crawl". Of all the songs to choose, it must have put Gabriel off as he gets some of the words mixed up. Near the end of the song there is a small drop-out – maybe the taper was clapping and hit the mic.

An uncharacteristically messy "32 Doors" receives only moderate applause from the not-so-excitable Dusseldorf audience. They enjoy the next story, especially the Banks-looks-like-the-"Slipperman" routine and the bit about cutting off of a certain organ.

Collins pulls out all the stops for "Lilywhite Lilith" in a very casual but confident way and then its time for the nightly dose of chaos. Hackett plays with his echo unit and Banks gets into oscillators and knob-twiddling while waiting for the arrival of Rutherford.

This time round the bass riff is faster and more straightforward, Gabriel is once again giving the oboe a bad name, so he quickly changes to flute and when the Hammond organ chords gradually build, the whole thing takes off. This is another classic "Waiting Room" with the band having sorted out the new approach and made it interesting again.

"Silent Sorrow" is sounding like something German ambient Krautrockers Popol Vuh would have dreamed up. "Arrival" – or 'delayed' as it should have be called – is over two minutes long and indicates someone had trouble getting into their rubberware. At least the band knew they were not playing to a script, so there was a touch less risk involved.

For some strange reason "Ravine" is missing from the recording – it's a strange place to turn a tape over so maybe there was a microphone problem. "Scree" gets almost funky in places until Collins unleashes another spectacular phased drum roll just to remind people he is still there. Both the standard encores are given a healthy workout with "The Musical Box" just winning by a short croquet mallet.

APRIL 7th, 1975

WESTFALENHALLE 3, DORTMUND, GERMANY.

Personnel: PG, TB, MR, PC, SH.

Set List: The Lamb Lies Down on Broadway, Fly on a Windshield, Broadway Melody of 1974, Cuckoo Cocoon, In The Cage, The Grand Parade of Lifeless Packaging, Back in N.Y.C, Hairless Heart, Counting Out Time, Carpet Crawl, The Chamber of 32 Doors, Lilywhite Lilith (cut), The Waiting Room, Anyway, Here Comes the Supernatural Anaesthetist, The Lamia, Silent Sorrow in Empty Boats, The Colony of Slippermen, Ravine, The Light Dies Down on Broadway, Riding the Scree, In the Rapids, It, The Musical Box.

A soundboard and a very good audience recording exist for this show; the latter has a great atmosphere and captures the real sound in the arena so this is the show in this review. The overall sound of this recording is reminiscent of the Italian shows from early 1974, lots of audience chatter and the feeling of a large concert hall.

After a competent introduction in German, Gabriel sets out his stall with another full-on declaration of who he is and what is going on, Hackett really hammers "Windshield" and the band back him all the way as he lays on a superb solo. Banks returns the favour during a rampant "In The Cage" after Collins has paved the way with a seriously good lightning-fast fill that sets up the synth solo as it leaps out of the speakers.

The next story is in English and goes on for ages with a lot more detail, especially about events involving the yellow plastic tube containing the recently removed appendage. Maybe the taper got bored because all of a sudden we jump in at the end of "Lilith" and at the start of the longest "Waiting Room" yet. The beginning is quite frantic with Hackett scratching his strings at full volume, Banks detunes the choirs in a swirl of disembodied voices, and Collins of course goes ballistic, first on the vibes, then his kit.

For the second show running the "Room" includes some backing tapes playing a strange spoken word piece, it only lasts a few seconds sounds like it is in German, and is followed by Gabriel's screeching oboe. The rhythm gets faster and louder and becomes almost organised, which in some respects steers it away from the original disjointed mayhem. Either way, it is still a startling ten minutes.

Gabriel gets a good deal with his vocals at this show, no hindrance from the "Slipperman" outfit and plenty of clout where it matters. The keyboards also sound up-front, and the "Scree" solo comes across even more fantastic than usual.

Some fans were obviously not listening to the encore story as a loud cheer of recognition goes up as the opening chords of "The Musical Box" ring out. This is a truly great version with the echo in the hall adding to the drama. It is so far removed from what has gone before that it is almost a concert within itself. The quintessential Genesis song.

APRIL 8th, 1975

CONGRESSHALLE, HAMBURG, GERMANY.

Personnel: PG, TB, MR, PC, SH.

Set List: The Lamb Lies Down on Broadway, Fly on a Windshield, Broadway Melody of 1974, Cuckoo Cocoon, In The Cage, The Grand Parade of Lifeless Packaging, Back in N.Y.C, Hairless Heart, Counting Out Time, Carpet Crawl, The Chamber of 32 Doors, Lilywhite Lilith (cut), The Waiting Room, Anyway, Here Comes the Supernatural Anaesthetist, The Lamia, Silent Sorrow in Empty Boats, The Colony of Slippermen, Ravine, The Light Dies Down on Broadway, Riding the Scree, In the Rapids, It, The Musical Box.

A fairly clear audience recording that seems to improve as the show progresses. There is some sound fluctuation at the start but that too settles down after the first few numbers, which is about as much time as the band take to get into their stride.

After a somewhat half-hearted attempt at the title track they launch into a meandering "Windshield" which doesn't really go anywhere but still sounds good. Things go astray at the end when Hackett plays some different chords from the others. Gabriel really goes for "Back in NYC" with an aggression rarely heard in the progressive rock scene.

Collins adds some nice touches to "Hairless Heart" and Hackett lets his funky solo on "Counting Out Time" continue for the last verse and the bizarre East End noises the drummer and vocalist make. The guitar wails beautifully during "Carpet Crawl" which suffers a jump in the tape but an improvement in the sound quality. When the drums kick in, it adds a whole new dimension to the piece.

Gabriel takes his time over the next story, and great pleasure in giving Hackett the Slipperman treatment. The audience finally make a noise when he talks about castration and they and Gabriel get really excited when he does his raven impression as the tale reaches its somewhat unfulfilled conclusion.

A truly astonishing "Waiting Room" sounds like John and Yoko for the first five minutes, then the manic vibes from Collins give way to a monolithic marching bass, some staccato guitar and that classic Hammond. Gabriel adds his now customary bad oboe, then flute, as the whole thing just keeps growing into a vast wall-of-sound before dying down to complete silence.

Gabriel sleazes his way through "Anyway", sounding more like a Las Vegas crooner than a leather-clad street punk. Hackett finally cracks both the "Supernatural Anaesthetist" and "The Lamia" solos in the same concert. This is all-the-more impressive as "Supernatural Anaesthetist" almost doesn't start, as Rutherford's guitar packs up for several seconds and the show momentarily stops.

"Rapids" is sung with typical Rael emotion and is a suitably dramatic lead in for the run-for-home feel of "It", which again sees Gabriel in fine voice.

Someone calls for "The Knife", which of course would appear later in the tour, but not here. The now fully-awake audience get a thunderous "Musical Box" which positively explodes when Hackett takes to the skies with a soaring solo full of distortion and shredded notes. The Old Man dies and lots of happy Germans sing their way home, a very good gig indeed.

APRIL 10th, 1975

MARTINIHAL CENTRUM, GRONIGEN, HOLLAND.

Personnel: PG, TB, MR, PC, SH.

Set List: The Lamb Lies Down on Broadway, Fly on a Windshield, Broadway Melody of 1974, Cuckoo Cocoon, In The Cage, The Grand Parade of Lifeless Packaging, Back in N.Y.C, Hairless Heart, Counting Out Time, Carpet Crawl, The Chamber of 32 Doors, Lilywhite Lilith, The Waiting Room, Anyway, Here Comes the Supernatural Anaesthetist, The Lamia, Silent Sorrow in Empty Boats, The Colony of Slippermen, Ravine, The Light Dies Down on Broadway, Riding the Scree, In the Rapids, It.

Stunning soundboard/ambience recording that misses the opening story and also some of the early lyrics to the title song, the latter is due to the usual microphone problems. That is soon sorted out, and the show continues into a classic "Windshield" with Hackett firing on all cylinders for a good three minutes.

A nice laid-back swing to "Hairless Heart" courtesy of Collins is quite different to the early shows in the tour, everyone is a lot more relaxed and this has definitely filtered through in their playing. Gabriel swaggers through "NYC" and turns on the comedy for "Counting Out Time".

"The Waiting Room" is again the star of the show, another marathon. Its nine-and-a-half minutes are packed full of surprises; bells, crashing cymbals, the Hackett cat impression, as well as his nod to "Moonlit Knight", Gabriel's awful oboe, and of course the sound of a Mellotron choir being manically detuned. There are some great Tangerine Dream moments that mostly involve various synthesiser sounds being put through the Echoplex.

The drums and bass kick in, the taped voices are played, then Banks wanders up and down the ARP. The way it was developing, it could have easily ended up as a new song. After all the excitement, the instruments gently fade leaving a second-or-two of silence before another Dean Martin-inspired "Anyway".

The soundboard tapes are always kind to Hackett, a lot of the audience shows lose his delicate work in the crowd noise Here every sustained harmony is heard; his "Lamia" solo is fluid yet aggressive without spoiling the mood, even during "Silent Sorrow" he contributes a wonderful series of notes.

Unfortunately the "Musical Box" only gets as far as the story stage which means we miss a possible classic rendition. On this form, that is a real shame.

APRIL 11th, 1975

AHOY SPORTPALEIS, ROTTERDAM, HOLLAND.

Personnel: PG, TB, MR, PC, SH.

Set List: The Lamb Lies Down on Broadway, Fly on a Windshield, Broadway Melody of 1974, Cuckoo Cocoon, In The Cage, The Grand Parade of Lifeless Packaging, Back in N.Y.C, Hairless Heart, Counting Out Time, Carpet Crawl, The Chamber of 32 Doors, Lilywhite Lilith, The Waiting Room, Anyway, Here Comes the Supernatural Anaesthetist, The Lamia, Silent Sorrow in Empty Boats, The Colony of Slippermen, Ravine, The Light Dies Down on Broadway, Riding the Scree, In the Rapids, It, The Musical Box.

Back to the audience recordings with this nice clear tape that has lots of crowd noise and a great all-round sound, especially in the bottom end department that is generally lacking on the desk recordings.

A steady beginning with the now customary 3-minute jam on "Windshield" and some slightly out-of-sorts flute at the end of "Cocoon". The volume increases somewhat during the first verse of "Cage", this is just what the tape needed and it coincides with the band steaming into the keyboard solo with a speedy Banks being pursued by a rampant Collins.

A poignant "32 Doors" ends the next section and Gabriel gets the crowd on his side with the Banks/Slipperman comparison and another animated Raven sequence. "The Waiting Room" is a slow-burner lots of spaced-out but not to frantic noises, before Rutherford starts a slight variation on the rumbling bass riff.

Some nice avant-garde jazz oboe follows, and all of a sudden we are into a real groove, Collins must have been grinning from ear to ear; then it's classic Hammond and Genesis are back again. The end comes too soon and leaves you wondering where they would take it next.

The sound quality comes and goes and is not too clever by the time the "Slipperman" comes in, although it improves by "Ravine" which washes over the audience as if time was standing still. The homeward stretch from "Light Dies Down" onwards always has a certain sad feel to it, a combination of the story and Gabriel's vocals he puts a lot into "It", to the point of his voice slightly breaking.

At last, after several badly cut versions in recent shows, a complete "Musical Box" appears – it's the trusty audience tape that comes up trumps. *The Lamb* was well played and received, but this epic from the past will always steal the show. It is another stirring performance, with the applause long and loud before the backing music starts up and the taper calls it a day.

APRIL 12th, 1975

VORST NATIONALE, BRUSSELS, BELGIUM.

Personnel: PG, TB, MR, PC, SH.

Set List: The Lamb Lies Down on Broadway, Fly on a Windshield, Broadway Melody of 1974, Cuckoo Cocoon, In The Cage, The Grand Parade of Lifeless Packaging, Back in N.Y.C, Hairless Heart, Counting Out Time, Carpet Crawl, The Chamber of 32 Doors, Lilywhite Lilith, The Waiting Room (cut), Anyway, Here Comes the Supernatural Anaesthetist, The Lamia, Silent Sorrow in Empty Boats, The Colony of Slippermen, Ravine, The Light Dies Down on Broadway, Riding the Scree, In the Rapids, It, The Musical Box, The Knife.

A poor audience recording, of which there are at least two different versions with a slight sound variation, but both with the same track listing. Poor sound aside, the band is on top form and the crowd are well up for the gig.

An upbeat "Lamb" and a slow and muscular "Windshield" get things off to a good start, the audience respond well at the end of "Cuckoo" and there seems to be some cheering at the start of the song, so something must have been happening on stage. There are a couple of changes in sound quality but they are very quick with little disruption.

Gabriel seems very confident at this show and handles the "Cage" with ease and almost swings his way through "Counting Out Time" with a swagger. Collins joins him for the drunken ending and the crowd get very excited. They get to join in with a rock'n'roll-style call-and-response shouting match with Gabriel at the start of the next story, told mostly in French, and another reason the crowd are so happy.

It's a shame the quality of this recording is not up to the standard of the usual audience tapes, as band errors are few and far between and the band have one hell of a trump card to play at the end of the show.

Some of the early parts in "The Waiting Room" sound like Tangerine Dream circa *Electronic Meditation* and nothing like Genesis at all, lots of treated electronics with delay and echo etc. Even after the Hammond makes an appearance, it still sounds like some heavy Krautrock album. The track is unfortunately cut in two, but even then it still sounds weird.

The second half of the show suffers from the poor sound, but Hackett acquits himself well at the end of "The Lamia" and Gabriel sounds suitably desperate in "The Light Dies Down". For the first encore he combines well with Collins for those wonderful harmonies while Hackett decorates the background with some delicate lead lines. The heavy section is dominated by a thundering Hackett solo, which soon returns for afters once 'Old King Cole', has gone.

The surprise of the evening comes in the form of the second encore, for the first time on the tour "The Knife" is wheeled out and given a good thrashing, it sounds fantastic and the crowd go completely ape. Lots of foot stamping during the mellow section and plenty of manic screaming at the end. Whether this was done as a try-out for the UK shows, or they just fancied a change, it was an inspired way to finish a great show.

APRIL 15th, 1975

EMPIRE POOL, WEMBLEY, LONDON, UK.

Personnel: PG, TB, MR, PC, SH.

Set List: The Lamb Lies Down on Broadway, Fly on a Windshield, Broadway Melody of 1974, Cuckoo Cocoon, In The Cage, The Grand Parade of Lifeless Packaging, Back in N.Y.C, Hairless Heart, Counting Out Time, Carpet Crawl, The Chamber of 32 Doors, Lilywhite Lilith, The Waiting Room, Anyway, Here Comes the Supernatural Anaesthetist, The Lamia, Silent Sorrow in Empty Boats, The Colony of Slippermen, Ravine, The Light Dies Down on Broadway, Riding the Scree, In the Rapids, It, The Musical Box, Watcher of the Skies.

The second of the two London shows but the only one to have surfaced so far, this was one of the first *Lamb* bootlegs to hit the collector's field mainly due to the radio broadcast of part of the gig and the subsequent mass of copies. The radio shows are of course excellent quality but only include a part of the concert and all seem to start with "Watcher", which is obviously a case of the radio station wanting a familiar number to start the broadcast with, so they tweaked the running order.

There is also a very good cleaned-up audience recording consisting of a complete *Lamb* and both encores, so this is the source covered here. The band are still enjoying a run of form and are handling the tiring set with an air of confidence that was most definitely lacking at the early part of the tour.

The usual highlights stand out from the start, a driving "Windshield" and a full-steam-ahead "Cage", which almost goes too fast for Banks, as he slurs a note or two in an incredibly fast solo. Collins is hot on his trail as they cruise their way to the serenity that is "Hairless Heart".

The applause rings out at the end of "Grand Parade" and Gabriel keeps the audience in his pocket during a moving "Carpet Crawl". The drums and Mellotron benefit from the sound in the cavernous arena and give "32 Doors" a big sound which suits its volume changes, and again you could hear a pin drop during the quiet sections.

Another mammoth "Waiting Room" packed with electronic bubbles and clicks, Jimmy Page-like guitar echo, and those strange backing tapes, which now incorporate an operatic female voice. The creeping riff arrives, backed by Banks who doodles away on his synth, while Hackett and Gabriel add some strange contributions on guitar and flute respectively. Collins goes double-time for a while as the peak is reached, then it all fades and the plaintive vocal of "Anyway" brings us back to earth.

As audience shows go this a very good recording and having heard a lot of shows from this particular venue, the clarity of this tape is to be marvelled at. The sound fractionally improves for a thunderous "Slipperman" played as if wearing a lumpy yellow costume had no bearing on the song at all.

Gabriel mentions croquet and the crowd roar, he names the song and they explode in a wave of applause. In return for this appreciation the band deliver a stunning version, with Collins battering his kit as the power chords ring out. "Watcher" is equally well received, as the fanfare threatens to lift the roof off and fly into the night.

APRIL 16th, 1975

GAUMONT THEATRE, SOUTHAMPTON, UK.

Personnel: PG, TB, MR, PC, SH.

Set List: The Lamb Lies Down on Broadway, Fly on a Windshield (cut), Broadway Melody of 1974, Cuckoo Cocoon, In The Cage, The Grand Parade of Lifeless Packaging, Back in N.Y.C, Hairless Heart, Counting Out Time, Carpet Crawl, The Chamber of 32 Doors, The Waiting Room, Anyway, Here Comes the Supernatural Anaesthetist, The Lamia, Silent Sorrow in Empty Boats, The Colony of Slippermen, Ravine, The Light Dies Down on Broadway, Riding the Scree, In the Rapids, It, The Musical Box.

Excellent board/ambience recording that begins with a solid run through of the title track and then grinds to a halt at the start of "Windshield" due to a complete power failure. Collins flexes his Latin wrists at the vibes then goes into a drum break which neatly cues the band back in for a shortened guitar workout, a vexed Gabriel unsurprisingly sounds a bit angry during "Melody 74".

"In the Cage" is easily one of the best-ever versions, with the whole band playing at 100 mph and Gabriel delivering a vocal full of passion with a hint of desperation. Collins is his usual incredible self, not missing a beat and adding a multitude of razor sharp fills as he generates enough energy for a whole band full of drummers.

Gabriel shouts his way out of the "Grand Parade" as the choir-heavy final chords crash and burn, then he gets super aggressive as they thrash their way through "Back in NYC".

A hesitant Hackett takes a while to get into "Hairless Heart", but then gets swamped by a sea of Mellotron as Banks takes control. Banks then gets all Elizabethan as he makes the electric piano sound like a harpsichord on "Counting Out Time". Hackett duly responds with a particularly quirky solo.

"Lilywhite Lilith" and the stories are missing from the desk recording so we jump from the end of "32 Doors" straight into another very lengthy "Waiting Room". Things begin with the usual collection of nightmare-inducing noises followed by a new backing tape which now has a sporting connection with a voice mentioning the England players. When the bass riff emerges Banks is playing a spooky drone-like synth line while Collins and Hackett are doing their best to hold back before eventually joining the others for a simply inspired build up, the peak of which even includes the odd Gabriel scream.

A very laidback "Lamia" has an almost bluesy feel to it and Hackett turns in a fine solo at the end where he is almost out-gunned by an inventive Collins. Some laughter and a wolf whistle greet "The Slipperman" who promptly fluffs his opening few words, and generally struggles as the song fails to get off the ground.

They cruise through the rest of the set with consummate ease and Banks and Rutherford seem to dominate the last few shorter numbers. Gabriel's vocals are full of emotion as he tries to rescue his brother John for the umpteenth time on the tour.

The encore is so good it makes all that has gone before seem like another band. Gabriel has the audience in the palm of his hand from the first mention of croquet, to the last desperate cry of 'Now', which is where the board tape is most annoyingly cut.

APRIL 19th, 1975

EMPIRE THEATRE, LIVERPOOL, UK.

Personnel: PG, TB, MR, PC, SH.

Set List: The Lamb Lies Down on Broadway (cut), Fly on a Windshield, Broadway Melody of 1974, Cuckoo Cocoon, In The Cage, The Grand Parade of Lifeless Packaging, Back in N.Y.C, Hairless Heart, Counting Out Time, Carpet Crawl, The Chamber of 32 Doors, Lilywhite Lilith (cut), The Waiting Room (cut), Anyway, Here Comes the Supernatural Anaesthetist, The Lamia, Silent Sorrow in Empty Boats, The Colony of Slippermen, Ravine, The Light Dies Down on Broadway, Riding the Scree, In the Rapids, It, The Knife.

A soundboard/ambience tape that is a bit more board than ambience and has a flatter sound than the Southampton show. That aside, it is a stunning recording that highlights the musicians if not the audience. The title track is missing its beginning as someone at the desk was a bit late with the record button.

Hackett's guitar features nicely during a storming "Windshield" and Gabriel's flute does the honours in a spacey "Cuckoo" that is awash with rolling piano and childlike harmonies. Gabriel comes in too early at the start of "In the Cage", then suffers a squeal of feedback as the funereal beat picks up the tempo when Collins shifts into gear and off they go.

However clear the sound of the desk recordings, they do lack the atmosphere of the audience shows, this tape is no exception. When you do hear the crowd they sound like they were recorded somewhere else and added at the last minute.

The vocals on "Grand Parade" are so clear you can hear the several different voices Gabriel uses on this strange song, he casually switches from Rael to suave crooner and back again in the same line – something you don't normally hear on an audience show.

Once again the stories have been cut, which makes you wonder if the UK sound crew only wanted to record the songs. Sadly this deprives us of the usual array of amusing anecdotes, but at least we get a complete encore, which in this case is essential.

Only the last few bars of "Lilith" survive the pause button then it's on with a very strange sounding "Waiting Room" – the stifled sound from the desk gives the weird noises section an almost claustrophobic feel which goes all haunted house when Banks fiddles with the choirs. An operatic male voice possibly from a radio or part of a strange tape put together for the piece soon gives way to several strange voices that all add a slightly unnerving feel to the whole thing. The band were obviously getting well into developing their improvisational and experimental sides as this astonishing rendition shows.

Some very clear but badly edited silent film footage from one of the Liverpool shows has lots of great images from throughout the set including a scary silhouette figure with long fingernails dancing during the "Waiting Room", this must have really added to the atmosphere of the show and makes essential if somewhat dizzy viewing.

The encore is a ragged romp through "The Knife". Banks is spot-on with the classic organ intro, but Hackett gets his fingers stuck on the fretboard in the first half of the song. The middle section is vintage Genesis and harks back to those 1972 shows when the mic stand wielding singer would charge across the stage and threaten anyone in reach. Hackett makes amends with his second solo which is note-perfect.

The "Old Man River" backing tape kicks in so it looks like only the one encore was played, so at last "The Musical Box" was given the night off.

APRIL 22nd, 1975

USHER HALL, EDINBURGH, SCOTLAND.

Personnel: PG, TB, MR, PC, SH.

Set List: Cuckoo Cocoon (cut), In The Cage, The Grand Parade of Lifeless Packaging, Back in N.Y.C (cut), Hairless Heart, Counting Out Time, Carpet Crawl, The Chamber of 32 Doors, Lilywhite Lilith, The Waiting Room, Anyway, Here Comes the Supernatural Anaesthetist, The Lamia (cut), The Colony of Slippermen, Ravine, The Light Dies Down on Broadway, Riding the Scree, In the Rapids, It, The Musical Box (cut), The Knife (cut).

The first of two shows at the Usher Hall, both are excellent board recordings, but this one suffers from some dreadful cuts due to the lack of concentration being paid to the recording of the show.

The last part of "Cuckoo" leads into another breathtaking "Cage" which, like the last few shows, is played at breakneck speed. Everyone is right on the button and all manage to keep up with a slave-driving Collins. The stories are again missing, as is the start of "Back In NYC", but at least the band are on top form and the audience in fine voice.

This is easily the most successful part of the tour, and despite all the technical mishaps, the band have finally got hold of the album, played it inside out, and are now stretching the songs as far as they will go. They even cross into the world of improvisation from time to time, something never encouraged in the ranks until now. The sound on this show has more of a live feel to it than the Liverpool tape, more ambience than desk and all the better for it.

"The Waiting Room" is once more the eye-opening performance of the whole gig, the longer the tour goes on the wilder it gets. This one has a very loud, almost angry beginning with everyone playing their trump cards from the start. Collins goes vibe-crazy, then the scary shit starts and the hairs on the back of your neck begin to rise, brilliant stuff indeed. Hackett, or maybe it's Rutherford, sounds like he is trying to land an aeroplane, before Banks leans on the Hammond and Gabriel screams some crazy screams while he dances the strange silhouette dance.

A horrendous edit at the end of "The Lamia" butchers the guitar solo and totally wipes out "Silent Sorrow". What was the sound engineer thinking of? Banks get a bit ahead of himself on "Scree", so Collins throws in some great new rhythms near the end, then goes drum fill crazy for the loud section.

The vocals get quite distant on "Rapids" and "It", but Gabriel is restored to normal for the two encores. The first is missing the opening couple of lines, but is otherwise intact and is one of the better versions played so far on the tour. Another workout for "The Knife" goes down well with the audience, who after wildly applauding the "Musical Box", almost raise the roof when the second encore grinds to a halt.

One of the better *Lamb* shows, with two classic encores, despite far too many cuts.

APRIL 23rd, 1975

USHER HALL, EDINBURGH, SCOTLAND.

Personnel: PG, TB, MR, PC, SH.

Set List: Fly On a Windshield (cut), Broadway melody of 1974,Cuckoo Cocoon, In The Cage, The Grand Parade of Lifeless Packaging, Back in N.Y.C (cut), Hairless Heart, Counting Out Time, Carpet Crawl, The Chamber of 32 Doors, Lilywhite Lilith, The Waiting Room, Anyway, Here Comes the Supernatural Anaesthetist, The Lamia, The Colony of Slippermen, Ravine, The Light Dies Down on Broadway, Riding the Scree, In the Rapids, It, The Musical Box.

The second night at the Usher Hall is a high-quality soundboard/ ambience recording, and once more a lot more enjoyable than some of the true soundboards due to the all-round sound quality and the audience interaction.

The record button is still a bit late as we join the show just as the band launch into the heavy bit in "Windshield". It's a red-hot version and it sets the tone for the rest of the set. Gabriel is a bit wayward with his flute at the end of "Cocoon" and there is some dodgy bass at the start of "Grand Parade", but otherwise everyone is on top form.

Lots of applause after "Parade", but the story is cut and a small part of "Back in NYC" is also missing, so at least the sound guys are cutting the songs in the same places! The sound quality dips during "Counting" but it seems like a tape problem due to age rather than one at the gig, this continues into "Carpet Crawl" and somewhat spoils the atmosphere.

"The Waiting Room" clocks in at a modest seven-and-a-half minutes but all the ingredients are there. It's the first section that is now becoming shorter, with the riffing coming in a lot sooner than usual. The heavy 'King Crimson' section has more Gabriel screams and all manner of percussion, while Banks ploughs away with a slightly monotonous synth line.

The tape problem gets worse as the second half of the show progresses, maybe this could be corrected with the right equipment but that seems very unlikely. Luckily "The Lamia" is unaffected and Gabriel holds the spotlight with a very emotional performance, Hackett is not at his best for the solo, the notes are there but they are not played with much conviction.

The encore is the star of the show; the story might be missing but the melancholy and the menace are very much in evidence. The power chord section is classic and the Old Man's appearance is greeted with cheers, so he caps it all by dying on stage in a most dramatic fashion, much to the delight of a very noisy crowd.

APRIL 27th, 1975

PALACE THEATRE, MANCHESTER, UK.

Personnel: PG, TB, MR, PC, SH.

Set List: The Lamb Lies Down on Broadway, Fly On a Windshield, Broadway melody of 1974, Cuckoo Cocoon, In The Cage, The Grand Parade of Lifeless Packaging, Back in N.Y.C, Hairless Heart, Counting Out Time, Carpet Crawl, The Chamber of 32 Doors, Lilywhite Lilith, The Waiting Room, Anyway, Here Comes the Supernatural Anaesthetist, The Lamia, Silent Sorrow in Empty Boats, The Colony of Slippermen, Ravine, The Light Dies Down on Broadway, Riding the Scree, In the Rapids, It, The Musical Box.

One of the better audience recordings from a show with its fare share of technical problems (no surprises there) but still a good all round performance from the band who are on a roll and obviously enjoy playing on home soil. The taper decides it's better to stand up to get a good recording, it's a wise decision as the sound quality is consistent and very atmospheric, especially on the quieter numbers.

The vocals go missing at the start of "Cage", but Banks carries on playing until Gabriel eventually drops back in, delivering a serious version full of feeling. Hackett plays a blinder on "Grand Parade" with that continuous high-pitched riff that seems to last for an age, the song descends into chaos and the audience express their appreciation.

The story involves lots of calling out from the crowd and an apology from Gabriel about the electrical failures. He skips through the relevant events then "Back in NYC" arrives and Mr. Angry is back.

The second story is now a lot more elaborate with several references to women from various parts of the country, Collins is once again the "Slipperman" comparison and the audience is definitely having a good time.

"Lilywhite Lilith" bounces along, before its gradual decent into the strangeness of "The Waiting Room", which has settled into some kind of order with the last few renditions following a similar pattern. The rhythmic section gets better as the band learn to experiment more. Collins jazzes up his fills and Banks times the organ to perfection. More manic screaming from Gabriel adds to the mayhem and keeps the madness going.

An excellent "Silent Sorrow" includes a fair amount of flute, lots of seagull guitars, and that dreamy Mellotron extending past the three-minute mark – so much packed into such a simple link-piece. Collins almost takes the spotlight away from Banks on "Scree" with an endless barrage of quite incredible drumming – he is relentless, but every fill is spot-on and not overbearing or flashy.

Gabriel gives his all during "It", and then a bit more for "The Musical Box" which, despite missing the story is still the ace in the pack. The band have played this song so many times, yet it still sounds fresh and full of menace at each performance. The vocals are a bit low in the mix for the first half of the song, but pick up for the 'Old Man' section, Hackett flies through his first solo, vanishes, then returns for the heavy bit in the middle.

The climax of the evening sees Gabriel lying prostrate on the stage while Hackett plays that famous closing riff which is immediately swamped with applause, a classic end to a very good night.

APRIL 28th, 1975

PALACE THEATRE, MANCHESTER, UK.

Personnel: PG, TB, MR, PC, SH.

Set List: The Lamb Lies Down on Broadway, Fly On a Windshield, Broadway melody of 1974,Cuckoo Cocoon, In The Cage, The Grand Parade of Lifeless Packaging, Back in N.Y.C, Hairless Heart, Counting Out Time, Carpet Crawl, The Chamber of 32 Doors, Lilywhite Lilith, The Waiting Room, Anyway, Here Comes the Supernatural Anaesthetist, The Lamia, Silent Sorrow in Empty Boats, The Colony of Slippermen, Ravine, The Light Dies Down on Broadway, Riding the Scree, In the Rapids, It, The Musical Box, Watcher of the Skies.

Manchester *Lamb* number two and another very good audience recording, possibly made by the same person as the previous night's show. The band warm up pretty quickly and by the time "In the Cage" and "The Grand Parade" strut their stuff, they are flying high with Hackett turning in some fine work.

An excellent "Back in NYC" is followed by a flawless "Hairless Heart", the guitar and Mellotron combine to produce the perfect instrumental. The Mellotron, in all its glory, sweeps back in for "32 Doors" and is again accompanied by a divine Hackett guitar line. Gabriel really turns on the emotion for this one and milks his solo vocal spots, truly a great performance.

The sound quality of this recording sounds like the taper was quite close to the stage as the story is so clear. It is also very long and has almost turned into a stand-up routine, which obviously works as there is lots of cheering and applause. Hackett also gets some applause for being the "Slipperman" comparison – a rare honour, as it usually goes to the drummer.

Some nice bendy choirs at the start of "The Waiting Room" are followed by lots of drum workouts and some bass synth oscillation. Collins starts the second section with some nice cymbal work then Rutherford joins him, Banks solos and the drums kick in. Nothing from Gabriel at this point then you can make out some crazed screaming in the background as he does the scary silhouette dance.

This is one of the gigs chosen by one of the many fan-based remastering groups who do their best to clean up various shows so they can be traded in the best possible condition. The original tapes had some sound problems during "It", so someone dubbed the version from the 27th in its place. This has since been corrected with the original "It" back where it belongs.

A lone cry for "Harold the Barrel" goes unheeded; we get "Musical Box" instead – althought it is marred by obvious tape speed difficulties. The crowd obviously enjoyed it though, and after several minutes of sustained applause they are rewarded with "Watcher". The Mellotron booms out as the old show-opener brings an excellent gig to a triumphant close.

APRIL 30th, 1975

COLSTON HALL, BRISTOL, UK.

Personnel: PG, TB, MR, PC, SH.

Set List: The Lamb Lies Down on Broadway, Fly On a Windshield, Broadway melody of 1974, Cuckoo Cocoon, In The Cage, The Grand Parade of Lifeless Packaging, Back in N.Y.C, Hairless Heart, Counting Out Time, Carpet Crawl, The Chamber of 32 Doors, Lilywhite Lilith, The Waiting Room, Anyway, Here Comes the Supernatural Anaesthetist, The Lamia, Silent Sorrow in Empty Boats, The Colony of Slippermen, Ravine, The Light Dies Down on Broadway, Riding the Scree, In the Rapids, It, The Musical Box, Watcher of the Skies.

A recently unearthed audience tape that was recorded by a friend, so it's definitely a genuine first-generation show. It is a great improvement on the rather poor quality recording that was doing the rounds. The sound improves after the first few numbers, dips a bit near the end, but has a nice balance to it.

A confident start with the usual highlights, "Windshield" and "In the Cage" being the two peaks. Gabriel takes ages with the stories and again develops them into a mini-comic routine. A superb "Carpet Crawl" and a Mellotron-heavy "32 Doors" keep up the tension before things go weird.

Hackett adds another guitar phrase from "Moonlit Knight" to his "Waiting Room" repertoire, an inspired interpretation matched by Collins and Rutherford staggering the beat as the pace picks up. Banks plays a classic Banks synth-line, and Gabriel screams into his microphone and generally sounds a bit demented.

The constant synth in "Anyway" is almost as loud as the vocals, but it does highlight the consistency of the keyboardist. A dodgy sounding lead connection threatens the calm of "The Lamia", but thankfully disappears before Collins responds to Hackett's solo with some powerful fills. The sound quality suffers during "Silent Sorrow" and dips a bit for "The Slipperman", not the band's fault this time, but a hiccup with the tape recorder, which would have been a bit of a beast in 1975.

Loud applause at the end of "Scree", rapturous applause after "It". No "Knife" sharpening in the encores, and even though someone with an amazing Welsh accent rather speculatively calls out for "Supper's Ready", the usual suspects are wheeled out once more and are naturally greeted with hysteria.

MAY 1st, 1975

HIPPODROME, BIRMINGHAM, UK.

Personnel: PG, TB, MR, PC, SH.

Set List: The Lamb Lies Down on Broadway, Fly On a Windshield, Broadway melody of 1974,Cuckoo Cocoon, In The Cage, The Grand Parade of Lifeless Packaging, Back in N.Y.C, Hairless Heart, Counting Out Time, Carpet Crawl, The Chamber of 32 Doors, Lilywhite Lilith, The Waiting Room, Anyway, Here Comes the Supernatural Anaesthetist, The Lamia (cut), Silent Sorrow in Empty Boats, The Colony of Slippermen, Ravine, The Light Dies Down on Broadway, Riding the Scree, In the Rapids, It, The Musical Box, The Knife.

The most recent audience recording to surface and it's a real gem, from the start of "The Lamb" to the play-out music, this is a top grade performance and a welcome addition to the archive. It also proves that there are always new shows out there just waiting to be found.

There is an almost casual feel to "Windshield" as Hackett solos and Collins swings, Banks is in fine form for "Cage" but Gabriel has technical problems and vanishes for half of verse two. The taper often keeps time by tapping his fingers very close to his own microphone – a bad habit for a bootlegger to have, but understandably a difficult one to stop.

The intro to "Counting Out Time" often sounds faster than the song itself; it's as if the band get carried away after the highs of yet another classic "Hairless Heart" – this version definitely slows down a bit when the vocals come in. "Carpet Crawl", on the other hand, is a perfect example of control and gradual build-up as each verse features that little bit more from all concerned.

The taper's tapping addiction becomes annoying during "32 Doors" – what a tune to choose! Gabriel brings back his bad oboe for "The Waiting Room" then adds some trippy flute, acting as a cue for the Collins drum and percussion factory to start up the rhythm. This he eventually does, and things start cooking. Banks adds some blissful Hammond and the strange radio tuning and voices kick in, the build up is stunning and you hardly notice the fade to grey before "Anyway".

Only a minute of "The Lamia" survives the changing of the tape (golden rule of taping; always have your next tape close at hand for a swift change-around) but we do get an excellent "Silent Sorrow". All sorts of problems at the start of "Scree" as several instruments seem to cut out then return, Rutherford's lead is the most likely source.

The encores cause great excitement. Even though calls for the "Hogweed" are ignored, they perform an emotional "Musical Box" and a ragged but energetic "Knife", both songs bring the house down and are a fitting end to a great night.

MAY 2nd, 1975

HIPPODROME, BIRMINGHAM, UK.

Personnel: PG, TB, MR, PC, SH.

Set List: The Lamb Lies Down on Broadway, Fly On a Windshield, Broadway melody of 1974,Cuckoo Cocoon, In The Cage, The Grand Parade of Lifeless Packaging, Back in N.Y.C, Hairless Heart, Counting Out Time, Carpet Crawl, The Chamber of 32 Doors, Lilywhite Lilith, The Waiting Room, Anyway, Here Comes the Supernatural Anaesthetist, The Lamia, Silent Sorrow in Empty Boats, The Colony of Slippermen, Ravine, The Light Dies Down on Broadway, Riding the Scree, In the Rapids, It, The Musical Box, The Knife.

The second Birmingham show is perhaps the most famous *Lamb* 'boot' of all. One of the first shows to appear, the legendary 'Swelled and Spent' vinyl gave us all an invaluable record of the tour. Several different versions exist but sadly no soundboard has yet seen the light of day. The sound quality is good all round, if a touch light on the keyboards, but all the stories and both encores are present.

"Windshield" lets Hackett wander off with his solo until he plays the key phrase and the band change chord on mass. This moment is definitely a *Lamb* moment and sounds fantastic. Another is the bass run just before Banks lets fly in "The Cage", unfortunately the synth is down in the mix so the effect is lessened.

Lots of handy work from Gabriel and Collins at the end of "Grand Parade", much to the amusement of the crowd, who also enjoy the funny voices used during the second story. Rutherford is "The Slipperman" twice and gets lots of applause. The Raven section of the story is lengthened with lots plastic tube references and some swooping bird noises. Eventually Collins counts in a bass-heavy "Lilith" which is powerful and a perfect contrast to what follows.

Collins arrives in the second half of "The Waiting Room" armed with a classic beat – the rest of band join in as the mood takes them. Gabriel makes some funny noises and they all shift up a gear and things get a bit scary.

A nice solo wraps up "The Lamia" as Hackett varies things slightly, and backed by some heavy drumming, adds real power to the lengthy coda. The inflating of the rubber genitals means "The Slipperman" takes a while to start and is laughed at a lot. A more soberly attired Gabriel runs through the final numbers without anymore rubberwear, that is until he dons the old man mask for the first encore.

After a mighty "Musical Box" the audience are finished off with a rousing "Knife" which crashes straight in without any warning. The middle section has plenty of flute and some classic Banks organ, then Hackett turns up to eleven and the riot begins. Gabriel pretends to bayonet the crowd before a barrage of heavy distorted power chords brings the show to a close.

MAY 10th, 1975

OSTSEEHALLE, KIEL, GERMANY.

Personnel: PG, TB, MR, PC, SH.

Set List: The Lamb Lies Down on Broadway, Fly On a Windshield, Broadway Melody of 1974,Cuckoo Cocoon, In The Cage, The Grand Parade of Lifeless Packaging, Back in N.Y.C, Hairless Heart, Counting Out Time, Carpet Crawl (cut), The Colony of Slippermen, Ravine, The Light Dies Down on Broadway, Riding the Scree, In the Rapids, It, The Musical Box.

As recordings go this audience tape is one of the worst. It is very muffled and quite distant, but the band is playing well and there is a reasonable amount of atmosphere. This show is another of the confusion tapes and is often labelled as Heidelberg from the 5th of April, and as there is no desk recording to back it up there is still a slight element of doubt.

Gabriel's vocals suffer the most at this show, with some of them being almost inaudible and when he does turn up the heat, songs such as "Cage" and "NYC" are just a mess. The drums are very heavy during both "Windshield" and "Melody of 1974", so much so, that they are almost the only instruments you can hear.

After a shaky start to the synth solo, the band take "The Cage" by the scruff of the neck and give it a good shake, it's just such a shame we can't really hear the results.

This was the first show of the second trip into mainland Europe after the UK gigs. The band were trying recoup some money on the tour which was running at a loss, and even though morale must have been at rock-bottom with Gabriel's imminent departure looming, they still carried on with a dozen or so shows.

Even with the dreadful sound, "Hairless Heart" still sounds great, with Hackett rising from the distorted hissing haze in his usual style, a feat Banks just about manages later on during "Scree". The end comes a lot sooner than expected, as a great chunk of the show is missing from the recording. The quality does not improve, and even "The Musical Box" is ruined, I guess they can't all be soundboards.

MAY 12th, 1975
RHEIN AM MAIN HALLE, WIESBADEN, GERMANY.

Personnel: PG, TB, MR, PC, SH.

Set List: The Lamb Lies Down on Broadway, Fly On a Windshield, Broadway melody of 1974,Cuckoo Cocoon, In The Cage, The Grand Parade of Lifeless Packaging, Back in N.Y.C, Hairless Heart, Counting Out Time, Carpet Crawl, The Chamber of 32 Doors, Lilywhite Lilith, The Waiting Room, Anyway, Here Comes the Supernatural Anaesthetist, The Lamia, Silent Sorrow in Empty Boats, The Colony of Slippermen, Ravine, The Light Dies Down on Broadway, Riding the Scree, In the Rapids, It, The Musical Box.

An audience recording that is quite clear but runs a bit fast, once the speed has been sorted out, it becomes quite a nicely balanced recording, there is a touch of distortion when things get a bit heavy but otherwise it runs very smoothly.

Nice applause for "Cuckoo" as the appreciative crowd quickly get into the show. They seem to be well versed in the story of Rael as they know exactly where to clap, and there seems to be a great deal of excitement in the Halle as if they were so happy that the band were back in Europe so soon.

"In the Cage" suffers a bit from the aforementioned distortion, but that does not stop Banks from conjuring up another masterclass solo, before laying down a blanket of Mellotron in "Hairless Heart" as Hackett comes over all delicate.

There is an annoying edit in "32 Doors" spoiling a great sequence of songs that culminate in a hypnotic "Carpet Crawl" which gradually builds as each surreal verse unfolds. Gabriel has the audience in the palm of his hand during the second story; he takes his time and gets lots of laughs. Banks is a rare Slipperman and then it's straight into "Lilith" which rocks its way into another trippy if slightly shorter "Waiting Room".

Collins practices his hi-hat technique as Rutherford works on a bass riff unlike any other he has tried before. When the organ arrives Collins engages his whole kit and things shift up several gears; Gabriel starts calling out as only he can and the band eventually unite in a frantic, but very together climax before the piece comes to an end.

An emotive "Lamia" is topped with one of Hackett's finest solos yet; he really gets the most out of his spotlight moment and adds plenty of felling to an already highly charged song. A blast of feedback during "Silent Sorrow" is only a minor distraction and the dreamscape atmosphere continues.

For some strange reason "Riding the Scree" is missing from this recording, not sure what happened here as it seems too late to be a tape change. *The Lamb* ends as per usual and "The Musical Box" is wheeled out to cast its spell over the audience. It does just that and everyone listens to the first half and then cheers loudly at the grand finale. The "Box" never fails to raise the roof and this one was blown clean off.

MAY 15th, 1975
PALAIS DES SPORTS, RHEIMS, FRANCE.

Personnel: PG, TB, MR, PC, SH.

Set List: The Lamb Lies Down on Broadway, Fly On a Windshield, Broadway melody of 1974,Cuckoo Cocoon, In The Cage, The Grand Parade of Lifeless Packaging, Back in N.Y.C, Hairless Heart, Counting Out Time, Carpet Crawl, The Chamber of 32 Doors, Lilywhite Lilith, The Waiting Room, Anyway, Here Comes the Supernatural Anaesthetist, The Lamia, Silent Sorrow in Empty Boats, The Colony of Slippermen, Ravine, The Light Dies Down on Broadway, Riding the Scree (cut), In the Rapids, It, The Musical Box.

A true audience recording that gives a genuine feeling of how the concert actually sounded. There is also a soundboard tape, but for some reason it sounds awful so it's best left alone. The audience are up for the gig from the start and applaud at any opportunity and, as the band are in superb form, that means quite often.

The size of the Palais means the drums have a sharp echo every time Collins belts them hard, the Mellotron sounds enormous and again stays in tune, while Hackett soars on "Windshield" with another deceptively simple solo.

By the time "In The Cage" gets going, the band are in top gear and deliver a seemingly effortless version. Banks sails through the solo with Collins snapping at his heals, a bare-chested Gabriel struts his stuff makes the song his own. The stories are handled in French but take ages as Gabriel struggles to translate the contents of his ever-so-strange mind.

Without doubt this is one of the best "Waiting Rooms" of the entire tour. Some frantic drumming and synth work are eventually interrupted by Rutherford's very slow bass refrain which is soon accompanied by Collins and Hackett both playing at speed, thus accentuating Rutherford's contribution. Gabriel screams his entrance as Banks brings some classic Hammond to the party. The climax is breathtaking and the piece fades like a passing storm leaving chaos in its wake.

The next few songs pass by in the shadow of the "Room" but "The Lamia" and "The Slipperman" stand out in the Genesis classic category. There is a neat edit in "Riding the Scree" that removes the vocal section leaving just the 'Here I go' line, it is expertly done but I'm not sure why, as it seems an odd place for a tape change-over.

The finale rolls along nicely as "Rapids" gives way to a spirited "It" which, for once, is kept to a sensible pace and not the usual hurried performance. The encore is a colossal performance of "The Musical Box" with a French story, lots of foot-stamping, a pre-song drum roll and another of those Gabriel/Collins double-acts.

The backing tape signifies that "Watcher" was not played, which is a great shame as it would have sounded amazing at this venue.

One of the better audience *Lambs* and one well worth a place in any collection. It's a shame about the desk recording though.

MAY 18th, 1975

VELODROMO ANOETA, SAN SABASTIAN, SPAIN.

Personnel: PG, TB, MR, PC, SH.

Set List: The Lamb Lies Down on Broadway, Fly On a Windshield, Broadway melody of 1974,Cuckoo Cocoon, In The Cage, The Grand Parade of Lifeless Packaging, Back in N.Y.C, Hairless Heart, Counting Out Time, Carpet Crawl, The Chamber of 32 Doors (cut), Lilywhite Lilith, The Waiting Room, Anyway, Here Comes the Supernatural Anaesthetist, The Lamia, Silent Sorrow in Empty Boats, The Colony of Slippermen (cut), Ravine, The Light Dies Down on Broadway, Riding the Scree, In the Rapids, It, The Musical Box (cut).

Back to Spain for one show and it's another atmospheric audience recording. It sounds like a fair sized arena, so it's heavy on atmosphere but a touch distant. The title track has the very beginning missing, but then it's all guns blazing, and when "Windshield" kicks in the power of the band echoes round the Velodromo.

"Hairless Heart" sounds great, but Banks and Hackett appear to be playing in two different time signatures, the drums pull them together and the majestic Mellotron fills the hall; just like those great Italian shows of three years earlier when "Salmacis" sent shivers down the spine. This is not quite in that league, but the effect is similar.

The next edit cuts "32 Doors" in two, accompanied by some dodgy tape noise that soon sorts itself out, before Gabriel's voice rings out bringing some semblance of order to the noisy crowd. Hackett is the "Slipperman", but probably does not fancy the cure Gabriel has in mind. Collins returns some of his heavy drum fills to "Lilywhite Lilith" which suits the surroundings and add that extra punch to the track.

Some heavily-echoed guitar fills and a whole host of drum rolls dominate the first half of "The Waiting Room" – it really is the Hackett and Collins show for the first three minutes. The bass rumbles along accompanied by some radio-style taped voices and a wave of trademark Hammond. Gabriel does his spooky shouting and the rhythm section pick up the pace until the eventual slow fade.

The sound quality goes downhill somewhat in the latter stages of the show with some distortion creeping in when things get loud. The encore gets cut after about eight minutes – so the last show to have turned up from this tour ends, like many of the others, in frustration.

A STATEMENT BY PETER GABRIEL

The following is a press statement released by Peter Gabriel in September 1975, some months after the final *Lamb Lies Down on Broadway* performance, detailing his personal reasons for announcing his departure from Genesis.

photo: Janet Macoska

I had a dream, eye's dream. Then I had another dream with the body and soul of a rock star. When it didn't feel good I packed it in. Looking back for the musical and non-musical reasons, this is what I came up with:

OUT, ANGELS OUT - AN INVESTIGATION

The vehicle we had built as a co-op to serve our songwriting, became our master and had cooped us up inside the success we had wanted. It affected the attitudes and the spirit of the whole band. The music had not dried up and I still respect the other musicians, but our roles had set in hard. To get an idea through "Genesis the Big" meant shifting a lot more concrete than before. For any band. transferring the heart from idealistic enthusiasm to professionalism is a difficult operation.

I believe the use of sound and visual images can be developed to do much more than we have done. But on a large scale it needs one clear and coherent direction, which our pseudo-democratic committee system could not provide.

As an artist, I need to absorb a wide variety of experiences. It is difficult to respond to intuition and impulse within the long term planning that the band needed. I felt I should look at / learn about / develop myself, my creative bits and pieces and pick up on a lot of work going on outside music. Even the hidden delights of vegetable growing and community living are beginning to reveal their secrets. I could not expect the band to tie in their schedules with my bondage to cabbages. The increase in money and power, if I had stayed, would have anchored me to the spotlights. It was important to me to give space to my family which I wanted to hold together and to liberate the daddy in me.

Although I have seen and learnt a great deal in the last seven years, I found I had begun to look at things as the famous Gabriel, despite hiding my occupation whenever possible, hitching lifts, etc. I had begun to think in business terms; very useful for an often bitten once shy musician, but treating records and audiences as money was taking me away from them. When performing, there were less shivers up and down the spine.

I believe the world has soon to go through a difficult period of changes. I'm excited by some of the areas coming through to the surface which seem to have been hidden away in people's minds. I want to explore and be prepared, to be open and flexible enough to respond, not tied in to the old hierarchy.

Much of my psyche's ambitions as "Gabriel archetypal rock star" have been fulfilled – a lot of the ego-gratification and the need to attract young ladies, perhaps the result of frequent rejection as "Gabriel acne-struck public-school boy". However, I can still get off playing the star game once in awhile.

My future within music, if it exists, will be in as many situations as possible. It's good to see a growing number of artists breaking down the pigeon-holes. This is the difference between the profitable, compartmentalised, battery chicken and the free-range. Why did the chicken cross the road anyway?

There is no animosity between myself and the band or management. The decision had been made some time ago and we have talked about our new direction. The reason why my leaving was not announced earlier was because I had been asked to delay until they had found a replacement to plug up the hole. It is not impossible that some of them might work with me on other projects.

The following guesswork has little in common with truth: Gabriel left Genesis.

1) To work in theatre.
2) To make more money as solo artist.
3) To do a "Bowie".
4) To do a "Ferry".
5) To do a "Furry Boa round my neck and hang myself with it".
6) To go see an institution.
7) To go senile in the sticks.

I do not express myself adequately in interviews and I felt owed it to the people who have put a lot of love and energy supporting the band to give an accurate picture of my reasons.

INTERVIEW AT FISHER LANE FARM

Photo: Paul Russell

TONY BANKS, MIKE RUTHERFORD AND ANTHONY PHILLIPS TALK TO PAUL RUSSELL, WINTER 2001

With special thanks to Carol Willis Impey at Hit&Run for getting everyone together and Dale Newman at The Farm for the coffee and sausage sandwiches. After a brief 'pre-switch the tape on' chat about the music for the first *Lord of The Rings* movie and how it could perhaps have been better, the conversation switched to Genesis live, circa 1969…

Ant Phillips. ...actually I was thinking about the types of gigs that we did... Are we on?

Tony Banks. Yes. Put on a serious voice, your radio voice (very stilted English accent).

Paul Russell. If we can go back to…

AP. I was thinking about that Peter Sellers thing – do you remember? I was listening to it the other day, *'That is the answer to another question .. the answer to this one is...'* Ah yeah, still very, very funny. Do you know that? *Songs from Swinging Sellers* – I think George Martin produced it. We used to listen to it at the Genesis cottage. It's a bit dated but it's got this take off of the rock star with the dodgy manager who is completely illiterate and he has been given this set of questions. He does this interview and gets them all mixed up and it is terribly funny. It was actually written by Frank Muir and Dennis Norden.

TB. It defines one of our early humour things.

AP. His name was Twit Conway, which is obviously a spoof on Conway Twitty. She was Nancy Lisbon and there was a judge called Nancy Spain, but it is very clever and I would thoroughly recommend it. A lot of other good sketches. A very good take off of critics all trying to out quote each other – so funny. Irene Handel of course was on it, Sellers doing all the voices.

PR: So this is what was going on at the MacPhail cottage?

AP. Yeah. In the evening we used to listen to that, King Crimson, and watch *Monty Python* and wondered what the hell was going on.

TB. It pretty much defined our lives from then on actually.

AP. I thought Graham Chapman was *Monty Python*, 'cos he was always rushing around in military kit and saying, 'Stop, this is getting silly,' and I just thought well this is his programme. It was so weird.

TB. Is that it, can we go now? (laughs)

PR. The very first live gig is generally accepted to be this gig in Cobham, September 1969. Mrs Balmes Dance – a private party?

TB. I don't consider that a gig. We did it because Pete's friend needed someone to play and we wanted a bit of experience. What did we play? "The Knife"? I was on a piano.

AP. I'm not sure that we had that stuff yet.

TB. I think we had written the basic "Knife".

PR. There is a list here that is apparently the very first set list Armando Gallo had, which claims to be one of the very early sets.

TB. It looks reasonable. I don't think we did "Babies" on stage, did we? Maybe we did actually.

AP. The reason why I'm getting confused is this gig was ahead of us moving to the cottage and we did a period of about 2-3 weeks at my parents' house where we really did actually motor. 2 or 3 of the big songs like "Looking for Someone" and "The Knife" were hammered out, but I don't remember storming through those at the Balmes Dance, but maybe we did. I can clearly remember we did "Babies" 'cos we just left Peter in the end. He was rambling on and we just got up and left him.

TB. We did do things like "Masochistic Man" cos we had written that, and "Stumble" obviously is the old Cream song.

AP. I think put that gig down as transitional.

TB. We don't think of that as our first gig. The first gig we did was at Brunel. The main university is in Uxbridge, but we played in a smaller part of it in Acton.

AP. Where all the agents came to see us. So the first one was like an acoustic set – we can't remember exactly which songs – it wasn't our proper set. The proper set emerged a couple of months later.

TB. Well, we say a "proper set", I think at Brunel we ended the show with "Pacidy".

AP. We didn't end with "The Knife"?

TB. No, we didn't have any clue how to put a set together. Having kind of rehearsed all this sort of stuff and it sounded pretty good in the living room – we then went onto a stage and of course we had never done this before. I always remember from the word go just playing at full volume throughout the whole thing.

PR. Did you have an organ then, or a piano?

TB. I had an organ through a Selmer Goliath and I had this home made Lesley. I had all these subtle volume changes all worked out in rehearsal. I just put my foot flat out – couldn't hear a thing and it distorted like mad 'cos this Selmer Goliath really couldn't handle all the stuff I was putting through it. But the audience liked it. We either did "Pacidy" as an encore or we ended the set with it. But we certainly did it at a totally inappropriate moment 'cos it is a very sort of, like you know, floaty kind of song.

AP. We started with that track called the "In The Wilderness". Yeah in those days we still did that. I clearly remember this because it was a nightmare for me. I had restrung just before the gig, which you don't do, and I had a loose machine head and we hit the first break and the string slipped on that dah dah (sings riff from song). It was completely out of tune and I just started turning willy nilly, I hadn't got a clue which one – I was so nervous – our first showcase gig. And then when we switched to the acoustic guitar things. Because we hadn't rehearsed it properly in the right set up, it started feeding back. Neither Mike nor I knew which one of us was feeding back.

Phone Rings

Dale Newman. That was Mike, he is now on his way here.

TB. How nice of him (laughs)

AP. We got this sort of funnel noise starting with the acoustic guitar and neither of us knew which one it was so we both switched down and there was no sound – it was absolute chaos.

TB. All I remember was that we thought we had played absolutely abysmally, but the audience seemed to like it.

AP. Well they wouldn't have booked us again would they?

TB. At that stage you did what you could get. Then we got this guy Marcus Bicknall booking us. We did this thing at some college, was it Queen Elizabeth College? Where they had a series of bands playing, and they brought in a lot of social secretaries to see whether they liked you or not. We just did a short thing and from that we got quite a few gigs.

PR. The Queen Mary College?

TB. When did Queen Mary's College I remember that one quite well because we played with that band that used a steel guitar – it was a lovely sound. Quite a big audience, it seemed to me that was the first time we really got through to an audience. We all came away on a real high after that gig. We felt we had really cracked something and of course the next show we did was terrible. You learn that is just how it was. The people we ended up being with [booking agents] were called the College Entertainments, wasn't it? I can't remember. Terry King was another one. We just went with anybody who would get us a gig and we would pay them a percentage. But it wasn't very much, 'cos half the time we were playing for a fiver or for expenses – a euphemistic term for not getting paid anything at all. Normally the more you got paid the less important the gig was really.

There was a teachers training college that we did in Birmingham and we got paid £50 I think, and he didn't want us at all. Our music used to stop and start and these people wanted something relaxing they could dance to and we were completely the wrong thing. We just did the ones we wanted to do and were important to us like the Marquee club.

PR. So did you play many tracks from the *Revelations* album then or was it already the newer stuff?

AP. We did a few, but not many. We did "In The Wilderness" for a little while.

TB. And we probably did "In Limbo", actually we had quite a heavy version of that.

PR. Obviously all those songs from the pre-*Trespass*, and post-*Revelations* era only ever got played live, and quite a few of those aren't even on the first box-set archive?

TB. No. Well, probably we did do one or two, but most of these got lost.

PR. Or are they under different names?

TB. No. We had one or two of these acoustic songs like "Stranger" which was Ant's song and "Little Leaf" which Mike and I used to sing on stage. We used to do this sort of harmony and we sounded beautiful like Simon and Garfunkel, – or at least we did in our own heads. But we soon realised that actually we didn't want to sing on stage.

AP. It is well known that we used to do this extraordinarily ludicrous thing of starting with the quiet ones didn't we, building up.

TB. It worked fairly well, people got to know that – it is when I think set construction became quite interesting. The first three or four songs I actually played guitar, so the thought was that we were a folky band. And then the first electric song we did was "Stagnation" from *Trespass,* and then "Little Leaf" which starts off with just guitar then I brought in the keyboard and after that the keyboard got bigger and bigger until we did "The Knife" which was keyboard-dominant and then the whole heavy electric quality had come in. I think people who liked it, really liked it, and it gave us quite a sort of cult thing.

AP. But as I recall a lot of those acoustic numbers had to go. 'Cos we were stopping and guitars were being handed around. There was one called "Grandma" and it went. I mean by the time we finished on the road nearly all the tracks that had survived were heavy ones and sadly, even "Let us now Make Love" went towards the end.

TB. That song was a special case, we intended to record that around the time of *Trespass* but we didn't do it 'cos we were keeping it as a single. We all thought it as a really strong song – it went through so many changes – there were about three different choruses I remember.

AP. We were under pressure to record the live set, there wasn't time.

TB. No there was. We had about twice as much material as we needed for *Trespass*. So we went in and recorded the songs that we had. We didn't record "Twilight Alehouse", I don't know why we didn't.

PR How far back does that go?

TB. "Twilight Alehouse" was right from that first gig. We didn't record it 'cos that meant we wouldn't be able to record one of the others which we felt at that time was more important. Looking back on it I think I could certainly have lived without "Dusk" actually. We had to restrict ourselves to certain songs and I think we knew we had to have things like "Knife" and "Stagnation". They were definites.

PR: Was "Going Out To Get You" battling with "The Knife" as a big number?

AP. Yeah. Well at one stage that was the one we used to kick off with because that would stop people talking. We could then quieten down and do "Dusk" and "White Mountain". Actually I can't remember at the end of my period with the band whether we were still doing that one first or not?

TB. I can't remember what we started with. I always thought we pretty much started with the quiet stuff. But "Going Out To Get You" and "The Knife" at certain points reached about 20 minutes length each. We went on and on, from bit to bit. In the end I think "Going Out To Get You" didn't transfer itself quite so well from piano/ guitar sort of stuff, into the band format with the organ. Whereas "The Knife" did. Immediately we played it on the organ it sounded great and so it became more dominant... whereas later on in Genesis' career we tended to do the album first and then toured the songs. *Trespass* was the only one where we played all those songs live and as I say we had twice as many songs in the set.

PR Was "Visions of Angels" played live?

AP. Yes and that survived because that was a sort of acoustic but electric. I don't think we ever did "Stranger", not during a proper gig. I would never have sung it, I would never have had the courage. I think at the Balmes Dance I'm sure we did it. All the very pretty emotional ones you couldn't really do during gigs we were doing.

TB. Things like "Digby", I used that a bit later on in something else, so "Digby" was out and "Jamaica Longboat" which was quite a good piece live.

AP. There was never any time to rehearse new stuff. "Stagnation" came during the period of the cottage, and we refined the others, but we didn't write after that period. I mean the last 4 or 5 months in the group for me was just playing exactly the same songs on stage every night apart from "Jamaican Longboat".

PR So that set list, the '69 one, which begins with "In the Beginning", "The Serpent" – would that be the kind of songs you were playing when you left?

AP. Absolutely not, no.

TB. We never played "Silver Song" either. I don't know.

AP. I don't think so. You were actually right we did "Dusk" and "White Mountain" in the first set.

TB. I remember doing things at Eel Pie Island where I wore gloves to begin with, it was so cold.

AP. He wore gloves. I had to stand up or move my chair when guys wanted to go past and have a pee. I had to stop playing virtually. We played opposite Free. Free were on the other stage in the middle of the "All Right Now" period. People were interested in them and not in us. One of the roadies dropped the mike in the river as well.

TB. Do you remember that? Very strange. Everything had to be taken over on this tiny little bridge, which was hell for the roadies, but we were our own roadies.

PR Did you have a road crew then?

TB. Well we had two guys who helped us. We had Richard MacPhail and David Roots, all friends of ours. Ant and his delicate fingers. We had to move our own stuff. I didn't do too well out of that!

AP. Upstairs at Ronnie Scott's we all had to do the organ, Ronnie Scott's was not the place to take the organ. Also the cottage, it was a snowy winter, the stuff used to have to come up a lot of steps right up to the cottage at the top of the hill, so the organ in the snow was interesting. It was a workers commune really, we were all on the same level really weren't we?

TB. Yes

AP. They were our mates really we couldn't order them about – we weren't paying them – nobody was paying us so I mean we were very much all in it together.

PR: So, when all the tuning and guitar passing was going on, is that when Peter started to get a bit impatient and started telling stories?

TB. It wasn't impatience, it just used to fill the gap 'cos we had complicated tuning. So while we were tuning he would tell a story or just mutter away and it developed. Peter is not really a 'natural' on stage – it was a way of getting through the time, to tell a formalised story rather than to lark about in the way that some people can. So it became quite a thing really and of course in the end the stories started taking much longer than the tuning.

AP. He was so nervous early on that Richard was going to have to do the announcements. As Peter Gabriel he was very unsure of himself, but once he assumed this other persona... It's like that actor, I can't remember his name, but he used to stutter all the time but when he acted he didn't stutter he became a different person. I wonder whether it would have happened in the same way if we hadn't played 12-strings.

PR: Did you have the flute at the very beginning?

TB. Oh, he always had the flute. The flute and the tambourine were things to hide behind, plus this bass drum.

AP. He felt very exposed there actually.

TB. Which was quite funny. Once Phil joined the band, we had to put more and more padding into this bass drum. He couldn't bear the fact that he was so out of time – bore no relation to anything. Pete would have been there with his tongue hanging out smashing this bass drum at the end of "The Knife". As far as the audience was concerned all they would hear was the great sort of fwacking sound in their faces...

AP. Not necessarily in time.

TB. Not a question of not necessarily! Not in time. Pete, he has great rhythm sense but he can't play in time, so his drumming was always a bit sort of – out.

AP. I played in a band with him as a drummer before anything else. We were in this holiday band. Although Pete was a reasonably good flute player he couldn't play in lots of different keys and he couldn't handle "The Knife" solo in A-flat minor. He had to pull the flute out in order to do an A minor and he would never remember. Tony had to always remind him, and he would do the announcement, the song was just about to start and Tony would say 'Flute'. The thing would quieten down for this moody solo and he was out of tune.

TB. Oh God, oh dear. The flute was actually rather a nice thing. I think in the group it was a nice sound quality, quite distinctive which gave it character. And the other thing – the nature of Genesis music right the way through has always been this thing to have quite a long instrumental periods and what does a guy do who is a singer? So those days he used to stay there playing flute or perhaps tambourine or something. Later on he'd tend to go, obviously during *The Lamb Lies Down*, he'd go off stage and wander about. It was a way of stopping him fidgeting all the time.

AP. Do you remember during "Stagnation" when he played the accordion? He used to put it on the floor and it would then fall over and squeal and do its own thing. Now that definitely happened.

PR. An accordion on "Stagnation"!

AP. You know about Mike Rutherford and the cello do you?

PR: I was going to wait to see if he remembered it

AP. Mike did very well. He was given this cello by Brian Roberts' granny and he was very good at picking up instruments and making a good sound, but he couldn't cope with it without the frets.

TB. Here's the man himself

Mike Rutherford arrives.

AP. We are just talking about your bloody cello playing.

MR. Ah! Good days.

AP. Yeah you would hear this squealing breaking out when the torch failed or the frets came off and the sound was whacked out of the PA.

TB. The best one was at Blaise's wasn't it? We were set up in a kind of phalanx with Mike at the front. What were we doing? Was it "Little Leaf" you used played on that?

MR. "Pacidy"?

TB. I know but there were a couple of others, wasn't it "Little Leaf" where it bowed up this girl's skirt they were so close! I don't know if you have been to Blaise's but it's a tiny little place, tiny.

AP. Extraordinary range of these gigs. We would go from huge colleges to pubs where we didn't really fit in. I mean the colleges we didn't really fit in cos they just wanted a lot of noisy stuff. We occasionally played in places that were very receptive like Farx and Friars, then we find ourselves at somewhere like the Sunderland Locarno, which is a bloody ballroom standing next to palm trees, and then these dodgy nightclubs like Revolution and Blaise's full of couples smooching and arms dealers. And we were still then doing these weird changes over of instruments and Mike on the cello and the whole thing was completely incongruous. It was very bizarre actually. You didn't know what you were coming up against next.

PR: Did people talk about how and where you set up in those early days – you didn't really know where to stand or put the PA?

TB. PA? We had one speaker!

AP. Wasn't there an argument with Peter at the first gig when Pete kept moving the PA?

MR. It was kind of weird. We hadn't thought about how to set up. We were playing at the cottage in a round and now it was in rows. Three in a row sort of Pete, me and then there was a drummer, it was very weird. We were trying to be very musical – that was our intention. I remember some of the college gigs we used to do, there was a roar from the bar until the drums came in and then they realised we were playing!

AP. Well that's why we had to toughen up and make more noise.

MR. I remember John Mayhew arriving just in time to play the drums on "Stagnation". Some college – he was late, remember, he arrived just in time.

TB. What about that one we played with The Who?

AP. I never played with The Who unfortunately. I would have loved to have done that.

TB. I don't think we stayed for them actually, (laughs). Maybe they didn't turn up or something or they had cancelled.

PR: There are quite a few interesting bands. Uxbridge Brunel with Fairport Convention?

AP. Yeah we did that. That was the one I really do remember because we got a better reaction then they did. That was one of those exceptional gigs when we went down very, very well.

TB. This was the thing you used to try to do as a support band – to blow the main band off stage, and I'd say that happened to us reasonably often actually. Certainly, it wasn't that rare a thing. It happened to us a couple of times – the other way around. I remember Amazing Blondel were playing with us somewhere when we were topping the bill and they went down a real storm. It was somewhere in the West Country – they loved them. And we came on afterwards and we were a total disaster by comparison. But normally the best thing was you went down well and then the main band came on and they went down well too because that kind of made a good show.

AP. We played with Mott The Hoople early on and they were very nice – they were very enthusiastic about us. That was quite early on and that gave us a lot of confidence.

TB. And very helpful too, they introduced us at the time to Guy Stevens, didn't they? But he wanted to control us more than we wanted to be controlled, and he wanted to change the name, do you remember?

AP Not to Revelation?

TB. No, not to Revelation

AP. What was his name? No we won't go down that road, Who else? I remember Rare

Bird were the front line Charisma Act, we were pretty impressed by them. I remember being impressed by Caravan, weren't we?

TB. We thought Caravan were good – well they had the best gear. I remember they had WEM gear, and we thought one day we were going to aspire to having that ourselves. And we did finally get the WEM gear actually. And it was good.

Mike studies an early Genesis gig listing.

MR. I just saw Deep Purple in Chatham. The amazing thing is that I remember that. I can picture the venue, I can picture Caravan, I can picture Deep Purple, and of course their volume too, but once you get later on in our career....

TB. It blends into one

MR. Each gig is less distinctive.

TB. I remember that gig where that guy borrowed your bass guitar – it was Coliseum wasn't it? Their bassist borrowed your guitar and he was kind of like abusing it. Our gear was pretty important to us, we couldn't buy another one and this guy was banging it into the speakers and we weren't feeling too good about that.

AP. Deep Purple was a shock for us because, although it was quite a big venue, it was the first time we saw a band put a lot of stuff through the PA. Quite a lot like squealing cats actually. I respected them, but I have to say it's not my favourite area of music, but the whole machine was big with all the women surrounding them and all the strutting poses and we were pretty naive, it was too much to handle at the time. Very overawed by them actually.

MR. The two roadies – do you remember that? They couldn't get the Hammond in the doorway. One roadie said, "We'll never get it in there," and the other said, "Of course we will." It was like a comedy skit.

PR: Were there any really early gigs when only one man and his dog showed up at the venue?

AP. Well there is the legendary South London one – have I got this right? – where there was this one guy in that pub in South East London and Gabriel said, "Are there any requests?" I may be wrong.

TB. We went to this club somewhere in South London, Bermondsey, and three girls had come and sat right at the back – I think they had basically come to meet some blokes. What they got was us lot on stage playing this weird stuff. The first thing Pete said was, "Come to the front, what's your name, I'm Peter."

AP. You reckon it was three girls, I thought it was one guy. Peter definitely said, "Are there any requests." It was so embarrassing. We stopped didn't we? We didn't do the whole set, did we?

TB. I thought we did we got paid for it. The real aim in those days was to get an advertisement in the back pages of *Melody Maker*, which showed 7 consecutive gigs, which meant you were really happening. With 2 or 3 you were looking good, there were no problems. Ronnie Scott's which were residencies, that was alright, and then you had to fill the other gap nights. We had quite a few shows with very small audiences, not enthusiastic audiences – we just shouldn't have been there.

AP. Sunderland Locarno was an extraordinary one. We actually did a demo with Tony Clark, the Moody Blues guy. Didn't we drive straight up there? I'm not sure we had any sleep at all.

PR: Yes the Sunderland Locarno Ballroom, January '70...

TB. We did a version of "Looking for Someone" and I remember we were seriously considering going to Threshold [The Moody Blues record label] but when we did this version in one take I had a bum note in it. There was no way we were going to use this as a track on the album with that note in it. We went back and tried to decide between Threshold and Island I think, wasn't it?

AP. I'd forgotten Island.

TB. And the other people we went to see were Chrysalis.

AP. I'd forgotten that too.

TB. Was that at that early stage? I remember them saying that you couldn't have women on the road and all that stuff.

AP. Let's put it all into perspective. We couldn't afford to stay anywhere. We drove a bread van that had no windows, so the guys in the back just sort of sat in a line surrounded by gear.

PR: Did Peter have his black cab then?

TB. Well yeah, but we couldn't take it on the road. Once we started travelling, we used the big van. I remember one time when we did our first gig staying away, we went up to Birmingham and Manchester it must have been Worley and Cheadle, I suppose. We were just about to go and Pete turned up with his mattress and threw it in the back. And he said, "Well I'm taking my mattress." And we said, "Well we can't all take our mattresses, there is no room." Pete said he had had the idea first and he was taking his bloody mattress! Worley Social Club and we stayed in....

MR. ....a changing room with under-floor heating. You remember these things.

TB. The under-floor heating came on in the middle of the night. So you'd put yourself down and it was all fine, pretty uncomfortable, and then suddenly about 1am, we all kind of thought, "Oh God," cos the floor had got burning hot.

AP. I will never joke about your memory again – I've been extremely impressed! I don't remember that at all!

TB. I remember Worley Social Club.

AP. Good heavens have you been swotting up? That's why he's late, he's been cribbing!

MR. Short term memories have been long term...

MR. There was no budget for hotels.

AP. And almost no budget for the van, we crashed the van at some stage, didn't we?

TB. Richard didn't drive it. Mike and I drove. Pete sometimes. Richard couldn't drive. Not in those days, not in the bread van.

AP. Did he not?

TB. He hadn't passed his test.

AP. Are you sure? Tony I'm not sure that's right.

MR. A roadie who doesn't drive, I love it!

TB. No it's right. Mike and I used to do most of the driving. And Peter did a little bit.

AP. Rich crashed it at some stage.

MR. First time out in the van, he crashed it, not badly.

TB. And obviously later on when we became a two-van band, then we all used to drive. All I remember about the driving was trying to keep awake. Obviously staying awake while I was driving and then when Mike was driving I had to stay awake as well to keep Mike awake! Occasionally I would look at him and his eyes were completely closed. And at that time we crashed Lindisfarne's van into those things on the M4, and he said, "I didn't fall asleep I didn't do it. One was sticking out further than the others and I didn't see!"

MR. One night, I remember I was driving and everyone was completely out cold in the back. I must have been going some and was nodding off, came to a roundabout – I went straight across it, and everyone went, "Waaaaaah! What was that?" And I said, "What, you must have dreamt it! I didn't hear anything."

AP. I remember handing you a cigarette in the car and putting it into your mouth the wrong way around!

MR. It's amazing at what one did! This is like three old codgers in a pub! I'm very conscious that a lot of people I know now, talking about their sort of teenage and early twenties years, and it's full of weekends going to football matches and doing things, you know what I mean? In our life, it was like, happily so, just driving around. We would drive from London to Newcastle unload the gear ourselves, do the gig, load it back in again and drive back to London.

TB. You've got to also appreciate this bread van had a governor on it. It was designed to stop people doing more than 45 mph, but if you moved the accelerator pedal to the right you could get it up to 48 mph! I don't quite know why this was the case! So we went into overdrive!

PR: Was it just one van or did anyone else have a car?

AP. No, absolutely not!

TB. Occasionally when we did Blues Playground we took Pete's Hillman Imp 'cos we spent the night. The thing about Hillman Imps if you remember, they have the engine in the back. It had this long accelerator cable and it broke and we spent the night with Caravan's roadie. It was the old joke, but he actually did do this. He went to sleep with a joint in his mouth and woke up in the morning and lit it! It was a pretty strange sort of thing.

AP. Like us in the cottage, pretty debauched!

TB. No, we were very clean living. Pretty clean living.

AP. We never went for any walks. We were in the heart of the most beautiful countryside – we just stayed inside all the time.

TB. Very conscientious.

MR. We were very serious young men.

TB. It was quite difficult for John Mayhew who had a slightly different approach to it all.

AP. He was married, his wife was left in London. We were toffs and he was not, and I think he felt slightly....

TB. And he didn't really get what we were trying to do with the music half the time. So there was an awful lot of shouting. We were very cliquey we had our own humour and everything. Tough, very tough for him.

MR. We seem to have this image of silver spoons and toffs. The whole truth was we couldn't afford to go to motorway cafés – we had to be self-catering.

TB. We chose him 'cos he could go da da da da (TB does drummer noises) that was the only reason. We desperately searched for someone who could do that.

AP. We had a dreadful time auditioning drummers, dreadful.

TB. I remember this guy we auditioned and he didn't have a cymbal stand and we had to hang the cymbal from the ceiling. Do you remember? The poor guy, I mean it was pathetic.

MR. John bought his own kit, I think.

AP. He had been with Steamhammer. He had been with a proper group.

TB. What he must have thought about us lot, I just have absolutely no idea!

MR. We must have been so odd when I think back to that time. What was around, what we were doing, our attitude. I think in a funny way that first bit in the cottage, six months of writing, we were so removed from the business we didn't get drawn into doing things this way or that.

TB. We tried getting all these people down to hear us to get interest either from record companies or management or from agents. I don't know what they made of us. Most of them made excuses. There was always this thing like their car had broken down, it just got so tedious.

AP. Quite a few liked us though, didn't they?

TB. Well, they said they like us.

AP. This guy came down and he said he was quite knocked out – do you remember that! Quite a lot of people reckoned we had potential. It was quite rough hewn in those days wasn't it? With tracks like "Stagnation", we were a bit odd to people I suppose.

TB. I just think, honestly these people didn't mind who they had on their books actually. They would give you a go and see how it went. And once they had signed a band they had a chance. There was nothing to lose particularly. No one put any money up until we got to Charisma when they gave us a tenner a week which was an advance against our future earnings. Actually when we went in there, they said, "£15 per week does that sound all right?" and John Mayhew said, "I can manage on £10."

AP. He didn't.

TB. Yes, he did!

TB. It was so wonderful to just to have *something*, 'cos it meant you could exist rather than have to bribe or beg off your parents.

PR: An early break on the live scene was when you hooked up with David Stopps and the band started doing the Friars shows. How did they come about and what was that like?

AP. I can't remember but that was just one of the few gigs where they were always very receptive. They loved us there.

TB. Yes he liked us really, because his audience liked us. They would tell us stories about how David Bowie broke from there and stuff like that. They liked progressive acts.

MR. We used to enjoy going to Friars gigs you know, even if they hadn't heard of the band they went along to see.

TB. That's right, you kind of trusted them. That's when the promoter's aspect would come in. He would be quite good at getting bands that they liked and that worked quite well. And the other place was Farx in Southhall, where we would go as a support act and then went back as a headliner. It had a very, very enthusiastic kind of crowd. Farx was quite small, wasn't it?

AP. Absolutely.

TB. Probably about 200-250 people?

AP. They were few and far between. You would have one of those for every ten of these weird and wonderful ones. The Revolution– that was where we played with Ginger Baker's Air Force.

TB. Well no, they were rehearsing.

AP. Matthews Southern Comfort played and we witnessed that totally..... Yes we'd better not go into that!

TB. We ended the first song and there was not a sound from the audience, and we had never been in a place like that – we didn't realise what these places were all about – we were stunned. Afterwards of course we got used to the fact that we didn't get any applause, and then somebody shouted out, "Play 'Whole Lotta Love'."

TB. There were the three nightclubs. The Speakeasy was considered to be a reasonable gig, I think. Blazes and Revolution were their sister clubs.

AP. They were dives, really.

TB. The Speakeasy might have been worth playing but we never played it. But the other two, the theory was you played them and you might be able to play the Speakeasy and of course we played the others.

AP. I got in as a roadie at the Speakeasy. That was where I had my long conversation with John Lennon. He came through and I said, "Excuse me," and he just went, "Hi!" It was back in the Cynthia days, he was very serious sitting there with Victor Spinneti. Anyway we didn't play there, despite my roadie-ing with whichever ever band it was.

PR: There are obviously quite a lot of gigs in the very early '70s at Ronnie Scott's. You got a residency there?

TB. That's right.

AP. That was the London showcase wasn't it?

TB. Yes it was a bit of experiment to have progressive music upstairs at Ronnie's. Most nights we played there, we just played to our friends and to the odd media person we could encourage to come. Through Rare Bird, who we got quite friendly with and we admired, their producer John Anthony came to see us. He liked us and was happy to have another band to produce, and he got Tony Stratton Smith to come along to one of the Ronnie Scott's evenings. He loved "Visions of Angels", he kept going on about it. Wonderful, wonderful!

AP. Oh you are camp, Tony! (laughter)

TB. He was very enthusiastic about that. You have to say also he was trying to get interesting new bands for his label, and I don't know how much he really liked us at that early stage. He had Rare Bird who were obviously his babies at that time. Van der Graaf Generator, who he had a sort of strong feeling for, and then there was us. And he got Lindisfarne, then Audience and stuff, but he was trying to get a stable of bands together which were a little bit different.

AP. I remember those gigs feeling quite pressured actually. I remember thinking, "God this is important." We had been on the road for six months and had a few bites here and there, but it started getting very serious at that point. Are they going to sign us or not? 'Strat' was a big name, so when he came along, it was like don't fuck up.

TB. Because we were playing a residency up there, we were able to try out one or two new numbers. I remember doing one song one night, which for a lack of a better title, was called "I've Been Travelling All Night Long", which didn't have any lyrics written at the time and we said to Pete, "Just go waaaaah! No one will know the difference." Because of the PA, no one could hear the vocals anyhow, and so he did that.

MR. There was a time when we would tour and write. It wasn't like later on, we would tour then we would take time off to write. Back then we did a bit of writing, then played a couple of new songs, do a bit more writing – it was an ongoing thing, gigging and writing at the same time. It's shame that later on in one's career that sort of dies. Block of touring, a block of writing.

TB. Yeah the last time we did that really was for the *Foxtrot* album – "Watcher of the Skies" we had done on stage before we recorded it.

PR. (to AP): Six months on the road, you were starting to feel the pressure of doing live gigs? Starting to build up to your final, the Haywards Heath moment?

AP. Yeah, I was. And that is all a long story, I mean we don't have to go into that really.

TB. Oh come on. (laughs)

AP. I was just thinking about the Marquee, we haven't mentioned the Marquee. That was somewhere where we used to go, well I certainly used to go and watch people and all these huge household names and suddenly we found ourselves there. Whereas a lot of the places we played we didn't know from Adam. But the stigma of the Marquee was fantastic.

TB. Our original first goal, I think, was the Marquee Club. Who did we support the first time? Was it Jackson Heights?

AP. Yes, yes, yes.

TB. And the audience actually seemed to really quite like us, so that was good.

AP. Didn't we hear that Jon Anderson was there once and he quite liked us?

MR. In those days the fact that someone famous came to see you, and you heard they liked you, cheered you up.

TB. Well we were desperate for something, 'cos we'd had the odd show where it seemed to go quite well, but it did seem like we didn't know where we were heading. We had to take morsels of comfort from where we could find them I think.

AP. Absolutely! Even if it was a second-hand opinion.

TB. Things were very up and down emotionally I think. We would get an incredible high from a good response and then we would just feel very depressed when it wasn't. Particularly when there were equipment problems. I had this home-made Lesley that John Mayhew made.

AP. John was a carpenter.

TB. Basically it was fine. I liked the slow Lesley sound I didn't like the fast stuff like the Brian Auger sound. So to get it moving really slowly was really difficult. You had to have a resistor which was OK, but we did not always have one, so we originally tried with a light bulb which was fine but it wasn't very accurate. Then we got a variable resistor which was quite technical and exciting in those days. You would get it set and it was great – it would move beautifully, then suddenly as it heated up the resistance lowered, and of course we were going faster and faster and you were playing this moody piece and suddenly it would turn into Mrs Mills.

MR. You were always getting up to fix it.

TB. That was the other thing, if you got it going too slow it would stop! Particularly when it wasn't miked up, or if the thing was facing the wrong way and the audience couldn't hear anything because it was stuck in this kind of mode, so I had to get up and give it a whack to get it started again.

MR. What was interesting too, there became a certain moment when suddenly lots of gear came out with sounds and effects. There was a period in our career when there was nothing much happening. So we had to try and find ways to make things happen – like with a fuzz box, just to be different, and then suddenly out came a chorus pedal and everything changed.

TB. That was quite a lot later actually. The Fuzz box and the Wah Wah didn't really suit our music.

PR: What would you do? Just stick your 12-strings straight into an amp or would it go into a PA?

AP. The 12-strings went into the amps so they were always feeding back – that was the problem. I remember we were too close to the amp. It was like at the Revolution Club, the way the stage was shaped we couldn't turn the guitars up as they would feed back. And it was a complete lottery. We wouldn't know which one of us was feeding back. When this noise started, both turned down and then both turned up again. Chaos, chaos.

TB. Talking about the PA thing, we didn't put anything through the PA at all, apart from the voice. The first thing we ever put through the PA was the Mellotron, after Ant left. And the thing that was so exciting, was that you just put it in one side and then the echo on the other side and then suddenly it was whoosh, a sound that I don't think the audience had ever heard before! It was stereo on stage and it was just a massive sound with the strings. It was just a wonderful, wonderful thing.

The opening of "Watcher of the Skies" was just a big, big chord sound. Making the most of what little equipment was actually available, using a little WEM Copycat, which is a loop of tape which used to go round and round and gradually get worse. So the PA was entirely just for the vocal and it couldn't handle that to be honest. Most of the time we were playing in fairly small places where it was all right, once we played a bigger hall I don't really know what sort of sound people were getting because it really depended so much on the speaker volume. I think the guitars would tend to always dominate the keyboards for example. The keyboards had this big bassy speaker.

PR: Did you play much lead in those days?

AP. I would have to go through song by song really. A fair amount.

TB. You didn't tend to improvise. We didn't improvise at all really.

AP. The only free solo was "The Knife" where there was a little bit of freedom.

PR: Were you a Strat man or a Gibson man?

AP. Strat actually, there was quite long chunks of electric. "Looking for Someone" was all-electric, "The Knife" was all-electric, "Going Out To Get You" was too. It all went through our own amps. I had a Vox AC 30, [to MF] what was your amp? Did your acoustic go through the same as the bass? It must have done. I can remember most of the set we were doing in my last few months. "Dusk", "Visions of Angels", "White Mountain", "Twilight Alehouse" would have all been 12-string.

TB. We did "Going Out To Get You" for quite a long time.

AP. "Stagnation" was acoustic, Mike was acoustic and then you would switch wouldn't you? You did quite a lot of switching… I can't remember.

PR: "Pacidy" and stuff, that was still around?

AP. We dropped "Pacidy" near the end didn't we?

TB. I think we did drop it after the *Trespass* album came out, then the set got a bit more streamlined, of course, but it still included "Twilight Alehouse" and I think "Going Out To Get You".

MR. "Pacidy" was never a live audience pleaser. Not a great live song.

TB. Not a great studio song, if we're honest about it.

AP. It was a nice tune, but I ruined it with some dreadful lyrics.

TB. Hey, there was nothing wrong with that!

PR: So you were doing *Trespass* and gigging all at the same time? Or did you take some time off to record it?

TB. We took a week, didn't we?

MR. The thing about *Trespass* was that we had played all the songs live for quite a long time before we recorded it. In a way it made it easier but in a way it meant you weren't very free – you were fixed with how you had played it live and you played it the same way really. And you couldn't drop in if you made a mistake!

TB. The thing was you had to go on until the drummer got it right. I remember with *Nursery Cryme*, and "The Return of The Giant Hogweed" – it wasn't a terribly easy song to play, it had lots of changes in it and stuff, and Phil couldn't get it right and we finally got it at take 27. That was how we had to do it really. We obviously over-dubbed some things. The idea was we put it down with the four of us playing at the same time and all battling with the headphone parts. Of course now no one would think twice about it, everyone would have their own headphone parts. But sharing say with the drummer, I wanted more keyboards and the drummer wanted more bass drum and it was just a nightmare!

PR: Did the sound of *Trespass* change a lot in the studio. The album has a very distinctive feel to it.

AP. We were reasonably pleased with it.

TB. I think we were all aware pretty quickly that we had put the vocals too soft on "Stagnation". Mainly the first part. I think we were reasonably pleased with what we had done, certainly things like "The Knife" sounded pretty good and the electric stuff seemed to be easier.

AP. I remember having a battle with Robin Cable (sound engineer) about how the 12-string was going to be recorded, as I had to go through this weird and wonderful way of recording. The guitar went through this tape recorder that Peter and I had some repeat echo on. And Robin Cable used to say that it did not sound like a 12-string, and it sounded much more harmonic than the usual strummed 12-string.

TB. He wanted a thinner sound than us. Did we end up using him or did we go with someone else?

AP. We did use him, but I had to dig my heels in.

TB. It was quite difficult as we felt he was professional and he knew how to do it.

MR. We knew what we liked, there was no question about that, so we stuck to our guns.

AP. I think I'm just about done really, my period is just about exhausted.

TB. It would be fair to say I think that the period with Ant was the crucial period for forming all aspects of the band, the musical direction and our approach to everything. Which was why, obviously when he left, it was very difficult.

AP. What was the name of the drummer you got after I left? (laughter)

PR. Did the gigs you played after *Trespass* was released include any later songs, like early versions of "The Musical Box", as some of that had been written back in 1969?

AP. We had lots of guitar bits that Mike and I had written, including those early chords from "Musical Box". It wasn't played live while I was in the band.

MR. After *Trespass* came out how long did you play (Ant)?

AP. Not for very long I think…

PR. Ant left in July 1970 after the Haywards Heath Gig.

TB. I remember it coming out to no great interest – there were a few decent reviews. But I remember that period as being pretty depressing, and we really weren't going anywhere. And particularly once Ant had decided he was going to leave, the whole thing seemed like it would probably fold. I think we assumed it would, as there was such a stong relationship between Ant and Mike. I also thought that out of all of us

Ant was the key person, as he was most into the live thing and was the motivator for us to become a live band. I thought there was a magic between the four of us.

PR. When did you decided to keep going?

TB. Richard (MacPhail) said we should keep going.

MR. I drove back after that gig with Pete and we had a conversation about the fact that we might carry on.

TB. You must appreciate how the band was originally formed. Ant and Mike were musical partners and so were Pete and I, and so it was such a big change. So I was really surprised when Pete and Mike and Richard said we should keep going. So I said, "OK, but we have to find another drummer."

MR. Ant had been the driving force at that point, especially at the early stage of being a band and writing songs, then Pete came on quite strong and he was very determined which was useful.

TB. When Pete set his mind on something, there was no shifting him, so he was quite useful at that point. It was very strange moment, kind of weird and you weren't quite certain what was going to happen. Trying to replace Ant was a real problem, but finding a new drummer wasn't.

AP. Did you decide immediately that John had to go?

TB. I said at the meeting that he was not going where we were going, or adding in the way that we were. We needed someone creative with more spark.

AP. The rest of us had an intuitive thing, I remember it was a bit of a plod at times with John.

TB. I had most problems with John, and I am a very patient person, but it would take him a long while to get things. Two or three of the fifteen or so of the drummers we auditioned were good, but Phil had a feel for it and he was just fantastic. But finding a guitarist was a much bigger problem, as we were trying to replace Ant, which is why we went out as a four piece for a while.

AP. I'm awfully flattered by what Tony was saying, the thought that I could have had the responsibility for what might have happened would have been awful.

TB. We needed that kind of shake up really, it stopped us living in a fantasy land. So we said let's change the drummer, and if we are going to do this let's do it in a more professional way. The four-piece thing made Mike and I mature a lot, I had to play a lot of Ant's parts on guitar, and Mike had to take on the role of some of the lead playing as well. I think Mike had lived somewhat in the shadow of Ant in those early days, so this made him come out of himself more. And we all got more self-confidence as musicians which was a good thing for the band.

PR. Then it was hunt the guitarist.

TB. It was difficult as most guitarists wanted to be rock gods and do the whole guitar hero bit. To try and find someone who could fit in with the ensemble was not easy at all.

PR. When did you know that the Haywards Heath gig was going to be your last, did it just happen or had that moment been some time arriving?

TB. We knew it was coming.

AP. I think I'd sort of plodded along trying to make a go of it after the album came out.

PR. Was the lack of interest in *Trespass* a factor?

AP. Not at all, it was personal stuff.

MR. I remember you driving me out in the van to the back of Kingston Rugby club with

Richard and telling me you were going to leave, or maybe Rich told me, I know someone told me in the back of the van.

TB. When we first started Ant was the most natural extrovert who liked being a bit of a show off. Certainly on stage he liked being up there.

AP. Let's face it, most singers and guitarists were like that, even Peter was once he started acting.

TB. But it seemed like you became totally uncomfortable being that show off. It was a funny period then, because the band was quite static and at that age – I was only 20 and you were 17 – life moves at a different pace and if nothing happens for a month or two you begin to wonder if you should be doing this at all.

MR. It was pretty gruelling physically then, you know what I mean?

TB. Definitely, and it didn't get any better as a four piece. We produced some nice music but it was such a sweat and there were endless arguments particularly between me and Pete, I remember storming out and walking round the block. Poor old Phil, who had just joined the band, he just wanted everyone to love each other, everybody to be nice (laughs).

AP. Some of the best stuff comes out under conflict, I remember at the end of my time Pete used to come in for a bit of stick, I think he felt a bit lost without an instrument, he didn't have a power base. He would come up with moments of genius and then stuff that wasn't genius, and he got shot down quite a lot. It was like he was assuming a position, rather perverse at times.

TB. With Peter, whenever he introduced an idea it meant everything stopped for a bit, because he would have to sit down at a piano or something to demonstrate the idea. Whatever flow we had going seemed to disappear at that point and it made the whole process somewhat difficult.

AP. For someone who was so articulate when he was acting, he couldn't articulate what he meant. A lot of the time he had these visions of arrangements and he couldn't get it across.

MR. Very soon after Pete left, his recording skills took off fantastically, but in our environment there was no room to breathe.

AP. He had this thing about all the thick chords we were playing, we all loved chords and chord sequences and there were loads of them, everyone playing at once, and I think he was ahead of his time in the respect of the way he was always trying to break it down.

PR. One gig that has been mentioned a lot recently is the Roundhouse show with Bowie, of which some black and white silent footage has been offered around various circles.

AP. Oh yes, we only did a couple of numbers.

TB. I used to really like David Bowie in the early days.

PR. He would have had "Space Oddity" out then.

TB. But it didn't go anywhere. I thought the actual show was pretty disappointing. I much preferred his Anthony Newley period and I didn't like all the showmanship. I thought the costumes distracted from the music, but I was a bit of a purist I suppose. Look what happened later.

AP. I remember a lot of bands being on, so we only did a few songs, and an old school friend of ours was there with some cameras.

MR. Someone's tried to sell it for a fortune.

AP. There was no sound on the film; it's the only visual proof that I was ever in the group actually (laughs).

TB. Talking of proof, poor old John Silver wasn't even on the cover of the repackage of the *Revelations* album. They used a picture of Chris Stewart instead. So his son is saying, 'Dad I thought you were in this group.'

AP. I'm trying to think of any other interesting gigs from that time.

PR. Chatham Central Hall with Deep Purple, Ewell Tech with Atomic Rooster.

TB. Vince (Crane) used to play all the bass parts on the left-hand side of the organ, and it was incredibly noisy – the loudest noise we had heard at that point. They were alright.

AP. I remember seeing Alan Price somewhere in London, and I hadn't heard a Geordie accent and his band was full of top session guys.

TB. The Angel in Godalming was a good gig for us actually.

AP. Fantastic, I remember seeing you guys there after I had left.

TB. There was a group called Nemesis.

AP. Was that where the tarpaulin fell on our heads?

PR. Where was this?

MR. An outdoor gig at Surrey University. The stage had this big tarpaulin, which must have filled with rain or something, and it fell down during our set.

TB. Didn't we play the Temple that same evening, I'm sure we did. It was the only time we had played to an audience that was all lying down, all completely stoned. We played our show and got the occasional clap – very bizarre.

AP. One constant was the Brighton Dome, where we were actually onstage and people were sitting down to watch us.

MR. That's right, who were we supporting?

TB. Was it Family? Didn't they come on late or was it the Bonzo Dog [Doo Dah] Band.

MR. I do remember the Dome as being the big thing when we actually got through to people.

AP. We did a gig with Noel Redding, post-Jimi Hendrix Experience.

MR. I can tell you where that one was, Fulham Town Hall, right next to the station.

TB. Blodwyn Pig?

AP. No, that was the guy from Jethro Tull.

PR. Fat Mattress.

TB. Fat Mattress (laughs), that was it.

MR. Those days, the more gear you had the better, and we helped them move their gear on stage and half the speaker cabinets were empty, just cabinets with no speakers inside.

TB. Fat Mattress, what a great name, not Black Cat something?

PR. Black Cat Bones.

TB. I'm sure they supported us once and they had this great bank of speakers, but when we went around the back they had one little speaker plugged in with a couple of dodgy leads.

AP. We did actually play with Nick Drake, and one of the sad things for me was that we just never really listened to him. And neither did the audience because he was painfully shy and you couldn't hear him. He was very nice, but very, very shy.

TB. I don't really remember him very well.

AP. I remember him coming up to us at Queen Mary's College I think, and saying to me about "Let us Now Make Love" how he thought it was 'Dangerous'. It was very nice of him. I feel guilty now.

PR. Ant's temporary replacement was Mick Barnard. Where did he come from?

MR. Friars area Aylesbury, recommended by Dave Stopps.

PR. He has always been the mystery man of early Genesis.

TB. The thing about him was he was OK, but not really forceful enough. I remember when we had already auditioned Steve but were still rehearsing with Mick which wasn't a very nice thing to do, we were doing the end part of "The Musical Box" and he was playing this little guitar phrase over the top of it and we thought this was really good. So just as we were about to boot him out he did something quite good.

MR. I think if we had not found Steve we could have made it work with him.

TB. He was good with sound, he had this Echoplex which he got some very interesting sounds out of and we liked that.

MR. It was a Vincent Echo not an Echoplex, I do remember these things, you know.

TB. Ronnie Caryl from Flaming Youth came down with Phil for his audition and the story goes that when they left, Ronnie thought he'd got the gig and Phil didn't.

PR. And Steve?

TB. We had let Mike do the auditions for a guitarist but it didn't get anywhere, so Pete and I saw this ad and went and met this guy, who of course was Steve, at his flat. We thought he was interesting. A different area from us, more classical and he did some nice things with his brother on flute and we liked the sounds and the way he approached playing. He was not the guitar-hero type and we thought he could blend with the group. If Mike had done the audition, we would never have got him (laughs).

MR. I was in bed for about a week which was no coincidence.

AP. I never knew that story, so you didn't choose him?

MR. They just needed me out of the way, because I was too fussy.

TB. I don't quite know what the problem with Mick was, I can't remember that now.

PR. There was an early TV appearance with Mick on.

TB. Yes, he mimed to Ant's part on "The Knife". We all mimed except Pete who had to sing live, but they wouldn't give him any echo. The tape has been wiped I think.

MR. Probably a good job I should think (laughs).

TB. Except it would have been quite good fun to see Mick, I remember what he looked liked vaguely.

MR. I had a blue screen behind my bass strings, a piece of card on which they showed War footage during the middle section. (Much laughter).

AP. That's my last story. Is it OK if I leave?

After a pause for photos, Ant takes his leave. Mike and Tony carry on.

TB. We can tell the truth about him now, how I kicked him out (laughs).

PR. Phil's early gigs were as a four piece?

TB. The four piece was not a good time for us. It felt really awkward. I remember having a terrible argument with Jill {Gabriel} outside a gig in Dunstable – not quite sure why though, things like that happened then.

MR. Just towards the end we glimpsed that we might have been able to do it, I am glad we didn't have to, but I think we could have managed it.

TB. "The Musical Box" was the only thing that really worked.

MR. Well, that was written as a four piece.

PR. Were some newer songs creeping in by then?

TB. Newer songs were easier. I think "The Hogweed" emerged at that point, but I just didn't think it ever really worked with just the four of us.

PR. Then Mr Hackett arrived.

TB. I remember his first gig as an exciting one. We were usually very disciplined, but at the University College gig, Phil, who is normally the most reliable member of the band and the best musician, had had a few drinks beforehand. He was just all over the shop and poor old Steve was trying to play in time, and Phil was just nowhere.

MR. Drunk drummer.

TB. Steve seemed to fit in quite quickly as we never had any problems on that score. We were still quite on our own, we didn't really mix with other bands until we did the tours with Van der Graaf Generator and Lindisfarne and then we were stuck with them.

PR. The 'six bob' tours of legend.

TB. I remember feeling pretty confident on those tours, we all felt quite good about it. We hadn't done *Nursery Cryme* by then had we?

PR. No, that came out in November '71. The live set at that time, was it still the *Trespass* material and songs like "Alehouse" and "Going Out to Get You"?

TB. We were doing "Musical Box" then and "Going Out to Get You" had gone, although we occasionally brought it back, also I think "Giant Hogweed" was, and maybe "Salmacis", I am not sure.

PR. Was it Steve that pushed for a Mellotron?

TB. We always wanted a Mellotron and Steve was keen to get one, I ended up buying one from King Crimson. We went to this place where they had three Mellotrons which was very impressive, so I bought one of those.

PR. Steve and Phil are now in, and it's off on the 'six bob' tour'.

TB. The good thing about that was that you were exposed to reasonably large audiences right across the country. Places like Newcastle, Manchester and Glasgow we were really strong.

MR. It was a proper tour.

TB. In Newcastle it was good for us, as well as Lindisfarne, who were obviously playing to a home audience. They were a great live band and everybody liked them. We were normally on first and if we did badly it was, "Oh well", but if we did well it was "Great". Then VdGG would come on and it was sometimes too much for the audience, but Lindisfarne seemed to go down well.

MR. We did Green's Playhouse in Glasgow which is a famous venue, and after we had finished "Stagnation" there was silence, and it was like Glasgow had decided that they didn't like us, but then after what seemed like an age there was this roar and it was fantastic.

PR. Three bands for 30p, was it Strat's idea?

MR. Yes, a clever idea and it worked.

PR. Talking to Peter Hammill about the shows, he remembers Genesis as being pretty reliable, whereas VdGG were not always on the case.

MR. I agree with that. Sometimes we saw them and they were fantastic and other times it was all over the place.

TB. One thing we seemed to have as a group was a really good idea of pacing, we were a long-winded group and some people will hate that and that's fine. We spent a lot of time on the set order and I think it makes a big difference. The way you juxtapose your songs can really sell them to an audience. You have to build people up then let them go, build them up again, and we had very dynamic music and the whole set structure was very important to us. When we played that first terrible show in New York, we thought we were terrible, but the audience liked us. So Strat came up and said, 'Look, 80% of Genesis is still pretty good,' so basically if we were 20% off we were still able to get it across to the audience.

PR. The first overseas gig was March '71 in Belgium.

MR. It was very exciting to travel abroad to do some gigs, and not only that, they liked us.

TB. We were amazed when we got there to this small club there was such a buzz. We had received some nice press in a trendy magazine so they knew we were coming. We had to set up in three rows as the stage was so small, and it was hot and sweaty and packed. The audience loved it, particularly "The Knife". They seemed to go for the pseudo-revolutionary thing which was very tongue-in-cheek from our point of view, but they seemed to take it seriously and they loved it.

PR. The show actually exists in collecting circles and is famous for having "The Light" on it.

MR. Oh really.

TB. I have a copy somewhere, it sounded awful.

PR. It's been cleaned up a bit since the early versions came out.

MR. Could you do me a copy?

TB. "The Light", of course, arrived when Phil first came in. We asked him if he had anything we could use, and he had this song called "The Light" with a slightly embarrassing lyric about Joe and Mary. It was to do with Jesus and was a bit kind of odd in that sense. It was quite a good melody so we constructed a big song around it. It had some good bits in the middle, the little triplet section.

MR. Did he sing it then?

TB. They sang it together, Pete and Phil.

PR. The guitar riff and the verse ended up in "Lilywhite Lilith".

TB. It was quite an interesting song. I don't really know why it didn't get recorded, too much material already I imagine.

PR. Was there any improvisation there? It almost sounds like some jamming is going on.

TB. It was all arranged improvisation, a bit like the end of "Looking For Someone" and "Can Utility". But thinking about it, the opening bass part (hums the intro to "The Light") came from "I've Been Travelling All Night Long" (hums more of the song).

PR. A second 'six bob' tour soon followed.

MR. That wasn't as much fun as the first one.

PR. The BBC sessions. How important were they to the band?

TB. From our point of view I don't rate any of those radio shows as important in our career. We did them because people asked us to. I don't think it made any difference at all.

PR. The infamous ankle-breaking Friars gig. Must have been exciting to say the least?

TB. We were big stars there, we didn't get this impression at many places we went, but we did there, and I think it just got hold of Pete actually. It wasn't the same night he asked them to boo was it? That was another night and a bad mistake. He said, "Instead of clapping everybody boo," and they did. And of course it created a very strange atmosphere which really didn't work at all.

At Friars, I remember him leaping off the stage and when we all came off the at the end, he was lying down going white saying, "I think I've hurt my leg." So we said, "Come on get up it's time to go." and of course he had broken his ankle.

PR. Then came the 'walking stick gigs'.

TB. I remember one gig Pete was going up and down in a wheelchair, I think at some teacher training college. The audience didn't understand at all. I think they thought it was a sick joke. That made us realise what an important visual element Peter was.

PR. Most of 1971 was spent touring, which I guess helped you perfect the stage show with Peter and his costumes.

TB. I think it's well documented about the Dublin gig when he appeared in this red thing and the fox's head. It got us on the front page of *Melody Maker* and so helped promote us.

MR. He had been doing the 'Old Man' for some while, but it really worked when we used the gauze sails at the Rainbow. We didn't want to see the amps, so we covered them with this gauze, then we shone UV light on them and it looked fantastic, the best value for money we have ever had.

PR. The Hobbit's Garden in Wimbledon with Roxy Music in Dec '71, an interesting gig?

TB. I think that was Roxy Music's first gig, and they had Davy O'List with them on guitar, he was with the Nice as well.

MR. Really?

TB. Yes, he was one of those guys that sort of left at the wrong time. The Nice were such a fantastic group when he was with them as guitarist – they really needed him. When he left, the whole emphasis of the band changed and I saw them live without him and they were only half the band they were. But in Roxy Music it wasn't so crucial when he left.

PR. The first Italian trip was in April '72 and was quite an eye opener for you.

TB. It was kind of strange for us, as over here we had receptive audiences but normally quite small. Then we went out to Italy and we were playing the Palasport in Rome to 20,000 people, or perhaps that was a bit later on.

MR. They had some very strange gigs in Italy, you had these packed afternoon discos out of town that had to be over by about six, and these places were crumbling old Palasports, very odd.

TB. The sound in some of these places was just lethal.

MR. It was very exciting being in a country for the first time and finding it likes you.

TB. They seemed to really like the *Nursery Cryme* album, which in England didn't sell any more than *Trespass,* but out there they loved it, and that was very important for us. They liked stuff like "Salmacis" and all the romantic stuff which still had a somewhat limited appeal over here. But saying that, there were still some poor gigs over there, I'm sure there was one when Richard didn't show up.

MR. It was tours like that when we started to appreciate being in a band. We had some days off and we were travelling the world. It was a sign of things to come I think. But we did work hard though.

PR. "Watcher of the Skies" came together in Italy.

TB. We were rehearsing it at Reggio Emilia, and it started to sound really good. I remember Mike and I writing the lyrics up in the hotel with the town looking deserted.

PR. On the way back from Italy there was one gig in the Zoom Club in Frankfurt.

MR. We were driving back from Italy through Germany, and that's where Steve met his wife.

TB. And Phil met Kiki, good old Kiki.

MR. Nearly his wife (laughs).

TB. The Zoom was a come-down after Italy because Germany didn't like us then, although in the later career of Genesis it proved to be the hottest place for us. It was a funny club in that it was L-shaped, so we played on the end of one side but most of the action was taking place round the corner.

PR. The Lincoln Festival in 1972 with Joe Cocker, Monty Python, the Beach Boys etc, was famous for the premier of "Watcher" and Peter's move into costume jewellery.

TB. They didn't like us. We were on in the afternoon and there was no atmosphere, nothing. It was raining, it was crap. I never felt we were a good festival band, the music was just too complex really.

MR. Also you need a bit of lighting, and in the cold light of day it killed the atmosphere.

TB. You needed to play something simple really.

MR. Lindisfarne were there.

TB. They actually taught us a lot about that sort of approach. There's nothing wrong with being direct, and they did it well and always had a good rapport with the audience. We used to think 'Bastards, they're going down much better than us'.

PR. Was there a process in which new songs were brought into the set?

TB. We were never afraid to try new songs, or in fact drop songs completely. For instance we always played "The Knife" at the end of a set, but we replaced it with "The Giant Hogweed" and moved "The Knife" to the encore. The "Hogweed" was very dramatic and used to get a good response. I think the audiences would take anything we chose to give them, but I think we overdid it with *The Lamb Lies Down*. It taught us that you could ditch a favourite and get away with it.

MR. As long as you give them a bit of old and mix it up a bit.

PR. With "Watcher" now in, and opening the set, the emphasis was now on 'big'.

TB. It was such an extraordinary sort of sound. Coming to see a Genesis concert that started with "Watcher of the Skies" meant you weren't coming to see anybody else, it could only be one group really. The Mellotron and those rock chords plus the look of the stage and Pete with his batwings and glowing eyes, this could not be the Rolling Stones, this had to be Genesis. Just those opening two chords set you up for the next ten minutes of the show, we could have done anything after that, a very, very strong beginning.

PR. The first Rainbow gig in Feb '73 with all the new costumes and the gauze sails and lighting must have been a special time for the band.

MR. The Rainbow was a very strong moment for us.

TB. It was lucky it worked as well as it did considering there were quite a few unknowns. Everything seemed to go right and we played well, it was one of the most exciting shows I can remember.

MR. By now we had a small cult following, it was a great feeling to have people excited about you appearing on stage.

PR. "Supper's Ready" was premiered at Brunel University on Nov 10th, 1972.

TB. I can't believe we hadn't played it before, because *Foxtrot* was out then, wasn't it? I know we recorded it in summer '72 at the same time as I got married, so I can always date that one.

PR. Was there ever any question about playing a 23-minute piece live?

TB. We knew it was so strong especially the second half, and our audience seemed to like the long complicated stuff we had been doing, it just used to go down really well right from the word go.

MR. It was always going to be in the set, we knew that as soon as we recorded it.

PR. By now the stage set and the costumes were getting more elaborate.

TB. The gauze curtains with the UV lighting effect was just stunning, the costumes were just sort of an addition to that which initially we were not 100% sure about really, although I don't remember there being any particular fights about that.

PR. The long instrumental sections in "Supper's Ready" were just made for a quick costume change.

TB. In the old days Pete would sit and play flute during the instrumental stuff, then it progressed to him running off to put a new costume on of some kind. Of course originally the end of "Supper's Ready" was without vocals, I had this idea of some heavenly choirs during the section that became '666', but Pete came in with the lead line and it sounded fantastic, I think the last section of that song is the strongest thing from our early career.

PR. With Steve and Phil in the group, did that create new writing combinations?

TB. The main writing contributions came from Mike, Peter and I. Steve would write some stuff but he tended to stay more in his own corner.

MR. Instrumentally it was the three of us; myself, Tony and Phil.

TB. Particularly things like "Cinema Show" and the 'Apocalypse' where the three of us just jammed ideas. Steve wrote, but got frustrated as an awful lot of what he wrote didn't get included, maybe he didn't shout as loud as the rest of us, I don't know. Phil didn't really write much then, but was very good at arranging and getting things together.

PR. The first live album came out as a budget release. Was that always the plan?

MR. It was Strat's idea – we had recorded for the King Biscuit Flower Hour but he pushed us into releasing a live album. It worked well as a filler, so you wouldn't have to wait six months for the next album.

TB. We had to make the decision to leave out our strongest song, which of course was "Supper's Ready", which seemed strange at the time but was the right move as it enabled us to include some of the older material.

PR. It's a very powerful album from "Watcher" through to the "Knife"

TB. I have never been a fan of our live albums, I didn't even listen to the remastered ones.

MR. I think most of us in the band tend to underestimate how much the fans enjoy the live albums, whereas it doesn't do it for us.

TB, I get most excitement when we have just recorded an album, after that I don't tend to listen to it much.

PR. The audience response on that album is very loud, you had obviously built up a strong following by then.

TB. It's amazing how it sounds when you put the crowd on afterwards (laughs). I think we used some old Yes audience.

PR. The *Selling England* tour was the biggest yet.

TB. We made a promotional film at Shepperton but they didn't let us have enough lights so it looked dreadful. Pete's make-up looked silly, which it did anyhow. I thought overall on that tour the costumes got a bit out of control at times with all that Bodicea stuff or Britannia – whatever it was at the beginning of "Moonlit Knight". It just looked silly to me, I didn't like that. Some things were great, like the simplicity of "I Know What I Like". Light-wise it wasn't as good as the previous tour, but we did have the back-projections with things like the two eyes for "Watcher" which was a very powerful image.

PR. On this tour Phil sang his first lead vocal on "More Fool Me".

TB. I used to go off and have a drink during that, it wasn't my favourite song. If I hear it now it sounds OK actually.

MR. For me "More Fool Me" was a song when there was a warm feeling from the audience towards Phil, he's that kind of a guy who has a presence on stage even as a drummer. It was a nice feeling, it also made it easier when Pete left.

TB. He always looked like a painter with no shirt under his dungarees.

PR. There was even a return for "Harold The Barrel" on this tour.

TB. Did we do that? You seem to know more than us – you don't need to talk to us (laughs); we did try to do some different songs on the tour.

PR. The live set was much longer on the *Selling England* tour.

TB. With "Cinema Show" and "Firth of Fifth" we had introduced two very good live songs which were exciting to play, and the Americans loved a bit of playing, and then we would play "Supper's Ready" at the end.

PR. *The Lamb* tour got off to a standing start with the cancelled UK gigs and Steve's injured hand.

TB. That was quite convenient, but absolutely genuine. We weren't ready for the tour then. So we started in Chicago before the album had come out, we played the whole bloody album.

MR. I found it one of the most difficult tours to do, because we had to play the whole album and some of it was not meant to be played live. Lots of little bits, and of course to start with, no one knew what we were playing anyway, It was a bit of an effort.

TB. It was ambitious and it didn't really work in lots of ways. People remember it being this glorious show, but for a start, technically, we were trying to be to adventurous and most of the time all the slides we had didn't work and that used to depress us. And we knew Pete was leaving and it was pretty awful.

MR. I'm sure the punters enjoyed it.

TB. It was my least enjoyable period in the group, some of the songs are great – some good writing. The Evil Jam (The Waiting Room) was the best thing, "Carpet Crawl" had a sought of feel about it. A few good things, but a bit laboured.

MR. A shame we didn't film it.

TB. That was a shame. We could have shown that twirly thing that went round, "The

Lamia", getting twisted up every bloody night (laughs). It was a pretty song and there's Pete fighting with this piece of gauze in the middle of the stage!

MR. It was a little restrictive in what we could play, as we always had some fun numbers in the set and we couldn't play them.

TB. I don't think it advanced our career in America at all. It was OK, but I don't think we won people over particularly. The album wasn't a great success, we have to be honest about this, it did alright and although some of the crowds were good, I don't remember it being as nearly as well received as the previous tour, because it didn't have as many good live songs. Some of the songs like "In The Cage" worked well live, but just kind of faded away, so you got most of your applause for "It" which wasn't the best of live songs.

MR. It was hard to play.

PR. Then of course there was the Slipperman.

TB. That's when we thought that the balance had gone the other way, I mean we were all involved with the slides and that was great fun, although the technology at that time was very limited so we couldn't always realise what we wanted to do.

MR. It was a sticky moment in our career, and coming back for the next one with Phil singing was much easier to do.

PR, The final *Lamb* show was not as originally billed, was it?

TB. The last show was in Besancon in France which was awful, and I think Poitiers and Toulouse were cancelled due to lack of interest, it was depressing anyhow.

MR. We did the second leg in Europe to try and make some money and pay some debts off, and of course we lost even more money (laughs).

TB. The crowds didn't come in France and I think the place where it went down best of all was England. With Peter leaving, again we were not sure what we were going to do, although we had made the decision we were going to try something, a lot of brave talking going on.

The interview ended with various live videos, including the Bataclan and Shepperton, being watched and laughed at.

IN PRAISE OF OLDER MELLOTRONS A PERSONAL COMMENT

I am a Mellotron fanatic. There I've said it now and I don't feel guilty in anyway, whatsoever. I bought my first one from a long-forgotten music shop in a part exchange deal with a string synth and fifty quid. It weighed a ton would hardly fit in the car and didn't sound anything like "In The Court of The Crimson King".

That first beast was eventually sold to a vicar from Birmingham, 'The Rev' for it was he, who was also a 'tron' maniac and a big Strawbs fan to boot. The church organ tapes on that one were right up his street.

My next beast was another 'white 400' model and in much better condition. It sounds great with some reverb through an old Marshall lead amp and cabinet. It currently resides in my dining room and I switch it on every so often. I recently found a dodgy video tape of said machine on stage in a London pub, being manhandled by yours truly as part of a slightly proggy band called Mage. (Where are you Mr Shutes?)

In the early years I used to hunt down vinyl that listed the Mellotron whether or not I knew who the artist was, I spent many a Saturday morning scouring record stalls in the local market for the next fix, it always seemed to work as I can't think of any really bad 'Tron' albums.

Genesis of course were up there with King Crimson, Yes, Greenslade, Barclay James Harvest, Strawbs, and all the other great 'Tron' bands but the undisputed heavyweights were the Moody Blues, Their seven albums from '67-'72 are essential masterpieces and should be in any 'tron' collection. Mike Pinder is the Godfather when it comes to spine tingling washes of sound, those albums still blow me away and no one has come close to getting the sounds he did.

With the advent of the synthesizer the mighty Tron started to vanish from the Prog Rock arena – the musicians generally hated their unreliability and untimely habit of packing up on stage, roadies hated the backbreaking work involved. The trouble was of course that the sound was so unique it could not be replaced, so in came lots a tinny sounding string synths and out went the mighty 'Tron'

This eventually sounded the death knell for the classic Prog Rock album, check out a band after they became Tron-less and put the theory into practice.

The recordings reviewed in this book are mostly packed with some of the best Mellotron-ship you will ever hear, Tony Banks is one of the few who really mastered the subtleties of the great beast and didn't just crank out the power chords, although a fired up 400 filling the hall with those opening bars from "Watcher of the Skies" does take some beating.

Paul Russell

GENESIS TOP TEN TIME

I can safely say that I have listened to more Gabriel era bootlegs than most. I of course had an unfair advantage and some shows reviewed here will most likely never be available. But seeing as everyone likes a good list I will endeavour to pick out ten shows for the list-lovers to argue about, so in no particular order we have:

1. Watford Tech, Mar 4th, 1972 – Nice sound and performance, great track listing.

2. Pavia Palsport Italy, April 14th, 1972 – Fantastic atmosphere and that version of "Can Utility", full blown Mellotron mayhem.

3. Bradford St Georges Hall, Oct 11th, 1972 – Short but very sweet topped by a thunderous "Weed".

4. The Rainbow Theatre, London Feb 9th, 1973 – Muddy recording of full-on performance, "Supper's" is scary.

5. LA Roxy, Dec 19th, 1973 – The late show is an absolute cracker, from start to finish Collins is on fire, whilst Gabriel freaks out L.A.

6. Rome Palasport, Feb 5th, 1974 – 20,000 go mad in Italy. The sound is massive "Supper's Ready" brings the house down.

7. Providence Palace Theatre, Dec 8th, 1974 – stunning sound quality and a very good all round performance. Hackett shines.

8. Rheims Palais des Sport, May 15th, 1975 – A true audience recording, massive sound very spooky "Waiting Room".

9. Lugo Hit Parade, Italy, April 15th, 1972 – "Stagnation" is spellbinding, "Salmacis" is vintage Genesis at its best.

10. Le Ferme, Belgium, Mar 7th, 1971 – Historic recording rough and not quite ready, "The Light" and "Going Out to Get You" make it a must have.

THE AUDIO FAKES

As with all live recordings there are Genesis shows in circulation that are not what they seem. The wrong date the wrong venue, sometimes both, some times the same recording is listed as several different shows.

The following selection is never going to be definitive but it should give the collector a good idea of what to look out for, and what not to get too excited about.

This list is bound to get some collectors shaking their fists at the page and shouting 'he's wrong, this tape is genuine', they might well be right which is why my address will not be appearing in this publication.

There are a couple of left over shows whose origin I am not sure about, so perhaps on a rainy day when I have nothing to do …

INCORRECT DATE & VENUE		CORRECT DATE & VENUE	
May 6th 1971	Marquee Club	Sep 19th 1972	Marquee Club.
Nov 22nd 1971	Watford Tech	Mar 4th 1972	Watford Tech
Jan 7th 1972	Bradford Tech	Oct 11th 1972	Bradford, St Georges Hall
Jan 16th 1972	Charleroi Festival	Jan 23rd 1972	Palais des Beaux Arts
Jun 16th 1972	Aylesbury, Friars	Jun 28th 1972	Watford Town Hall
Jun 26th 1972	Paris, Olympia Theatre	Sep 30th 1972	Kennington Oval
Sep 30th 1972	Paris, Olympia Theatre	Sep 19th 1973	Paris, Olympia Theatre
Oct 4th 1972	Aberdeen Music Hall	Sep 19th 1972	London, Marquee Club (Real Oct 4 exists)
Oct 30th 1972	Oval Hyde Park	Sep 30th 1972	Kennington Oval
Oct 30th 1972	Edmonton, Cooksferry Inn	Sep 30th 1972	Kennington Oval
Nov 10th 1972	London, Marquee Club	Sep 19th 1972	London, Marquee Club
Dec 17th 1972	New York, Philharmonic Hall	Feb 24th 1973	Manchester, Free Trade Hall
Feb 12th 1973	Plymouth Guild Hall	Dec 20th 1973	Midnight Special (2 tks)
Mar 8th 1973	Carneige Hall, USA	A dodgy version of the Genesis Live album	
July 6th 1973	Paris, ORTF Studios	Feb 12th 1974	Paris, TV Show
Oct 16th 1973	Bristol, Colston Hall	Jan 13th 1974	Bristol, Colston Hall
Nov 11th 1973	Buffalo, State University	Dec 1st 1973	Buffalo, State University
Dec 12th 1973	Miami, Gusman Hall	Mar 9th 1974	Miami, Gusman Hall
Apr 17th 1974	Evanston McGraw Hall	Dec 3rd 1973	Chicago, Kahn Auditorium
Apr 18th 1974	Quebec Centre de Congress	Nov 7th 1973	Quebec, Capitol Theatre
Apr 27th 1974	Buffalo, State University	Dec 3rd 1973	Chicago, Kahn Auditorium
Apr 29th 1974	Cleveland, Allen Theatre	Apr 28th 1974	Cleveland, Allen Theatre
Jun 23rd 1974	Wembley Arena	Apr 15th 1975	Wembley, Empire Pool
Oct 29th 1974	Newcastle City Hall	Dec 7th 1974	New York
Jan 29th 1975	San Diego	Jan 11th 1975	Florida, Lakeland
Feb 19th 1975	Norway, Oslo	Apr 15th 1975	Wembley Empire Pool
Feb 26th 1975	France, Cambrai	Mar 3rd 1975	Paris, Porte de Versailles
Mar 1st 1975	Dijon, Palais des Sports	Mar 3rd 1975	Paris, Porte de Versailles
Mar 2nd 1975	St Etienne, Palais des Sports	Mar 3rd 1975	Paris, Porte de Versailles
Apr 12th 1975	Connecticut, USA	Jan 11th 1975	Florida, Lakeland
Apr 24th 1975	Newcastle City Hall	Dec 7th 1974	New York, Academy
May 21st 1975	France,Cambrai	Feb 26th 1975	France, Cambrai
May 27th 1975	St Etienne, Palais des Sports	Mar 3rd 1975	Paris, Porte de Versailles

GENESIS LIVE – AS IT WAS

A fantasy live compilation possibly released on the 'Not Bloody Likely' label

CD1

01. HAPPY THE MAN	Rome Piper Club Italy Apr 18th 1972
02. HARLEQUIN	Watford Tech UK Mar 4th 1972
03. STAGNATION	Lugo di Ravenna Italy Apr 15th 1972
05. THE FOUNTAIN OF SALMACIS	Rome Palasport Italy Jan 21st 1973
06. ROCK ME BABY	Verona LEM Club Italy Apr 9th 1972
07. THE RETURN OF THE GIANT HOGWEED	Newcastle City Hall UK Feb 22nd 1973
08. SEVEN STONES	Genoa Teatro Alicone Italy Aug 22nd 1972
09. TWILIGHT ALEHOUSE	Reading Festival UK Aug 8th 1972
10. THE MUSICAL BOX	Medford Tufts University USA Nov 17th 1973

CD2

01. WATCHER OF THE SKIES	Rome Palasport Italy Feb 5th 1974
02. GET'EM OUT BY FRIDAY	London Lewisham Odeon UK Oct 29th 1972
03. SUPPER'S READY	New York Academy of Music USA May 4th 1974
04. DANCING WITH THE MOONLIT KNIGHT	Los Angeles Roxy USA Dec 19th 1973 (2nd show)
05. FIRTH OF FIFTH	Boston Music Hall USA Apr 24th 1974
06. HAROLD THE BARREL	Reggio Emilia Palasport Italy Feb 4th 1974
07. I KNOW WHAT I LIKE	Detroit Ford Auditorium USA Apr 16th 1974
08. THE CINEMA SHOW	New York Felt Forum USA Nov 20th 1973

CD3.

01. THE LAMB LIES DOWN…	Oklahoma Music Hall USA Jan 19th 1975
02. FLY ON A WINDSHIELD	Groningen Martinihal Centrum Holland Apr 10th 1975
03. IN THE CAGE	Cambrai Palais des Grottes France Feb 26th 1975
04. THE GRAND PARADE..	Liverpool Empire Theatre UK Apr 19th 1975
05. BACK IN NYC	Nurnburg Messezentrum Germany Mar 27th 1975
06. HAIRLESS HEART	Providence Palace Theatre USA Dec 8th 1974
07. CARPET CRAWL	Kansas Market Square USA Dec 14th 1974
08. CHAMBER OF 32 DOORS	London Wembley Empire Pool UK Apr 15th 1975
09. THE WAITING ROOM	Rheims Palais des Sports France May 15th 1975
10. THE LAMIA	Wiesbaden Rhein am Main Halle Ger May 12th 1975
11. THE COLONY OF SLIPPERMEN	Dortmund Westfalenhalle Ger Apr 7th 1975
12. RIDING THE SCREE	Dusseldorf Philipshalle Ger April 6th 1975
13. IN THE RAPIDS	Oslo Ekerberghallen Norway Feb 19th 1975
14. IT	Dijon Palais des Sports France Mar 1st 1975
15. THE KNIFE	Birmingham Hippodrome UK May 2nd 1975

GENESIS GIG LIST 1969-1975

Compiled from many sources, including Pete Morton, the Official Genesis website and Phil Collins.
Shows depicted in bold are reviewed in the book.

Date	Venue	Town/city	County/state	Country	Comments
23/09/69	Mrs Balmes Dance	Chobham	Surrey	UK	Private Party
01/11/69	**Brunel University,**	**Acton**	**London**	**UK**	**First 'proper' gig**
15/11/69	Technical College	Twickenham	Middlesex	UK	
23/11/69	Kingston Hotel	Kingston	Surrey	UK	
14/12/69	Worley Social Club	Birmingham	West Midlands	UK	
16/12/69	Cheadle Hulme Social Club	Manchester	Gtr Manchester	UK	
00/12/69	Brunel University	Uxbridge	Middlesex	UK	Support to Fairport Convention
00/12/69	Technical College	Twickenham	Middlesex	UK	
00/12/69	Kingston Hotel	Kingston	Surrey	UK	Support to Piblokto
00/12/69	Rolleston Youth Club	Rolleston		UK	
00/12/69	Eel Pie Island	Twickenham	Middlesex	UK	Genesis were paid £5 to perform
04/01/70	Haverstock Hill Country Club		London	UK	
17/01/70	Technical College	Watford	Hertfordshire	UK	Support to Spirit of John Morgan
24/01/70	Technical College	Ewell	Surrey	UK	Support to Atomic Rooster & Nick Drake
28/01/70	Technical College	Kingston	Surrey	UK	
29/01/70	Technical College	Leicester	Leicestershire	UK	
30/01/70	Locarno Ballroom	Sunderland	Tyne and Wear	UK	
04/02/70	Queen Mary College	London		UK	Band played two shows
12/02/70	Brunel University	Uxbridge	Middlesex	UK	
13/02/70	Technical College	Uxbridge	Middlesex	UK	Support to John Bummer Band
14/02/70	The Dome	Brighton	Sussex	UK	Support to T-Rex
15/02/70	Kingston Hotel	Kingston	Surrey	UK	
00/02/70	Hurlingham Tennis Club		London	UK	
22/02/70	**BBC Studio No. 4,**	**Maida Vale**	**London**	**UK**	**Nightride Session**
25/02/70	Revolution Club		London	UK	
26/02/70	Blaises Club		London	UK	
27/02/70	Brunel University	Uxbridge	Middlesex	UK	
28/02/70	Essex University	Colchester	Essex	UK	
01/03/70	Farx Club	Southall	Middlesex	UK	Support to Mott The Hoople
02/03/70	The Mistrale Club	Beckenham	Kent	UK	
03/03/70	Ronnie Scott's Club		London	UK	
10/03/70	Ronnie Scott's Club		London	UK	
11/03/70	**The Roundhouse**	**Chalk Farm**	**London**	**UK**	**Support to David Bowie (filmed)**
14/03/70	Technical College	Watford	Hertfordshire	UK	Support to Atomic Rooster
17/03/70	Ronnie Scott's Club		London	UK	
22/03/70	Farx Club	Southall	Middlesex	UK	
24/03/70	Ronnie Scott's Club		London	UK	
31/03/70	Ronnie Scott's Club		London	UK	
07/04/70	Ronnie Scott's Club		London	UK	
09/04/70	The Cooksferry Inn		London	UK	
10/04/70	**Eel Pie Island**	**Twickenham**	**Middlesex**	**UK**	
11/04/70	Central Hall	Chatham	Kent	UK	Support to Deep Purple
13/04/70	Friars Club	Aylesbury	Buckinghamshire	UK	Band played two shows
14/04/70	Ronnie Scott's Club		London	UK	
17/04/70	The Temple		London	UK	
18/04/70	Farx Club	Potters Bar	Hertfordshire	UK	
19/04/70	The One Oak Inn	Camberley	Surrey	UK	
25/04/70	Imperial College		London	UK	
05/05/70	Ronnie Scott's Club		London	UK	
08/05/70	Elliott College	Canterbury	Kent	UK	
09/05/70	Ronnie Scott's Club		London	UK	
16/05/70	Great Hall, Surrey University	Guildford	Surrey	UK	
24/05/70	Marque Club		London	UK	
06/06/70	Lyceum Theatre		London	UK	
14/06/70	Marquee Club		London	UK	
15/06/70	Borough Assembly Room	Aylesbury	Buckinghamshire	UK	
20/06/70	Carlshalton College	Carlshalton	Surrey	UK	
23/06/70	Ronnie Scott's Club		London	UK	
27/06/70	Surrey University	Guildford	Surrey	UK	Free Festival, Afternoon Show
27/06/70	Technical College, Hackney		London	UK	Evening Show
28/06/70	Farx Club	Southall	Middlesex	UK	
30/06/70	Ronnie Scott's Club		London	UK	
03/07/70	College For Distributive Trades		London	UK	
09/07/70	Kingston Polytechnic	Kingston	Surrey	UK	
11/07/70	St. Joans	Rickmansworth	Hertfordshire	UK	
17/07/70	Star Hotel	Croydon	Surrey	UK	
18/07/70	King's Arms, Haywards Heath		Surrey	UK	Anthony Phillips' last show
06/08/70	Gaumont Cinema	Doncaster	South Yorkshire	UK	

Genesis

08/08/70	Parish Hall	Dudley	West Midlands	UK	
13/08/70	Central Methodist Hall	Coventry	West Midlands	UK	
27/08/70	Transport House	Bristol	Avon	UK	
28/08/70	New Imperial Hotel	Birmingham	West Midlands	UK	
29/08/70	Metropole Hotel	Colwyn Bay	Conwy	UK	
30/08/70	Marquee Club		London	UK	
03/09/70	Assembly Rooms	Rotherham	South Yorkshire	UK	
10/09/70	The Polytechnic	Huddersfield	West Yorkshire	UK	
17/09/70		Wakefield	West Yorkshire	UK	
02/10/70	Medway Technical College	Chatham	Kent	UK	Phil Collins' first show
03/10/70	Technical College	Farnborough	Hampshire	UK	With Bram Stoker
04/10/70	Marquee Club		London	UK	Support to Stackridge
06/10/70	British Legion Hall	Princes Ris'boro	Buckinghamshire	UK	Ronnie Caryl on Guitar
07/10/70	Birdcage Club	Harlow	Essex	UK	
08/10/70	ABC Theatre	Blackpool	Lancashire	UK	
09/10/70	Club Liscard	Wallasey	Merseyside	UK	
10/10/70	Corn Exchange	Colchester	Essex	UK	
13/10/70	Fishmongers Arms,	Wood Green	London	UK	Support to Trapeze
16/10/70	Rex Cinema	Cambridge	Suffolk	UK	Support to Matthews Southern Comfort
23/10/70	Friars Club Addison Centre	Bedford	Bedfordshire	UK	Support to Medicine Head
03/11/70	Resurrection Club	Hitchin	Hertfordshire	UK	Mick Barnard on guitar
06/11/70	University	Salford	Grt Manchester	UK	Support to Curved Air
07/11/70	Brunel University, Uxbridge		London	UK	Support to Argent
08/11/70	Eyes Club	Chelmsford	Essex	UK	
10/11/70	Marquee Club		London	UK	Support to Jackson Heights
13/11/70	Kent University	Canterbury	Kent	UK	Support to Fairport Convention
14/11/70	Technical College	Watford	Hertfordshire	UK	Support to Steamhammer
14/11/70	BBC Studio Disco Two		London	UK	"The Knife" mimed Peter sings live, lost
20/11/70	Herriott Watt College	Edinburgh		UK	
21/11/70	Gamp? Club	Edinburgh		UK	
22/11/70	Kinema Ballroom	Dunfermline		UK	
25/11/70	Resurrection Club	Hitchin	Hertfordshire	UK	Support to National Head Band
26/11/70	Dead End Club	Blackpool	Lancashire	UK	
27/11/70	Neville's Cross College	Durham		UK	
28/11/70	Imperial College		London	UK	With Van der Graaf Generator
29/11/70	Farx Club, Northcote Arms	Southall	Middlesex	UK	
30/11/70	Youth Club	Letchworth	Hertfordshire	UK	
04/12/70	College of Education	Worcester	Worcestershire	UK	
06/12/70	Mother's Club	Birmingham	West Midlands	UK	Support to Rare Bird
09/12/70	Marquee Club		London	UK	Charisma Xmas Party
11/12/70	Café Royal		London	UK	Support to East of Eden
16/12/70	Grammar School	Aylesbury	Buckinghamshire	UK	
17/12/70	Civic College	Ipswich	Suffolk	UK	
18/12/70	Hatton Centre			UK	
19/12/70	Wintergardens	Cleethorps	Lincolnshire	UK	
20/12/70	Angel Hotel	Godalming	Surrey	UK	
28/12/70	Lyceum Theatre		London	UK	Steve Hackett attends show
03/01/71	University Arts Laboratory	Manchester	Gtr Manchester	UK	
08/01/71	Slough College	Slough	Berkshire	UK	Support to Hawkwind
09/01/71	Technical College	Ewell	Surrey	UK	Support to Kevin Ayers and Queen
10/01/71	Farx Club	Southall	Middlesex	UK	
14/01/71	University College		London	UK	Steve Hackett's first gig
15/01/71	Technical College	High Wycombe	Buckinghamshire	UK	
17/01/71	Tower Theatre	Blackpool	Lancashire	UK	
19/01/71	Assembly Rooms	Derby	Derbyshire	UK	
22/01/71	City University	London		UK	Support to Steamhammer
24/01/71	Lyceum Theatre	London		UK	Start of Charisma tour with Van der Graaf Generator & Lindisfarne
25/01/71	Town Hall	Birmingham	West Midlands	UK	
26/01/71	Colston Hall	Bristol	Avon	UK	Afternoon gig
26/01/71	Town Hall	Watford	Hertfordshire	UK	Evening gig. Support to Johnny Winter
27/01/71	City Hall	Sheffield	Yorkshire	UK	
28/01/71	St George's Hall	Bradford	Yorkshire	UK	
30/01/71	Free Trade Hall	Manchester		UK	
31/01/71	City Hall	Newcastle	Tyne and Wear	UK	
05/02/71	?	Hatton	Aberdeenshire	UK	
06/02/71	Frias Club	Aylesbury	Buckinghamshire	UK	
09/02/71	Rainbow Theatre		London	UK	
11/02/71	The Dome	Brighton	Sussex	UK	
13/02/71	Winter Gardens	Bournemouth	Hampshire	UK	
18/02/71	City Hall	Hull	Yorkshire	UK	
20/02/71	University	Southampton	Hampshire	UK	
22/02/71	Colston Hall	Bristol	Avon	UK	
23/02/71	Blaises Club		London	UK	Support to Paladin
25/02/71	Mountford Hall	Liverpool	Merseyside	UK	
28/02/71	University	Durham		UK	

04/03/71	Tower Theatre	Blackpool	Lancashire	UK	
05/03/71	University Great Hall	York	Yorkshire	UK	
06/03/71	Lyceum Theatre	Birmingham		UK	Support to Steamhammer
07/03/71	**La Ferme**	**Woluwe St Lambert**		**Belgium**	**Band's first overseas gig**
08/03/71	TV Studios	Brussels		Belgium	
09/03/71	TV Studios	Brussels		Belgium	
13/03/71	University Great Hall		Essex	UK	Support to Curved Air
00/03/71	East Street Hall	London		UK	
00/03/71	Sophia Gardens	Cardiff		UK	
02/04/71	Dacorum College,	HHempstead	Hertfordshire	UK	
03/04/71	Technical College	Farnborough	Surrey	UK	
00/04/71	?	Godalming	Surrey	UK	
09/04/71	Lyceum Theatre	London		UK	with Van der Graaf Generator, Audience, Bell and Arc, Patto
11/04/71	Fairfield Hall	Croydon	Greater London	UK	Start of 'Six Bob Tour' with Van der Graaf Generator, Lindisfarne, Bell and Arc.
13/04/71	Guild Hall	Portsmouth	Hampshire	UK	
15/04/71	Civic Hall	Guildford	Surrey	UK	
22/04/71	Floral Hall	Southport	Merseyside	UK	
23/04/71	Greens Play House	Glasgow		UK	
24/04/71	Caird Hall	Dundee		UK	
25/04/71	Caley Cinema	Edinburgh		UK	
26/04/71	Free Trade Hall	Manchester		UK	
30/04/71	Arts College	Kingston	Surrey	UK	
01/05/71	Resurrection Club	Hitchin	Hertfordshire	UK	
04/05/71	Guildhall	Portsmouth	Hampshire	UK	
06/05/71	Marquee Club		London	UK	
07/05/71	University of East Anglia	Norwich	Suffolk	UK	
08/05/71	Clarences	Halifax	Yorkshire	UK	
10/05/71	**BBC Studios, Shepherds Bush**		**London**	**UK**	**Sounds of the 70s**
21/05/71	Youth Centre	Bletchley	Yorkshire	UK	
22/05/71	Hydraspace	Watford	Hertfordshire	UK	
04/06/71	TV Studios	Brussels		Belgium	Pop Shop
05/06/71	TV Studios	Brussels		Belgium	
06/06/71	TV Studios	Brussels		Belgium	
08/06/71	Lyceum Theatre		London	UK	
12/06/71	Queen Margaret College	Edinburgh		UK	
18/06/71	Cheltenham Girls College	Cheltenham	Gloucestershire	UK	
19/06/71	**Friars Club**	**Aylesbury**	**Buckingshire**	**UK**	**Peter Gabriel breaks his ankle at gig**
22/06/71	Kingston Hall	Watford	Hertfordshire	UK	
26/06/71	Reading Festival	Reading	Berkshire	UK	
02/07/71	Friars Club Addison Centre	Bedford	Bedfordshire	UK	
03/07/71	Farx Club	Southall	Middlesex	UK	
09/07/71	Marquee Club		London	UK	
14/07/71	Lyceum Theatre		London	UK	
07/08/71	Jemelle	Brussels		Belgium	
08/08/71	Jemelle	Brussels		Belgium	
28/08/71	Weeley Festival	Clacton on Sea	Essex	UK	with VdGG, King Crimson,
05/09/71	Pavillion	H Hempstead	Hertfordshire	UK	
16/09/71	New Lord Lee Civic Centre	Gravesend	Kent	UK	
18/09/71	The Temple		London	UK	
22/09/71	Surrey Rooms		London	UK	
23/09/71	Kensington Town Hall		London	UK	
25/09/71	Sevens The Leas	Letchworth	Hertfordshire	UK	
09/10/71	Kingham Hall	Watford	Hertfordshire	UK	
12/10/71	William Street Club	Windsor	Berkshire	UK	
14/10/71	Lyceum Theatre		London	UK	start of Charisma tour with VdGG, Lindisfarne,Bell & Arc, Audience
16/10/71	Guildhall	Preston	Lancashire	UK	
19/10/71	The Halls	Dorking	Surrey	UK	
21/10/71	Town Hall	Oxford	Oxfordshire	UK	
22/10/71	University Great Hall	Exeter	Devon	UK	
23/10/71	University of Essex		Essex	UK	
26/10/71	GuildHall	Southampton	Hampshire	UK	
27/10/71	Town Hall	Birmingham	West Midlands	UK	
28/10/71	City Hall	Newcastle	Tyne and Wear	UK	
29/10/71	Lake Hall	Birmingham	West Midlands	UK	
31/10/71	Guildhall	Plymouth	Hampshire	UK	
01/11/71	The Dome	Brighton	Sussex	UK	
02/11/71	Starlight Club	Crawley	Surrey	UK	
03/11/71	Kings Hall	Derby	Derbyshire	UK	
04/11/71	Tower Theatre	Blackpool	Lancashire	UK	
06/11/71	College of Technology	Slough	Berkshire	UK	support to Redwing
07/11/71	City Hall	Salisbury	Wiltshire	UK	
19/11/71	Community Centre	Slough	Berkshire	UK	
20/11/71	Sevens The Leas	Letchworth	Hertfordshire	UK	
22/11/71	Surrey Rooms		London	UK	

24/11/71	Lyceum Theatre		London	UK	support to Lindisfarne
25/11/71	Corn Exchange	Cambridge	Cambridgeshire	UK	
26/11/71	Eton College	Windsor	Berkshire	UK	
28/11/71	City Hall	Newcastle	Tyne and Wear	UK	
30/11/71	City Hall	Sheffield	Yorkshire	UK	
02/12/71	Lyceum Theatre		London	UK	support to Lindisfarne
03/12/71	Red Lion, Leytonstone		London	UK	
04/12/71	Lawns Centre	Cottingham	Northamptonshire	UK	
07/12/71	Hobbits Garden	Wimbledon	London	UK	supported by Roxy Music
08/12/71	Technical College	Kings Lynn	Norfolk	UK	
09/12/71	Teeside Polytechnic		Middlesborough	UK	
10/12/71	Culham College	Abingdon	Oxfordshire	UK	
11/12/71	Cranbrook School	Cranbrook	Kent	UK	
12/12/71	Windrush Club	High Wycombe	Buckinghamshire	UK	
15/12/71	Big Brother Club	Greenford	Middlesex	UK	
16/12/71	Grammar School	Weymouth	Dorset	UK	
21/12/71	South Parade Pier	Portsmouth	Hampshire	UK	
23/12/71	Hydraspace Kingham Hall	Watford	Hertfordshire	UK	
01/01/72	The Roundhouse	Dagenham	Essex	UK	
07/01/72	Technical College	Bradford	Yorkshire	UK	
08/01/72	Baths Hall	Epsom	Surrey	UK	
09/01/72	**BBC Studios Shepherds Bush**		**London**	**UK**	**John Peel session**
15/01/72	Technical College	Cambridge	Cambridgeshire	UK	
19/01/72	College of Education	Coventry	West Midlands	UK	
20/01/72	St Johns College	Manchester		UK	
22/01/72	L'Athenee Royal de Woluwe	St Pierre	Brussels	Belgium	
23/01/72	**Palais des Beaux Arts**	**Charleroi**		**Belgium**	
24/01/72	Trocadero	Liege		Belgium	
27/01/72	Toby Jug	Tolworth	Surrey	UK	
28/01/72	Town Hall	High Wycombe	Buckinghamshire	UK	
29/01/72	Surrey Univeristy	Guildford	Surrey	UK	
30/01/72	The Black Prince	Bexleyheath	Kent	UK	
04/02/72	Queen Elizabeth Hall	London		UK	support to Lindisfarne
05/02/72	College of Technology	Luton	Bedfordshire	UK	
06/02/72	Lancing College		Sussex	UK	
11/02/71	Winter Gardens	Penzance	Cornwall	UK	
12/02/72	Van Dyke Club	Plymouth	Hampshire	UK	
14/02/72	University College of Wales	Aberystwyth	Ceredigion	UK	
17/02/72	City Hall	Sheffield	South Yorkshire	UK	
18/02/72	Medway College	Maidstone	Kent	UK	cancelled due to power cut
19/02/72	Alex Disco	Salisbury	Wiltshire	UK	
20/02/72	Greyhound	Croydon	Surrey	UK	
21/02/72	Winter Gardens	Cleethorpes	Lincolnshire	UK	
23/02/72	Polytechnic	Leicester	Leicestershire	UK	
24/02/72	Town Hall	High Wycombe	Buckinghamshire	UK	
25/02/72	Lorcano Ballroom	Sunderland	Tyne and Wear	UK	
26/02/72	Sports Centre	Bracknell	Berkshire	UK	
01/03/72	Civic Centre	Chelmsford	Essex	UK	
02/03/72	**BBC Paris Studios**		**London**	**UK**	
04/03/72	**Technical College**	**Watford**	**Hertfordshire**	**UK**	
10/03/72	South Parade Pier	Portsmouth	Hampshire	UK	
11/03/72	Friars Club	Aylesbury	Buckinghamshire	UK	
16/03/72	Princes Theatre	Hull	Yorkshire	UK	
17/03/72	Aston University	Birmingham	West Midlands	UK	
18/03/72	Fete Saint Gratien	Troyes		Belgium	
20/03/72	**TV Studios**	**Brussels**		**Belgium**	**Pop Shop**
21/03/72	**TV Studios**	**Brussels**		**Belgium**	**Pop Shop**
24/03/72	Essex University	Chelmsford	Essex	UK	
25/03/72	Carshalton College	Carshalton	Surrey	UK	
06/04/72	Palasport	Belluno		Italy	
07/04/72	Apollo 2000	Treviso		Italy	
08/04/72	Dancing Paradiso	Trieste		Italy	cancelled by the police
09/04/72	**LEM Club**	**Verona**		**Italy**	**2 shows**
10/04/72	Palasport	Pesaro		Italy	
12/04/72	Palasport	Reggio Emilia		Italy	
13/04/72	Dancing Le Rotonde	Courgne Turin		Italy	
14/04/72	**Palasport**	**Pavia**		**Italy**	**2 shows**
15/04/72	**Hit Parade**	**Lugo di Romagna**		**Italy**	**2 shows**
16/04/72	Supertivoli	Travagliato,	Brescia	Italy	2 shows
17/04/72	Palasport	Siena		Italy	
18/04/72	**Piper Club**	**Rome**		**Italy**	**2 shows (radio & TV)**
19/04/72	**Teatro Mediterraneo**	**Naples**		**Italy**	**2 shows**
22/04/72	Festival	Arlon	Brussels	Belgium	
23/04/72	Zoom Club	Frankfurt		Germany	
25/04/72	Greyhound	Croydon	Surrey	UK	
26/04/72	Van Dyke Club	Plymouth	Devon	UK	
28/04/72	Polytechnic	Kingston	Surrey	UK	

Date	Venue	City	County	Country	Notes
29/04/72	Polytechnic	Isleworth	Surrey	UK	
30/04/72	Civic Hall	Guildford	Surrey	UK	
05/05/72	Red Lion, Leytonstone		London	UK	
06/05/72	University	Bangor	Gwynedd	UK	
08/05/72	Essex University	Chelmsford	Essex	UK	
09/05/72	Town Hall	Oxford	Oxfordshire	UK	
11/05/72	Cleopatra's	Derby	Derbyshire	UK	
19/05/72	Mecca Ballroom	Newcastle	Tyne and Wear	UK	
20/05/72	City Hall	St Albans	Hertfordshire	UK	
21/05/72	Youth Centre	Bletchley	Buckinghamshire	UK	
25/05/72	Winter Gardens	Penzance	Cornwall	UK	
26/05/72	Van Dyke Club	Plymouth	Devon	UK	
27/05/72	Technical College	Farnborough	Hampshire	UK	
28/05/72	Great Western Festival	Lincoln	Lincolnshire	UK	VdGG, Beach Boys, Monty Python, Joe Cocker, Status Quo, Sandy Denny
02/06/72	The Pier	Hastings	Sussex	UK	
03/06/72	Technical College	Luton	Bedfordshire	UK	
04/06/72	Lyceum Theatre	London		UK	
06/06/72	The Rock Club	Wellingborough	Northamptonshire	UK	
09/06/72	Polytechnic	Leeds	Yorkshire	UK	
11/06/72	Argus Butterfly	Peterlee	Durham	UK	
12/06/72	Corn Exchange	Cambridge	Cambridgeshire	UK	
16/06/72	Friars Club	Bedford	Bedfordshire	UK	
17/06/72	The Rock Club	Wellingborough	Northamptonshire	UK	
19/06/72	Top Rank	Swansea	Glamorgan	UK	
23/06/72	Durham Castle	Durham	Durham	UK	
24/06/72	Pier Pavillion	Felixstowe	Suffolk	UK	
26/06/72	Olympia	Paris		France	
28/06/72	**Town Hall**	**Watford**	**Hertfordshire**	**UK**	
29/06/72	Shoreditch Town Hall	London		UK	
30/06/72	Community Centre	Slough	Berkshire	UK	
02/07/72	The Greyhound	Croydon	Greater London	UK	
07/07/72	Carre Hotel	Amsterdam		Holland	
08/07/72	Carre Hotel	Amsterdam		Holland	
14/07/72	Lyceum Theatre		London	UK	with Audience, Capability Brown
16/07/72	Coatham Hotel	Redcar	Yorkshire	UK	
21/07/72	"Red Lion, Leytonstone"	London		UK	
22/07/72	Alex Disco	Salisbury	Wiltshire	UK	
23/07/72	The Wake Arms	Epping	Essex	UK	
25/07/72	Civic Hall	Solihull	Yorkshire	UK	
27/07/72	Winter Gardens	Cleethorpes	Lincolnshire	UK	
28/07/72	Archer Hall	Billericay	Essex	UK	
11/08/72	**Reading Festival**	**Reading**	**Berkshire**	**UK**	
15/08/72	Palasport	Reggio Emilia		Italy	
16/08/72	Corte Malatestana	Fano		Italy	
18/08/72	Dancing Lago delle Rose	Monselice		Italy	
19/08/72	Jolly Club	Ravenna		Italy	two shows
20/08/72	**Piper 2000 Club**	**Viareggio**		**Italy**	**afternoon show**
20/08/72	**Piper 2000 Club**	**Viareggio**		**Italy**	**evening show**
21/08/72	Palasport	Albegna		Italy	
22/08/72	**Teatro Alcione**	**Genoa**		**Italy**	
23/08/72	La Locanda del Lupo	Rimini		Italy	two shows
01/09/72	Civic Hall	Merton		UK	with Fruup
02/09/72	Friars Club	Aylesbury	Buckinghamshire	UK	
03/09/72	Chelsea Village	Bournemouth	Hampshire	UK	with Capability Brown
09/09/72	Seloncourt festival	Montbeliard		France	
13/09/72	Big Brother Club	Greenford	Middlesex	UK	
16/09/72	Bracknell Sports Centre	Bracknell	Berkshire	UK	
17/09/72	The Greyhound	Croydon	Greater London	UK	
19/09/72	**Marquee Club**		**London**	**UK**	
22/09/72	Friars Club	Aylesbury	Buckinghamshire	UK	
23/09/72	Tait Hall	Kelso		UK	
25/09/72	**BBC Studios, Shepherds Bush**		**London**	**UK**	**Sounds of the '70s**
28/09/72	**Dublin Stadium**	**Dublin**		**Ireland**	**with Lindisfarne**
29/09/72	Friars Club	Aylesbury	Buckinghamshire	UK	
30/09/72	**Kennington Oval**	**London**		**UK**	**Melody Maker poll awards, ELP etc.**
01/10/72	City Hall	Newcastle	Tyne and Wear	UK	
03/10/72	City Hall	Sheffield	Yorkshire	UK	support to Lindisfarne & Rab Noakes
04/10/72	**Music Hall**	**Aberdeen**		**UK**	**as above**
06/10/72	Greens Play House	Glasgow		UK	as above
07/10/72	Empire Theatre	Edinburgh		UK	as above
10/10/72	Free Trade Hall	Manchester	Gtr Manchester	UK	as above
11/10/72	**St George's Hall**	**Bradford**	**Yorkshire**	**UK**	**as above**
12/10/72	De Montfort Hall	Leicester	Leicestershire	UK	as above
13/10/72	Winter Gardens	Bournemouth	Hampshire	UK	as above
14/10/72	Kingston Polytechnic	Kingston	Surrey	UK	as above
15/10/72	Colosseum		London	UK	as above

16/10/72	Top Rank	Liverpool	Merseyside	UK	as above
17/10/72	City Hall	Hull	Yorkshire	UK	as above
18/10/72	Top Rank	Watford	Hertfordshire	UK	as above
19/10/72	Trentham Gardens	Stoke	Staffordshire	UK	as above
20/10/72	Top Rank	Bristol	Avon	UK	as above
21/10/72	New Theatre	Oxford	Oxfordshire	UK	as above
22/10/72	Guildhall	Preston	Lancashire	UK	as above
24/10/72	Guildhall	Portsmouth	Hampshire	UK	as above
25/10/72	Odeon Theatre	Birmingham		UK	as above
26/10/72	Top Rank	Cardiff		UK	as above
27/10/72	Top Rank	Brighton	Sussex	UK	as above
29/10/72	**Odeon Theatre**	**Lewisham**	**Kent**	**UK**	**as above**
30/10/72	Cooksferry Inn	Edmonton		UK	as above
02/11/72	Hard Rock Concert Theatre	Manchester	Gtr Manchester	UK	
03/11/72	Civic College	Ipswich	Suffolk	UK	
04/11/72	University	Leeds	Yorkshire	UK	
05/11/72	The Wake Arms	Epping	Essex	UK	
06/11/72	Winter Gardens	Cleethorpes	Lincolnshire	UK	
10/11/72	Brunel University	Uxbridge	Middlesex	UK	"""Supper's Ready"" premiered"
11/11/72	Alex Disco	Salisbury	Wiltshire	UK	
12/11/72	Fairfield Hall	Croydon	Surrey	UK	with Capability Brown
15/11/72	Civic Hall	Guildford	Surrey	UK	
17/11/72	Essex University	Chelmsford	Essex	UK	with Capability Brown
18/11/72	**Imperial College**		**London**	**UK**	**with String Driven Thing**
19/11/72	Town Hall	Cheltenham	Gloucestershire	UK	
24/11/72	Corn Exchange	King's Lynn	Norfolk	UK	
25/11/72	The Belfry Hotel	Sutton Coldfield	West Midlands	UK	
26/11/72	Lord's Club Civic Hall	Gravesend	Kent	UK	with Jumping Jack's Experiment
06/12/72	Sundown Club, Mile End		London	UK	with Capability Brown
07/12/72	Southampton University	Southampton	Hampshire	UK	
11/12/72	Guildhall	Plymouth	Devon	UK	
16/12/72	Brandeis University	Boston	Massachusetts	USA	first gig in USA
17/12/72	Philharmonic Hall	New York City	New York	USA	
19/12/72	Salle D' Expositions	Mulhouse		France	uncertain if gig took place
20/12/72	Salle Penfield	Strasbourg		France	as above
06/01/73	The Greyhound	Croydon	Greater London	UK	
07/01/73	Roundhouse	Dagenham	Essex	UK	
09/01/73	Place D' Hiver	Marseilles		France	
10/01/73	**Bataclan Club**	**Paris**		**France**	**TV Show**
13/01/73	Congresshalle	Hamburg		Germany	
14/01/73	**Festhalle**	**Frankfurt**		**Germany**	
15/01/73	**Stadhalle**	**Heidelberg**		**Germany**	
16/01/73	Stadhalle	Offenbach		Germany	
17/01/73	Philipshalle	Dusseldorf		Germany	
20/01/73	**Palasport**	**Reggio Emilia**		**Italy**	
21/01/73	**Palasport**	**Rome**		**Italy**	
02/02/73	Arts Festival	Lancaster	Lancashire	UK	
04/02/72	Hippodrome	Bristol	Avon	UK	with String Driven Thing
09/02/73	**Rainbow Theatre**	**London**		**UK**	**as above**
10/02/73	The Dome	Brighton	Sussex	UK	as above
12/02/73	Guildhall	Plymouth	Devon	UK	as above
14/02/73	University Great Hall	Exeter	Devon	UK	as above
16/02/73	**Greens Play House**	**Glasgow**		**UK**	**as above**
17/02/73	**City Hall**	**Sheffield**	**Yorkshire**	**UK**	**as above**
18/02/73	Town Hall	Birmingham	W. Midlands	UK	as above
19/02/73	New Theatre	Oxford	Oxfordshire	UK	as above
21/02/73	**Bishop Holgate School**	**York**	**Yorkshire**	**UK**	**as above**
22/02/73	**City Hall**	**Newcastle**	**Yorkshire**	**UK**	**as above**
23/02/73	University Great Hall	Lancaster	Lancashire	UK	as above
24/02/73	**Free Trade Hall**	**Manchester**	**Gtr Manchester**	**UK**	**as above**
25/02/73	**De Montfort Hall**	**Leicester**	**Leicestershire**	**UK**	**as above**
26/02/73	Civic Hall	Dunstable	Bedfordshire	UK	as above
01/03/73	USA Bob Harris Radio Show			USA	Venue not known
02/03/73	Carneige Hall	New York City	New York	USA	
03/03/73	**Grand Theatre**	**Quebec City**	**Quebec**	**Canada**	
04/03/73	Montreal Forum	Monteal	Quebec	Canada	
05/03/73	Gusman Hall	Miami	Florida	USA	
08/03/73	Carneige Hall	New York City	New York	USA	
10/03/73	Tower Theatre	Upper Darby	Pennsylvania	USA	
31/03/73	Seton Hall University	South Orange	New Jersey	USA	
02/04/73	Philharmonic Hall	New York City	New York	USA	
03/04/73	Philharmonic Hall	New York City	New York	USA	
06/04/73	Grand Theatre	Quebec City	Quebec	Canada	
08/04/73	Community Centre	Sherbrooke	Quebec	Canada	
09/04/73	Maple Leaf Gardens	Toronto	Ontario	Canada	
11/04/73	?	Rochester	New York	USA	
13/04/73	Alpine Arena	Pittsburg	Pennsylvania	USA	

14/04/73	Case Western University	Cleveland	Ohio	USA	
17/04/73	Henry Levitt Arena	Wichita	Kansas	USA	
20/04/73	Aragon Ballroom	Chicago	Illonois	USA	support to Richie Havens
22/04/73	Princeton University	Princeton		USA	
23/04/73	Brandeis University	Waltham		USA	
07/05/73	**Olympia Theatre**	**Paris**		**France**	**for French Musicorama radio show**
08/05/73	Ancienne Belgiquie	Brussels		Belgium	
06/07/73	Ortf TV Sessions	Paris		France	
07/07/73	Olympia Theatre	Paris		France	with Peter Hammill
26/08/73	**Reading Festival**	**Reading**	**Berkshire**	**UK**	
19/09/73	**Olympia Theatre**	**Paris**		**France**	
25/09/73	Munsterhaller	Munster		Germany	
26/09/73	Congresshaller	Hamberg		Germany	
27/09/73	?	Darmsdorff		Germany	
29/09/73	**Halle Des Fetes Beaujoire**	**Lausanne**		**Switzerland**	
30/09/73	Festhalle	Frankfurt		Germany	
05/10/73	Apollo Theatre	Glasgow		UK	
06/10/73	Opera House	Manchester		UK	
07/10/73	New Theatre	Oxford	Oxfordshire	UK	
09/10/73	**Apollo Theatre**	**Glasgow**		**UK**	
11/10/73	**Gaumont Theatre**	**Southampton**	**Hampshire**	**UK**	
12/10/73	Winter Gardens	Bournemouth	Hampshire	UK	
15/10/73	The Dome	Brighton	Sussex	UK	
16/10/73	Colston Hall	Bristol	Avon	UK	
18/10/73	De Montfort Hall	Leicester	Leicestershire	UK	
19/10/73	Rainbow Theatre	London		UK	
20/10/73	**Rainbow Theatre**	**London**		**UK**	
23/10/73	**Empire Theatre**	**Liverpool**	**Merseyside**	**UK**	
25/10/73	City Hall	Sheffield	Yorkshire	UK	
26/10/73	**City Hall**	**Newcastle**	**Tyne and Wear**	**UK**	
28/10/73	**Hippodrome**	**Birmingham**	**W. Midlands**	**UK**	
30/10/73	**Shepperton Film Studios**	**Shepperton**	**Surrey**	**UK**	
31/10/73	**Shepperton Film Studios**	**Shepperton**	**Surrey**	**UK**	
07/11/73	**Capitol Theatre**	**Quebec**	**Quebec**	**Canada**	
08/11/73	**Massey Hall**	**Toronto**	**Ontario**	**Canada**	
09/11/73	Queen's University	Kingston	Ontario	Canada	
10/11/73	**University Sports Arena**	**Montreal**	**Quebec**	**Canada**	
11/11/73	State University Auditorium	Buffalo	New York	USA	
13/11/73	Cosh Auditorium	Lawrence	Massachusetts	USA	
15/11/73	Tower Theatre	Upper Darby	Pennsylvania	USA	
17/11/73	**Tufts University**	**Medford**	**Oregon**	**USA**	
18/11/73	Bergen Community College	Paramus	New Jersey	USA	
22/11/73	**The Felt Forum**	**New York**	**New York**	**USA**	
24/11/73	McCarter Theatre,	University	Princeton	USA	
26/11/73	Gusman Hall	Miami	Florida	USA	
27/11/73	Institute of Technology	Rochester	New York	USA	
29/11/73	The Agora	Columbus	Ohio	USA	
30/11/73	The Allen Theatre	Cleveland	Ohio	USA	
01/12/73	**The State University New Gym**	**Buffalo**	**New York**	**USA**	
03/12/73	**North Western University**	**Chicago**	**Illonois**	**USA**	
07/12/73	Perdue Regional Ballroom	Fort Wayne	Indiana	USA	
08/12/73	**The Peace Auditorium**	**Ypsilanti**		**USA**	
09/12/73	The Hara Theatre	Tolido	Ohio	USA	
17/12/73	**Roxy Theatre**	**Los Angeles**	**California**	**USA**	**Early Show**
17/12/73	**Roxy Theatre**	**Los Angeles**	**California**	**USA**	**Late Show**
18/12/73	Roxy Theatre	Los Angeles	California	USA	Early Show
18/12/73	**Roxy Theatre**	**Los Angeles**	**California**	**USA**	**Late Show**
19/12/73	**Roxy Theatre**	**Los Angeles**	**California**	**USA**	**Early Show**
19/12/73	**Roxy Theatre**	**Los Angeles**	**California**	**USA**	**Late Show**
20/12/73	**The NBC Studios**	**Burbank**	**California**	**USA**	**TV Show - Midnight Special**
13/01/74	**Hippodrome Theatre**	**Bristol**	**Avon**	**UK**	
15/01/74	Theatre Royal Drury Lane		London	UK	
16/01/74	Theatre Royal Drury Lane		London	UK	
18/01/74	Theatre Royal Drury Lane		London	UK	
19/01/74	Theatre Royal Drury Lane		London	UK	
20/01/74	**Theatre Royal Drury Lane**		**London**	**UK**	
26/01/74	**Vorst Nationale**	**Brussels**		**Belgium**	
27/01/74	Congresshalle	Hamburg		Germany	
28/01/74	**Eulach Halle**	**Winterthur**		**Switzerland**	
29/01/74	Victoria Concerthalle	Geneva		Switzerland	
30/01/74	**Philipshalle**	**Dusseldorf**		**Germany**	
31/01/74	**Stadhalle**	**Offenbach**		**Germany**	
03/02/74	**Palasport**	**Turin**		**Italy**	
04/02/74	**Palasport**	**Reggio Emilia**		**Italy**	
05/02/74	**Palasport**	**Rome**		**Italy**	
06/02/74	**Teatro Mediteranno**	**Naples**		**Italy**	
08/02/74	Salle Vaubier	Winterthur		Switzerland	

Genesis

09/02/74	Palais des Sports	Marseilles		France	
10/02/74	Palais d'Hiver	Lyon		France	
12/02/74	**ORFT TV Studios**	**Paris**		**France**	**"Melody" Show**
01/03/74	Capitol Theatre	Passaic	New Jersey	USA	
02/03/74	Tower Theatre	Upper Darby	Pennsylvania	USA	
03/03/74	**Tower Theatre**	**Upper Darby**	**Pennsylvania**	**USA**	
04/03/74	East Wind Ballroom	Baltimore	Maryland	USA	
05/03/74	TP Warner Theatre	Washington	Washington DC	USA	
07/03/73	**Sports Arena**	**Fort Wayne**	**Indiana**	**USA**	
08/03/74	Fox Theatre	Atlanta	Georgia	USA	
09/03/74	**Gusman Hall**	**Miami**	**Florida**	**USA**	
12/03/74	Muthers	Nashville	Tennesse	USA	
13/03/74	North Hall	Memphis	Tennesse	USA	
17/03/74	Armadillo World Headquarters	Austin	Texas	USA	
20/03/74	Civic Plaza Assembly Hall	Phoenix	Arizona	USA	
21/03/74	**Civic Reunion Centre**	**Santa Monica**	**California**	**USA**	
24/03/74	Winterland Arena	San Francisco	California	USA	
26/03/74	Arena	Seattle	Washington	USA	
27/03/74	Garden Auditorium	Vancouver	British Columbia	Canada	
02/04/74	Philharmonic Hall	New York City	New York	USA	
03/04/74	Orpheum Theatre	Davenport	Iowa	USA	
05/04/74	Embassy Theatre	Fort Wayne	Indianapolis	USA	
06/04/74	**Student Union Auditorium**	**Toledo**	**Ohio**	**USA**	
07/04/74	**The Agora**	**Columbus**	**Ohio**	**USA**	
08/04/74	Centre Cultural Grande Salle	Sherbrooke	Quebec	Canada	
09/04/74	Guthrie Theatre	Minneapolis	Minnesota	USA	gig cancelled
10/04/74	The Spectrum	Philadelphia	Pennsylvania	USA	
11/04/74	Auditorium Theatre	Chicago	Illinois	USA	
12/04/74	Convention Centre	Indianapolis	Indiana	USA	
13/04/74	Kiel Theatre	St. Louis	Missouri	USA	
14/04/74	Memorial Hall	Kansas City	Missouri	USA	
15/04/74	**Palladium Theatre**	**New York City**	**New York**	**USA**	
16/04/74	**Ford Auditorium**	**Detroit**	**Ohio**	**USA**	
17/04/74	McGraw Hall	Evanston	Illinois	USA	
18/04/74	Centre de Congress	Quebec		Canada	
19/04/74	Civic Centre	Ottawa	Quebec	Canada	
20/04/74	**University Sports Arena**	**Montreal**	**Quebec**	**Canada**	**with Peter Hammill**
21/04/74	**University Sports Arena**	**Montreal**	**Quebec**	**Canada**	**as above**
22/04/74	Auditorium Theatre	Rochester	New York	USA	
23/04/74	**Civic Centre**	**Quebec**		**Canada**	
24/04/74	**Music Hall**	**Boston**	**Massachusetts**	**USA**	
25/04/74	AG Hall	Allentown	Pennsylvania	USA	
27/04/74	Century Theatre	Buffalo	New York	USA	
28/04/74	**Allen Theatre**	**Cleveland**	**Ohio**	**USA**	
29/04/74	**Allen Theatre**	**Cleveland**	**Ohio**	**USA**	
02/05/74	**Massey Hall**	**Toronto**	**Ontario**	**Canada**	**Early Show**
02/05/74	**Massey Hall**	**Toronto**	**Ontario**	**Canada**	**Late Show**
03/05/74	Syria Mosque	Pittsburgh	Pennsylvania	USA	
04/05/74	**Academy of Music**	**New York**	**New York**	**USA**	
06/05/74	**Academy of Music**	**New York**	**New York**	**USA**	
20/11/74	Auditorium Theatre	Chicago	Illinois	USA	
21/11/74	Auditorium Theatre	Chicago	Illinois	USA	
22/11/74	**Indiana Convention Centre**	**Indianapolis**	**Indiana**	**USA**	
23/11/74	Ambassador Theatre	St Louis	Missouri	USA	
25/11/74	**Allen Theatre**	**Cleveland**	**Ohio**	**USA**	
26/11/74	**Allen Theatre**	**Cleveland**	**Ohio**	**USA**	
27/11/74	Veterans Memorial Coliseum	Columbus	Ohio	USA	
28/11/74	**Masonic Temple**	**Detroit**	**Ohio**	**USA**	
29/11/74	National Guard Armoury	Fort Wayne	Indiana	USA	
30/11/74	**Syria Mosque**	**Pittsburgh**	**Pennsylvania**	**USA**	
01/12/74	**Lyric Theatre**	**Baltimore**	**Maryland**	**USA**	
02/12/74	Warner Theatre	Washington	Washington DC	USA	
04/12/74	**Mosque Theatre**	**Richmond**	**Virginia**	**USA**	
05/12/74	**Tower Theatre**	**Philadelphia**	**Pennsylvania**	**USA**	
06/12/74	**Academy of Music**	**New York**	**New York**	**USA**	
07/12/74	**Academy of Music**	**New York**	**New York**	**USA**	
08/12/74	**Palace Theatre**	**Providence**	**Rhode Island**	**USA**	
09/12/74	Music Hall	Boston	Massachusetts	USA	
11/12/74	Palace Theatre	Albany	New York	USA	
12/12/74	**Palace Theatre**	**Waterbury**	**Connecticut**	**USA**	
13/12/74	**Capitol Theatre**	**Passaic**	**New Jersey**	**USA**	
14/12/74	**Market Square Arena**	**Kansas City**	**Missouri**	**USA**	
15/12/74	**The Forum**	**Montreal**	**Quebec**	**Canada**	
16/12/74	**Maple Leaf Gardens**	**Toronto**	**Ontario**	**Canada**	
17/12/74	**The Dome**	**Rochester**	**New York**	**USA**	
18/12/74	Century Theatre	Buffalo	New York	USA	
10/01/75	**Convention Hall, West Palm Beach**		**Florida**	**USA**	

11/01/75	**Civic Centre**	**Lakeland**	**Florida**	**USA**	
12/01/75	**Municipal Auditorium**	**Atlanta**	**Georgia**	**USA**	
15/01/75	**Music Hall**	**New Orleans**	**Louisiana**	**USA**	
17/01/75	Music Hall	Houston	Texas	USA	
19/01/75	**Civic Centre Music Hall**	**Oklahoma City**	**Oklahoma**	**USA**	
20/01/75	McKey Auditorium	Boulder	Colorado	USA	
22/01/75	**Community Centre**	**Berkley**	**California**	**USA**	
23/01/75	Old Waldorf Astoria	San Francisco	California	USA	
24/01/75	**Shrine Auditorium**	**Los Angeles**	**California**	**USA**	
25/01/75	**Fox Theatre**	**San Diego**	**California**	**USA**	
28/01/75	**Civic Centre**	**Phoenix**	**Arizona**	**USA**	
29/01/75	Golden Hall Community Centre	San Diego	California	USA	
01/02/75	Kansas Memorial Hall	Kansas City	Missouri	USA	replaced cancelled Vancouver gig
02/02/75	**Grand Valley State College**	**Grand Rapids**	**Michigan**	**USA**	
03/02/75	Memorial Coliseum	Fort Wayne	Indiana	USA	
04/02/75	**Arie Crown Theatre**	**Chicago**	**Illinois**	**USA**	
19/02/75	**Ekerberghallen**	**Oslo**		**Norway**	
21/02/75	**Falkoner Theatrit**	**Copenhagen**		**Denmark**	
22/02/75	**Niedersachsenhalle**	**Hannover**		**Germany**	
23/02/74	**Eissporthalle**	**Berlin**		**Germany**	
24/02/75	**Carre Hotel**	**Amsterdam**		**Holland**	
26/02/75	**Palais des Grottes**	**Cambrai**		**France**	
28/02/75	**Salle des Expositions**	**Colmar**		**France**	
01/03/75	**Palais des Sports**	**Dijon**		**France**	
02/03/75	**Palais des Sports**	**St Etienne**		**France**	
03/03/75	**Palais des Sports**	**Paris**		**France**	
06/03/75	Pavihao dos Desportos	Cascais		Portugal	
07/03/75	**Pavihao dos Desportos**	**Cascais**		**Portugal**	
09/03/75	**Pabellon Nuevo**	**Barcelona**		**Spain**	
10/03/75	Pabellon Nuevo	Barcelona		Spain	
11/03/75	Pabellon Real Madrid	Madrid		Spain	
17/03/75	**Palais des Sports**	**Paris**		**France**	
22/03/75	**Salle D'Expositions**	**Annecy**		**France**	
24/03/75	**Palasport Parco Rufino**	**Turin**		**Italy**	
26/03/75	**Stadhalle**	**Offenbach**		**Germany**	
27/03/75	**Messezentrum**	**Nurnburg**		**Germany**	
29/03/75	Festhalle	Berne		Switzerland	
30/01/75	**Saarlandhalle**	**Saarbruken**		**Germany**	
01/04/75	**Fredrich Ebert Halle**	**Ludwigshafen**		**Germany**	
02/04/75	**Killesberghalle 14**	**Stuttgart**		**Germany**	
03/04/75	**Jahrhunerthalle**	**Frankfurt**		**Germany**	
04/04/75	**Circus Krone**	**Munich**		**Germany**	
05/04/75	Stadhalle	Heidelburg		Germany	
06/04/75	**Philipshalle**	**Dusseldorf**		**Germany**	
07/04/75	**Westfalenhalle 3**	**Dortmund**		**Germany**	
08/04/75	**Congresshalle**	**Hamburg**		**Germany**	
10/04/75	**Martinihal Centrum**	**Groningen**		**Holland**	
11/04/75	**Ahoy Sportpaleis**	**Rotterdam**		**Holland**	
12/04/75	**Vorst Nationale**	**Brussels**		**Belgium**	
14/04/75	Empire Pool Wembley	London		UK	
15/04/75	**Empire Pool Wembley**	**London**		**UK**	
16/04/75	**Gaumont Theatre**	**Southampton**	**Hampshire**	**UK**	
17/04/75	Empire Theatre	Liverpool	Merseyside	UK	
18/04/75	Empire Theatre	Liverpool	Merseyside	UK	
19/04/75	**Empire Theatre**	**Liverpool**	**Merseyside**	**UK**	
22/04/75	**Usher Hall**	**Edinburgh**		**UK**	
23/04/75	**Usher Hall**	**Edinburgh**		**UK**	
24/04/75	City Hall	Newcastle	Tyne and Wear	UK	
25/04/75	City Hall	Newcastle	Tyne and Wear	UK	
27/04/75	**Palace Theatre**	**Manchester**	**Grt Manchester**	**UK**	
28/04/75	**Palace Theatre**	**Manchester**	**Grt Manchester**	**UK**	
29/04/75	Colston Hall	Bristol	Avon	UK	
30/04/75	**Colston Hall**	**Bristol**	**Avon**	**UK**	
01/05/75	**Hippodrome**	**Birmingham**	**West Midlands**	**UK**	
02/05/75	**Hippodrome**	**Birmingham**	**West Midlands**	**UK**	
10/05/75	**Osteehalle**	**Kiel**		**Germany**	
11/05/75	Grugahalle	Essen		Germany	
12/05/75	**Rhein am Main Halle**	**Wiesbaden**		**Germany**	
13/05/75	Stadhalle	Bremen		Germany	
15/05/75	**Palais des Sports**	**Rheims**		**France**	
16/05/75	Palais des Sports	Rheims		France	
18/05/75	**Velodromo Anoeta**	**San Sabastian**		**Spain**	
20/05/75	Palais des Sports	Paris		France	
21/05/75	Palais des Grottes	Cambrai		France	
23/05/75	Salle des Expositions	Colmar		France	
25/05/75	Palais des Sports	Dijon		France	
27/05/75	Palais des Sports	Besancon		France	Peter Gabriel's last show

ABOUT THE AUTHOR

Paul Russell has written numerous magazine articles on such luminaries as Genesis, Jethro Tull, Yes, Peter Gabriel, Phil Collins, David Bowie Todd Rundgren, Peter Hammill and Van Der Graaf Generator, and the Moody Blues amongst others, for *Record Collector*, *Record Buyer*, *Top Magazine*.

He has contributed sleevenotes for albums by The Nice, Tangerine Dream, Yes, Gillan, ELP (as well as supplying some recordings for the box set), Rick Wakeman and various progressive rock compilations.

He assisted Peter Hammill compiling the tracks for the Van Der Graff Generator box set, and interviewed the band members for a comprehensive history included in the package.

He was the only UK writer present at the Genesis Heathrow Airport reunion for the first *Archive* box set, where he interviewed and photographed all seven members.

He continues his work as a garden designer, and freelance Professor of Progressive Rock.

SAF and Firefly Books

Order Online

For the latest on SAF and Firefly titles, or to order books online, check the SAF website. You can also browse the full range of rock, pop, jazz and experimental music books we have available, as well as keeping up with our latest releases. There are also:

Special pre-publication offers
Signed copies
Monthly offers
Book reviews and extracts
Competitions

You can also contact us via email, and request a catalogue.

info@safpublishing.com
www.safpublishing.com

Recent titles:
Morrissey, Devo, Mountain, Alex Harvey, The Pretty Things, Cabaret Voltaire, Coil-Current 93-Nurse With Wound, U2 Encyclopedia (updated), Thin Lizzy, Shirley Collins.

Forthcoming titles:
Gentle Giant, Nirvana recording sessions, Hawkwind, Suicide, Kraftwerk, amongst others.

Backlist titles:
From Frank Zappa to Alice Cooper, from Captain Beefheart to Prince, from Robert Wyatt to The Residents, from Kraftwerk to the Ramones,
and many, many more.....

saf publishing

www.safpublishing.com